PRAISE FOR FEED YOUR LIFE

"Based on several true experiences, the author presents a series of engaging life lessons, often with humorous examples. This is a fun and valuable read."

> Brad J Kerbs
> Former President of Purina Mills LLC

"Brad's book delivers a GPS guidance system to the destination "A Life Well-lived". Landmarks are identified and brought into focus with humor, fun and poignant interludes. Told as the story about the learnings of Shane, a college intern for a prestigious animal nutrition company, the content creates a powerful and timeless How-to resource on building a successful, fulfilling career and living a happy life. What could be more important?"

> Mary Claire Wall
> President and Founder of Snail Mail Forever

"Intuitive…Inspiring…Thought Provoking. An easy read for current Agribusiness Sales Professionals and those contemplating a career in any kind of Sales"

> Dale Bowman Co-Owner of R.D. Bowman and Sons (One of America's Great Feed Retailers)

"Everybody is in sales, no matter what type of job you have, you are selling something to somebody. This book is a composite of 40 years of experience on how to build productive relationships, by understanding what makes people tick and helping them win. To be successful, you must invest in talking and connecting with people, some think this has become a "dead language" in today's technology-driven world. But no matter how digital your world is, people will always buy from people, and you will do much better following the formula offered in this reading."

>Mark Chenoweth
>Retired Animal Nutrition and Animal Health Executive

"Whether your career leads you into sales or down any other path, the life lessons contained in this book are invaluable to every college graduate."

>Amy Butler
>Dealer Development Manager, Purina Animal Nutrition

"Chock full of thoughtful and heartfelt business and life advice. I couldn't put it down". In "Feed Your Life", Brad Schu masterfully packs his decades of hard work and experiences into Shane's summer internship with Alumni Feed. I enjoyed these relevant and timely lessons that apply to everyone whether you are a young person considering a sales role with an agriculture firm or a seasoned high-tech executive. Nuggets like "Thee Before Me" will make the time spent breezing through this book well worth the investment.

>Steve Storgion
>Enterprise Account Executive, Amazon Web Services

FEED YOUR LIFE

BRAD SCHU

Copyright © 2023 by Brad Schu

All rights reserved.

No part of this book may be reproduced in any form or by any electronic or mechanical means, including information storage and retrieval systems, without written permission from the author, except for the use of brief quotations in a book review.

This work is dedicated to my loving and ever-supportive wife, Margo, and my two wonderful children, Daniel and Connie. You are the three most important people in my life. My youthful and colorful Mother-in-Law, Mary Constance McManus. My father, Ed (who was a role model by action more than by word); my brother Mike (may he be at peace), brother Dick (the most dedicated working man and farmer I know) and his supportive wife, Debbie. My flight-loving sister Mary (the safest pilot on the planet) and her husband, Gary. My mother, Mary Jean, who passed too soon, and Leila Van Dyke and Betty Johnson, who filled the void of her passing as well as anyone could.

I want also to thank the many people who helped with the content or construction of this book. Without their input and encouragement, this would not have happened. That list, in no order, includes Mark Chenoweth, Brad Kerbs, Kent Phalen, Jim Jarvis, Jay Carter, C. Robin Brock, Steve Storgion, Mike Krakoviak, Roberta Gleicher, Dale Bowman, Kenny Russell, Danny Naegle, Teresa Miller, Jay Carter, Mary Claire and Ed Wall, Larry and Linda Miller, Craig Palubiak, Max Fisher, Ed McMillan, Lynn McCord, David Nelson and of course my wife Margo.

It is the right thing to do to recognize a distinguished list of bosses, co-workers, or key influencers that shaped various learning opportunities and developed countless successes through observing each one's unique style. My first 2 bosses Roger Schaefer (RIP) and Wendell Law had the biggest impact at an early age in my life. Bruce Baker (RIP) made an impact by teaching me the fundamentals of sales management. Mark Chenoweth for all he taught me about strategy, was a Superman in that arena. Brad Kerbs taught me leadership principles and how to fight through adversity. Brian Gier taught me the importance of integrity as a part of your personal life strategy. I learned so much from so many others that it would fill pages. Thanks to you all. You are all on the Mount Rushmore of great bosses.

In dedication...

To every high school ag teacher that inspired a kid to experience something different and, as a result, gained self-confidence and an increased sense of worth. Larry McKay was one of those that did that for many, including this brash young punk at Rosalia High School. If there is an Ag Teacher Hall of Fame. He would be a first-ballot selection.

To every Agricultural Salesperson who has 'carried a bag,' ventured to the farmgate, and has helped the American Farmer become the most productive food generator the world has ever known through your help and expertise.

To every Sales Manager who has to be a coach, psychologist, parent, mentor, cheerleader, and emotional bail bonds person.

And maybe most importantly, it also is for the most complex working people in American agriculture...the people who own or work in a feed store. Creating a Top Ten List would be impossible. They are all great. THANK YOU ALL!

CONTENTS

FEED Your Life	ix
1. Palouse	1
2. McCutcheon	16
3. Bootch and the Dreamweaver	26
4. The Odor of Strangers	63
5. "Moses Wears Carhartt"	106
6. Three Little Words for the Bell Cow	138
7. "How About Some Cobbler with That Magpie?"	151
8. Connie Mack Goes to Ephrata	166
9. The Day That Art Appreciation Class Came in Handy	178
10. Surgery with a Backhoe	203
11. "There's a Feeling I Get When I Look to the West" – Led Zeppelin	237
12. The Lost Tribe and the Harmony of the Crickets	259
13. Put the Potato in the Front	282
14. The Seven Words You Can't Say in a Feed Store	304
15. A Million Years of Angel Tears	329
16. Maslow Meets the Jackals	351
17. Carving a Totem Pole on a Toothpick	379
About the Author	409

FEED YOUR LIFE

PREFACE

My name is Brad, and I am a "Feedstoreaholic."

I love FEED STORES, agricultural supply centers of any kind. I have visited thousands in all parts of the United States and Internationally. I love the complex aromas and the imperfectly merchandised randomness of products and remedies meant to nourish the earth, animal, and the occasional human.

Many more tenured agricultural retail entities have historically impacted their community, lasting much longer than each growing season. Store owners have important side gigs, such as a Justice of the Peace who has married thousands of couples. Several are mayors, council people, and school board members. Most are involved heavily in youth agricultural development or church governance. A select few have become Senators or Representatives at our government's State and Federal levels.

Looking back over forty years of involvement with the owners and employees, I view them collectively and individually as unaccredited centers of higher learning. There are all kinds of agronomy, fertilizer, and grain-handling retail centers worldwide. I pay reverence to all of them. However, each trip to a feed store offers an advanced excursion toward wisdom and a reflection of the cadence of a community.

That enlightenment one can get at a FEED STORE is what this book is about. With respect and deference to the great Robert Fulghum book about critical learning in kindergarten, I could proclaim and paraphrase….

"Everything I learned worth knowing I learned in a FEED STORE."

The general population's predominant perception of the FEED STORE would rarely mirror my enthusiasm for this underappreciated segment of merchants. What often follows when I tell the unfamiliar person that I interact with feed or agricultural store owners: "Those places are dirty." "Aren't those people a little dense?" "Seems like a backward or primitive industry."

Let me counter this ignorance.

With nearly 7 billion people expanding on our planet, there have been, and will be, conflicts, learning, creation, destruction, and more than a few moments of inspiration and happiness. None of this happens without human fueling. A sustainable and high-quality food source that nourishes all nations, bonds villages, and sustains our happiest family events is essential. Yet food is often taken for granted.

Many of the moments we spend on this earth are better because of our relationship with animals. Numerous studies point out the human health and wellness benefits we receive through pets, from dogs to domesticated condors. The FEED STORE "feeds 'em all" and guides how to enhance your pet's appreciation as only they can.

Let me provide more evidence of agricultural retailers and FEED STORES' impact on the world.

To emphasize the magnitude of demand, consider it: "A lot can happen in one second." Agricultural officials report that approximately 10 &1/2 tons of meat are consumed worldwide every second. Forty-eight thousand pounds or 24 tons of milk are consumed or processed every second. Over 100 dozen eggs and 91 tons of grains are eaten or further processed to be included in other food ingredients every second. I was told that in the United States alone, over 4 acres of pizza are consumed every hour. That's nearly 250 slices per second! No cave dweller, an early settler, or a ruling Royal could have foreseen the demand for such a vast and diverse food source in the world's future.

Maslow's study of the human hierarchy of needs highlights the sheer importance of a consistent food supply to people. His logic (paraphrased) is, "Until your food and shelter needs are met, little else matters." Food is important. That is genius stuff, huh? Additional evidence of the benefits of a plentiful and high-quality food source is illustrated throughout history in a quick review of some societal metrics. A shortage of food has caused the premature end of wars and, conversely, was the spark that ignited wars. A significant by-product of our food system is has extended life expectancy of humans. When teamed with the applied breakthroughs in human medicine, life expectancy has nearly doubled in less than a hundred years. Interestingly, the animals' nutritional needs used in studies to promote reliable and effective drug commercialization were supplied by; you guessed it, a FEED STORE.

Many accolades will be passed out to those who have generated the luxury of our World Food Supply. Albeit in most cases for a profit. There are scientists, botanists, nutritionists, Land Grant Universities, animal caregivers, veterinarians, Vocational Agricultural teachers, food companies and their marketers, bankers, railroad and barge workers, truckers, local extension agents, and last and maybe most important, the farmers themselves. No doubt, essential members of the chain have been overlooked. Unfortunately, they are used to it. Let's focus on specific leaders in this great success.

While there are agricultural participants all over the planet, the American farmer is collectively recognized as the standard by which most agriculture participants are measured. Regarding production, the American farmer and rancher is now less than 2% of the population they operate amongst. They feed over 150 people in addition to themselves. Metrics show production has increased eight-fold since the 1920s, and nearly the exact multiple has reduced food cost per consumer dollar. Most agricultural operations are family-owned versus the growing but over-emphasized corporate farming we hear much about from the media.

Another even more significant and less obvious contributor and leader is the previously mentioned success. That is the FEED STORE. These INDEPENDENT AGRICULTURAL RETAILERS were pioneers and catalysts for much of the unprecedented growth of the world's food over the last century. In today's agriculture, diverse specialized agricultural entities, including agronomy centers, fertilizer depots, machinery and implement stores, and integrated, high-production animal feed mills dominate the sale of inputs to production agriculture operations. The specialization of AG RETAILERS has been economically and scope driven. Today the focused nature of these large and diverse input suppliers has evolved into more farmer-owned cooperatives. I highlight the FEED STORE because, before this specialization of agriculture retailers, the FEED STORE sold most of the supplies a farmer needed to improve their productivity.

Growing up in a family that participated in this agricultural food system, I observed agricultural evolution at the end of a pitchfork, cleaning a hog or cattle barn in the seat of a combine, grain truck, or tractor. I can tell you there are millions more consumer misunderstandings of farmers than there are farmers themselves.

Let me help with a few specifics that help set a baseline for the rest of the message in this book:

> Farmers work hours that only some would attempt or even understand.
> Farmers are as concerned about their crops and animals as the gardener or the pet owner.
> Farmers are proud of their work and consistently seek to improve.
> Farmers are often generous to their community.
> Farmers are highly creative in solving problems.
> Farmers tend to be EXTREMELY independent.
> Farmers are not leaders in change management. Like many, change only comes when the pain becomes so great that they must adapt.
> Farmers rarely trust the unfamiliar and what they can't see or experience.
> Farmers deal almost exclusively with Mother Nature like no other business.

The FEED STORE owner recognizes, accepts, and adapts to all of the strengths and "warts" of their customers. The scientist, the University, the nutritionist, and the botanist create many advances and innovations that move food production and animal ownership to revolutionary status. However, if no one knows about it, the benefits of it, or how to apply it effectively, it will have little success.

The FEED STORE owner remedies this knowledge gap thousands of times daily with the wit of a bartender, an insurance provider's finesse, and a clergyman's foundation. So how does one capture in the written word the under-explored collection of complex and "raw-bone simple" feed store wisdom so that you can apply it to your life, family, or business? I wrestled with this in multiple approaches. First, I thought, "What about a musical? "*FEED STORE the Musical*" didn't seem like it would ever grace the moniker of a Broadway theater. Expecting the reader to trudge through the blow-by-blow of my 40-plus-year career would be an adequate remedy for insomnia. In addition, it is hard to write about oneself without complete reader rejection unless you have some unusual circumstance, such as "I was raised by a herd of pygmy goats and won a cactus-eating contest." The last option, a "step-by-step how-to book," seemed to read a lot like a software installation manual.

The only viable approach was to lead you through a story of learning by someone else. Shane is an imaginative and capable college intern responsible for a summer assignment of working with feed stores. He is charged with learning how his company can do more for the feed stores they service. So, how can a college intern's story capture and deliver meaningful insights if you are wondering? While naïve and raw, Shane is inquisitive and dangerously bold with his inquisition and has a valuable wit to help absorb and regurgitate his learnings. His innocence, desire to achieve, and curiosity is emblematic of so many agribusiness leaders who started the way he did and achieved greatness by learning from their customers the way Shane did.

The period of this story is the spring and summer of 1980. The 80s were a decisive period for the success of family agriculture. It was also a period untethered by today's modern satellite-driven technology and social media. Thus, human interaction and communication were essential to be successful. Today's social media has many benefits. One could argue that if the power of social media had been available in the 1940s, the unthinkable tyranny of Nazi Germany would have met a more humane resolution more rapidly. The more recent world of hashtags, tweets, posts, Insta-stories, likes, and unsecured truth news stories has had unfavorable effects on trust for others. It has deteriorated the language of getting along with one another.

The adjacent point to be learned today is that in our high-speed technology-saturated connections, the fundamentals of human interaction and practices can be improved if we recognize and exercise elements that made people successful in the 80s when communication tools were much more technologically primitive. The FEED STORES are preserving a LOST LANGUAGE of caring about others. Together with Shane, they provide a road map for connecting and benefitting from this language.

How the book is laid out in each chapter adds to Shane's story. At the end of each chapter is a list of his most pertinent learnings and occasional commentary from me. I hope both add to your reading experience and your chance for future recall.

I want to thank the agriculture industry, colleagues, friends, customers, and family for their support and willingness to supply personal stories and feed store experiences to add to Shane's colorful renaissance.

And in respectful summation, I want to salute and commend the American Farmers, including my family. I would also like to show appreciation to anyone who has ever worked in an agricultural retail outlet. Most of all, the incredible men and women of the FEED STORES have improved this world through their service and leadership.

Brad Schu

1

PALOUSE

The world in 1969 was cycling through its ever-accelerating list of achievements, such as a man from rural Ohio stepping onto the formerly human-repellent sphere known as the moon. A pasture in the bucolic Finger Lakes region of New York became a concert venue that put the term "Woodstock" and "organizational disaster" in the same sentence. And the four most significant musicians of all time, The Beatles, played their last live public performance on a rooftop during a lunch break in Central London.

While all that transpired in 1969 Whitman County, Washington, the soft white wheat price was $2.29 per bushel, and the local high school basketball team missed the state tournament for the 7th year. Those were the two significant watermarks that all years were measured against. A rural community's surroundings and spirit can align your DNA for a lifetime. This is how a young citizen of rural America learns from leaders in the world's most crucial industry, agriculture. Rural living is not for everyone. Those who have lived it understand it but often have difficulty explaining it. Those thrust into it rarely embrace the details they must know to enjoy it.

Shane was his given name as a hangover of his parents falling in love with the main character's name in some B western movie about a manic bounty hunter. He had a handful of nicknames such as "Barnacle," "Gopher," and "8 Penny.""8 Penny" referred to a relatively small carpenter nail size and correlated to Shane packing a hammer with him all over the farm where he grew up. He was constantly swinging all four ounces of the toy hammer with the authority of Thor, simultaneously chanting in savage toddler diction, "Me fixin, me fixin."

Nicknames were a cultural foundation within Shane's family because of the tireless handy work in the craft of "alternative branding" by Shane's Uncle Bo. He was the most overly qualified hired man who ever roamed a wheat field. Uncle Bo was a Renaissance man who could fix any piece of farm equipment with maple syrup and tin foil, knock out a Bohemian stew in a "Dutch oven," and in a single meeting with a stranger, drop an "affectionate epithet" a moniker that might end up on your tombstone. He was the king of the nickname.

He was a valuable asset to Shane's dad, "Boxcar," to the whole farm operation, and most everyone in town knew it. He often heard, "If you were to leave, Boxcar's whole operation would fall apart." Uncle Bo was as loyal as he was humble, which would illicit the same standard response when someone questioned his indispensability. Bo would discount that nonsense by saying, "Irreplaceable? Hell, they replaced Kennedy in half an hour." This response would get the point across with minimal argument.

As a kid, Bo raised a stray infant raccoon found in the hayloft. Bottle raised with a tendency to chew Bo's tinker toys, and Lincoln logs into sawdust, so the raccoon became "Chainsaw." As a reverse penance to Bo, he was known as "Warbucks" because of his love of

Sears & Roebuck's catalog. He often said he would have bought his wife and kids through Sears, but he said there would be way too much assembly required. Uncle Bo had distinct rules about nicknames: 1. A naming outcome could never intend malice, and thus the name primarily dealt with actions and not appearance 2. Assigning one's own nickname was never acceptable 3. The adhesion of the name was often tied to creative absurdity. That last part was what addicted him the most.

By ten years of age in 1969, Shane had amassed nearly one hundred pounds of body weight and a similar number of friends in his school and community. He was mildly successful and passionate about his local youth sports. Shane wanted to emulate his two brother's success in basketball. When either brother made a basket in a high school game, a 300-lumen smile and a 90-decibel celebration were sure to follow. In school, Shane was the dependable leader of the "C students." Not because he wasn't brilliant, but Shane made sure that life's more critical decisions were based on a different set of criteria than someone with a teaching certificate. He reasoned that he didn't want to be significant at anything because no one liked Goliath in the Bible. He allowed the correlation of not wanting to get big to augment the action of not getting substantial grades. The excellent news.... this corrected itself years later.

It was a mile-and-a-half walk from the combination grade school and high school to 'Elk's house. Elk's nickname centered on his affection for Santa's reindeer as a child, which he called 'Elk.' This was because he couldn't pronounce Rudolph. Elk was a good friend to Shane, and Shane liked his carefree attitude and big-city sense of humor, and maybe what he envied most was that Elk lived in town. Elk was the opposite of the more athletic Shane. Elk was skinny enough to tread water in a garden hose, plus he had the "teen magazine cover" long hair to hide his larger-than-normal ears.

The term "town" may have been a stretch with a population of about 650 people. Most were multi-generation citizens of the agricultural-themed carnival in Whitman County, Washington. The glacially enhanced soil of this impressive expanse earned Whitman County the title of "white wheat capital of the world." The county is approximately 650 square miles and has around 400 dedicated historically immigrated farm families. Their farms clustered a similar crop shipping radius of the twelve strangely uniform small towns. These dozen towns had many similarities: They all had a main street with family-run businesses supporting the neighboring farm families. Each had a grain handling cooperative that marketed their crops. Each had a proud grade school and high school with an over-zealous parental athletic obsession. Each had a convenience grocery store the size of the produce section of today's modern supermarkets. They all had at least one tavern and always more churches than drinking establishments.

The town Shane and Elk walked through that day was considered blessed versus the other smaller 'Whitman burbs.' They walked by a lumber yard, two hardware stores, a tire shop, an auto parts store, a bank, two taverns, five churches as per the rule, an eight-lane bowling alley, two restaurants, doctor and dental offices, car dealership, jewelry repair, and two barbers. Both barbers scared Shane and were foreign to the long-locked Elk. Unless you were the county seat, most other towns had few amenities. On this particular day, the two comrades were walking by the tallest fixture in the city, the grain elevator feed mill. The aroma coming out of the mill grabbed Shane by the nostrils. It may have been what subconsciously seduced him into a future life of service in the animal nutrition industry that he could never have imagined. The feed mill used steam to roll barley and added molasses to make steer feed. The slightly fermented sweet fragrance could be savored seven city blocks away or, in other words, clear across town. If Shane had been the corporate leader of Old Spice, he would have sent the scientists to figure out how to make a cologne out of this heavenly sweat. We usually never know what stimulus to our senses have directed our future. Agriculture has some great smells.

Elk, living in town and Shane able to hang out with him, was a little like a sailor on shore leave. Shane lived 5 miles straight from town and 7 miles by vehicle. The reason for the extra distance is that there are no straight lines in Whitman County. It is known as the Palouse Country garnering its name from the Palouse Native Indian tribe, which inhabited this region as late as 100 years ago. The unusual topography of this land was a continuous carpet of 200 to 800 ft. elevation hills from their base that only was occasionally interrupted by a tree on the property boundary line. Near the center of the county was a 3,600-foot monolith peak that stuck out of the earth like a pimple on prom night. Steptoe Butte was the tallest point for nearly 60 miles in every direction and was a constant landmark if you were ever lost. It was named after a United States Cavalry Colonel who battled Indians in the 1800s. The silty loess soil in the Palouse was formed by a volcano and ice age pressures that made a crop medium that an average farmer could brag about 'Eighty bushels per acre' of dry-land wheat. The actual results may have been seventy bushels, but eighty sounded better to peer farmers in the coffee shop.

Shane's seven-mile distance from town allowed developmental learning in school bus riding. You must adhere to etiquette and pecking order in an 18-passenger mass transit. There are undocumented imperatives of rural yellow bus transit. One decree was that the meanest and most obnoxious elder rider made the rules of who got to sit where and when they could roll a window up or down. They always sat in the back with the comfort of an entire seat and access to a window. The bus-riding associates were always enthusiastic when one of these evil bus tyrants turned sixteen and got a car. That meant less oppression and shuffling the leadership deck. When the bus wasn't running, the distance also made for regular bicycle and mini-bike trips to town for little league and football practice. There was also the occasional snowmobile ride to town to an important winter-time basketball tourney when the country roads were snowed shut. Those vehicles, while technically not legal on the gravel-based roads they traveled, provided valuable freedom from hours of farm work and a way to escape the smell of the family hog operation. The porcine sewer was physically close enough to the house that Shane thought the hogs were in the closet of his room at night. While Shane had no issue with the hogs themselves, he held them in high regard for the revenue and the tasty output they provided, but the odor was non-habit forming. .…. Not "every" smell in agriculture is pleasingly robust.

The Palouse Country was considered the end of the world by many people from the more populated and less tolerant Seattle area. But for the people that lived in this hilly habitat, the Southeast end of the county housed the higher learning center of the wheat monarchy, Pullman. Pullman was the proud home of Washington State University. It was revered in the Palouse for the significant economic impact WSU crop research had on improved wheat yields for the farmers of Whitman County. Many of the bachelor farmers loved the substantial bounty gained by the work of the University so much that they would bequeath their farm ground to WSU upon their death. Washington State athletics was the other dedication they gave religiously and emotionally. Much like Shane's grade school report card, the Washington State Cougars (Cougs) achieved more than their share of mediocrity on the athletic field. This lack of dominance did not deter the farming hoards. There wouldn't be a Saturday in the fall when a tractor radio on the Palouse wasn't tuned to the famous voice of Bob Robertson as he broadcast the achievements and the more than occasional disappointments of Cougar football. Shane's neighboring family's father, 'Sky King,' was rumored to have co-authored the Cougar Fight Song in the 1920s. One of the cooperative grain elevator operators in town where Shane's family would take their grain, "Shovelhead" (yep, Uncle Bo named him), always wore a hard hat with the WSU Cougar logo. He often said, "That whole Coug thing can get a holt' of ya." A no more encompassing statement could be made.

Shane's family lived in a house that was once a barn with a hay loft. The structural recovery happened sometime in the 1930s, and other than the necessary sporadic painting not much had been done to it since. A two-story gambrel design contained a curving and creaking staircase that would, later in life, get him in trouble for getting home way too late, awakening his dad. This late arrival certainly conflicted with one of his dad's famous sayings, "Nothing good happens after midnight." Shane felt he had heard that phrase in his lifetime more than all the beer commercials ever heard on the radio. In the future, he tested the efficacy of those words and, in reflection, found them more often right than wrong.

The family included two brothers, fourteen and fifteen years older, respectively, and his sister, who was ten years older than Shane. The brothers mentioned earlier for their basketball prowess were a big help on the family farm. In high school, his sister represented the town as the queen on the community float, was a cheerleader, and an active pleasure horse rider. At only 12, she was more challenging than a nickel steak and could drive farm equipment and cook meals between laps on the tractor around the field. Everyone pitched in because that is what farm families do. The youngest, Shane, was two years old when their mother died of cancer. He had very little recollection of her or her passing. He also had no way of understanding the emotional scar tissue such an event would have on his family's other remaining members.

A father in his 50's, Ed was now trying to deal with farming 1800 acres and overseeing a 100-sow hog operation. Ed was one of 3 children, an older sister of 8 years and a younger brother of 4 years. They were born to German immigrants who had initially settled near the center of South Dakota. Ed's road to the Palouse had unique twists and turns. Much despair hung over Ed's family as he grew up in a small Dakota farming community. The family adversity and the economic depression of early childhood were convenient historical references when dealing with his wife's passing. He had been well-conditioned.

Ed's Dakota relatives were mostly unsuccessful grain farmers who had a stretch of 8 years where they never saw a crop. His family and most others found consistent misfortune as agricultural participants during the dust bowl. This eight-year-running weather phenom routinely saw relentless winds blow crops out of the ground across most of South Dakota. Their father worked part-time with horses as a draftsman. He dealt with the poverty the dust bowl created through alcoholism. The abuse from her husband's addiction, mixed with "agricultural deficiency depression," eventually drove their fragile mother to seek psychiatric support, but she never recovered. She died in her forties.

All this put a cumbersome burden on Ed's older sister, "Yam." Her real name was May, but the boys spelled it and said it backward just to irritate her. Yam, the eldest child with little assistance from their intoxicated father, was thrust into motherly service at thirteen and put her life on hold to get the boys through grade school.

As mentioned earlier, Shane's dad was named Ed. People that knew him in the Palouse called him "Boxcar." Because of the misery in the Dakotas, he and other young men and occasionally some women would "hop a freight" and ride on the railroad boxcars looking for new life adventures and improved commerce. Ed did this directly after graduating high school, leaving home with $7.42 in his pocket, which constituted his life savings. He had many stories about riding the rails, living in the hobo jungles, and nimbly constructing ways to stay alive.

The nickname Boxcar came to him from what happened on one of his adventures. He jumped into a wooden slatted, temperature-controlled railroad car nearly full of lemons that were being hauled from Los Angeles to Seattle. As he hid away silently in a dark corner on the top of the car, trying to avoid detection from the train marshal, the expected and unexpected happened. The investigator closed the door. That was the desired part, but he didn't know until later that the marshal had put a lock on the door. Three days after a steady diet of tart citrus, he emerged with a phobia of lemons and a lifetime of tightened underjaw muscles. He eventually ended up in Whitman County, Washington, employed by various farmers and the local co-op grain elevator. Once he got to the Palouse, he very seldom left. He saved money, met his future wife, and pursued his farmer dream. He achieved this through share-cropping and longer-term farm property leases, eventually purchasing his farmland. The only detour in his plan was the tragic loss of his spouse in her early 40s. Uncle Bo was a fantastic asset through all of this. He was a great listener and teacher to the whole family and the most patient worker that has ever been employed.

When you have dealt with as much turmoil and challenge as Boxcar had in South Dakota, one can understand his propensity to want to control everything around him. Shane greatly respected him and loved to challenge his sense of humor from time to time. An example was when Shane was about fifteen and on hog manure-spreading duty. The John Deere 4030 tractor he was driving to pull the 3-yard manure spreader had a power take-off that could be switched on and off from the driver's seat. The manure spreader could be managed strategically to spread hog manure on demand. Shane decided to make his job more artistic by making the tractor and spreader the paintbrush, and the long sweeping slope of the Palouse his canvas. He thought what better way to honor his father than to spell the letters *E* and *D* in manure side by side in a configuration the size of a football field. Shane and his brothers thought it was hilarious. Boxcar was less amused but happy if that was what it took to move the manure. It was worth the temporary embarrassment.

Ed could also be a witty and unpredictable fun character. He and several friends had created unique rituals and creative exchanges that not all mainstreamers could grasp. An innocent but unexpected stunt like flipping a coin for the final payment of the groceries might often make thirty dollars of food cost sixty when he would lose the double-or-nothing convert to the local merchant. And, of course, the provisions were free about an equal number of times. Probabilities would, in their lifetimes, show an even split, but it was a way to put a bit of a rush into small-town grocery procurement. And the grocer also realized that this was a magnet to keep a $30 return customer.

Then there was 'Wiley.' He was the local crop-dusting daredevil pilot whose given name was Sinclair. Ed had a good idea of where that name's first part came from. Ed called him Wiley after the famous pilot and aviation legend Wiley Post. Sometimes creativity and better judgment never coalesce, and Wiley was the sponsor of many near-perilous outcomes. Once when he and one of the town leaders went for a ***joy flight*** in his pleasure plane one Sunday afternoon, they reportedly ran the ice chest out of beer about an hour into the flight. So what do you do when your thirst outraces your good judgment? They landed the plane on the main street in a small and secluded Northern Idaho town. He taxied the plane in front of the local tavern and scurried in. The look on the patron's faces had to be priceless when Wiley purchased two six-packs to go and sprinted off to continue their journey.

Wiley was a gymnast in a Grumman Ag cat spray plane. He would whisper along with a contour less than 20 feet off the hardpan, up, down, over hills, and into valleys like a spatula applying frosting to a cake. He often went under power lines and telephone wires to accomplish his spray and fertilizer regimens.

Wiley loved to use the Grumman as a wakeup and hello to 'Boxcat' as he liked to edit Ed's nickname. Ed wanted to start his tractor fieldwork early morning, right after sunrise. This coincidently was almost always an ideal time to spray from an airplane because the lack of wind resulted in less unwanted excess drifting of the spray.

When driving a tractor with implements behind you, you focus on keeping your equipment in line with your last pass or mark. You are looking backward and sometimes forward to avoid running into equipment or power poles with the implement you are towing. The tractor's rampaging diesel engine and the violent screeching and rhythmic thumping music from the Caterpillar tractor's steel tracks can put you at ease. Ed's open cockpit D-6 was a comfortable ride, but extended use could affect kidneys and hearing. Of course, he would wear no ear protection.

Wiley, in his airplane, had an unfair height and visual advantage over a guy riding 5 feet off the ground in a crawling tractor kicking up dust. He would see Ed chugging along at 3 miles an hour, audio impaired and keenly focused on his mark execution. Wiley would descend the Grumman behind a hill and try to time his morning greeting for arrival at about the same time Ed would bring the tractor to the top of the hill. This, of course, created a blind spot for the tractor driver. The Grumman with Wiley in control was about 30 feet off the top of the tractor, catapulting by over 120 miles per hour. Now the Caterpillar is a noisy machine, but the Grumman, as it climbs, will make neighboring counties take notice. The surprise, the speed, and the organ-jarring noise are a surefire way to prepare for your colonoscopy. Wiley loved this prank; conversely, it would nearly make Boxcar see the holy lights approaching him. This would occur at least once a year and sometimes even more frequently.

One early fall morning, as he was driving his D-6 plowing with a six-bottom moldboard plow, he glimpsed out of the corner of his eye the wingtip of the Grumman dipping behind a hill. He threw the Caterpillar out of gear, which brought it to an immediate halt, and shut off the engine. He quickly jumped to the ground and secured one of the newly plowed dirt clods. It was about half the size of a loaf of homemade bread. With the tractor engine turned off and a slight ringing in his ears, he could still make out the sound of fury from the Grumman engine as it banked, turned, and accelerated toward him. Ed crouched behind the fuel tank between the tractor and the plow, holding his dirt clod. Here came the high pitch of a plane accelerating toward the stopped tractor less than 25 feet up from the plowed field. Ed was a hell of a good pheasant hunter and knew it was:

>*Best to keep both eyes open when shooting.*
>*Keep the gun moving ahead of the pheasant.*
>*The critical thing is to "lead" your shot by shooting where the bird will be.*

When the Grumman was about eight plane lengths away from the front of the tractor, Boxcar slung the 2-pound dirt clod from between his legs like an underhand free throw as high as he could heave it. The dirt clod appeared to float lifelessly until the top of the propeller ran into it and made a thumping noise, followed by several Oreo cookie-sized clods peppered Wiley's windshield. The

Grumman tipped its wings back and forth to simulate being stunned, and that nonsense never happened again.

Because of his wife's premature passing, Ed was unexpectedly thrust into corralling two pre-college-age boys and trying to support a 12-year-old daughter going through her life's most significant changes, all without her closest role model. This upheaval was capped off by trying to find the instruction manual on how to raise his toddler, Shane.

The soil in the Palouse is transformational. It can sprout, nurture and grow the world's bounty while asking for very little in return. Similarly, this happens to the people that live on it. Farmers who are fiercely independent rally together around a fellow farmer that has cancer or is ill and will plant or harvest their crop without hesitation, even if they are behind in their own work. This happened to Shane's family. Mothers stood in line to offer maternal care. This led to his involvement with the caring Mother's brood and the activities and rituals that made them a family. Shane's sister was embraced and schooled in 'all things woman' by one of the ladies who lived a mile down the road from the farm. The older boys had basketball to distract the pain. However, they were also guided by community parents with more experience in the mysterious world of college enrollment. A guy who rode freight trains from South Dakota knew nothing about that.

No one asked the community members to engage in this help for Shane. No one made any contracts to limit liability or risk. The community assembled around others that needed help. This statement also defines the power of the Palouse...... wonderful people doing what's right.

Shane's Learnings

On nicknames: When applied with positive intent, nicknames are one of the World's great ways to express love.: 1.) A naming outcome could never intend malice (that is why the name primarily dealt with actions and not appearance) 2.) No self-respecting person can ever give "themselves" a nickname 3.) The adhesion of the name was often tied to creative absurdity.

On governing dumbass behavior: "Nothing good happens after midnight" .... It seems like it would be difficult to quantify the number and frequency of "dumbass" things that occur by the hour each day. However, it may be a safe estimation that the "dumbass activity" ranging from dangerous, illegal, potentially immoral, or even borders on self-selection is most prominent when most of the world is asleep. The phrase *Nothing good happens after midnight* is a handy and memorable mind nugget passed from parent to offspring to remind them not to be a "statistic" because of their nocturnal behavior.

On rural school bus transportation: School bus etiquette is more conducive to dictatorships than democracies. The caste system of rural public-school transportation is filled with oppression and intimidation of the younger riders. The social lessons one learns here can prepare you for life's toughest outputs.

On the fragrance of farming: Agriculture has a lot of great smells.

. . .

On the idea of being irreplaceable: Uncle Bo would always dismiss that by saying, "Remember, they replaced Kennedy in half an hour."

On unauthorized train travel: Don't plan to spend your whole life in a "lemon car."

On the generosity of neighbors: People in sparsely populated areas tend to help their fellow man.

On hunting pheasants: Three tips on hunting pheasants: a) Best to keep both eyes open when shooting b) Keep the gun moving ahead of the pheasant c) The critical thing is to "lead" your shot ahead of the bird by shooting where the bird is going to be.

On the diversity of pet selection: Raccoons have been known to make an affectionate pet.

2

MCCUTCHEON

"DON'T TAKE THE LID OFF THE GO JO!...DON'T TAKE THE LID OFF THE GO JO!...DON'T TAKE THE LID OFF THE GO JO!". Those were the cadenced words powerfully delivered in a baritone drawl hidden in a hint of disgust by Shane's 25+ year veteran high school agricultural teacher known by one name. 'McCutcheon'. The go-jo hand cleaner in the high school ag shop was above the shop sink. The hand soap dispenser was extremely cumbersome and slow. Students would take the lid off to get hand cleaner to get more materials and use way too much of this expensive soap. Much like the mononym names of Cher or Elvis, the name McCutcheon in northern Whitman County was familiar to almost everyone. He was a most colorful and vital figure in the lives of many high school students and their parents whom he had also taught.

Shane wove his way through the grade school experience with minimal shrapnel, developing two things: more friends like 'Finch, Gook, and Stag' and above-average athletic skills. Being in high school meant his sister was off to college and soon to be married.

Both brothers were college graduates from the only school worthy of their attendance, Ole Wazzu (Washington State University). One brother joined the army, and the other the corporate jungle. His dad, Ed, was 60+ and indeed senior to all the parents in Shane's class of 30. With siblings away, no one else could hear his fatherly prophet-driven messages such as "So much could get done if no one cared who got the credit." Among his most famous, that statement came out almost every time he talked about the ridiculous nature of politics. Much of his rural-powered, life-altering philosophies were illuminating, but the repetition wore thin on Shane. Elk had moved with his widowed mom to the big city. Shane missed him but knew that move would happen someday. Now Shane was navigating the hallways of a world full of caste system traditions of initiation rituals that accompany being a freshman in high school. The pranks and bully-driven calisthenics had tamed dramatically from the stories Shane heard from his brothers. One that concerned him most was the basketball initiation for incoming first-year students known as the "marshmallow cradle" ... The senior ball players would kick all the observers out of the gym, including the coaches. Sentinels guarded the entrance doors. The freshmen basketball players were commanded to strip to their jockstraps and tennis shoes and line up on the end line to run wind sprints. Once in place, they were blindfolded and handed a marshmallow. They were told by the head bully to "Take the marshmallow and cradle it in your butt cheeks" ... They were instructed to use their sphincter strength to hold their marshmallow while they ran a wind sprint to the other end of the gym. Further instruction was "the first to drop your marshmallow ... or cross the end line last, must eat everyone else's marshmallow". If you resisted, they would escort you blindfolded outside the locked high school entry with nothing on but your jockstrap and your hands taped behind your back. Like most rural scholastic legends, it grew with each event recall. Marshmallow consumption never happened, but the blindfold perpetuated the intrigue surrounding the hoax. Shane and Finch often talked about how they would fight the seniors like John Wayne in a Green Beret movie if this had happened to them. The prank didn't happen, but the visual orchestration and embellishment by Shane's brothers certainly did stimulate angst for their little brother.

McCutcheon was a self-selected bachelor in his early fifties. His appearance conjured thoughts of what 'Pig Pen' in the Peanuts cartoons looked like as an adult. He had an old growth mustache that caught at least a ¼ pound of pipe tobacco when he chewed. Occasionally he smoked it too. He would spit, often with surprising accuracy, into a gray steel, 5-gallon office trash can. While driving the school's half-ton 'vocational-ag' pickup, which he used like a personal vehicle, he imagined the gray can in the cab with him targeting the brown lumpy saliva somewhere close to the floor. This often included the dash, steering wheel, horn button, and heater controls resulting in rubber floor mats that looked like brown, short pile carpet when the expulsion had dried. One can see evidence of why he was single.

He was known for his off-the-record teachings about carnal intelligence and human propagation. Yet he was frank about how you were to treat the creatures of the opposite sex properly. All conversation was made with positive intent. While these off-curriculum lessons bordered on inappropriate and limited political correctness, Shane and the boys appreciated them. The reality was that these public service moments might be the only exposure to the ways of the world that most of them would get, except for listening to tawdry senior class locker room seminars. Once every four years, McCutcheon took students to visit the State Penitentiary under the auspices of learning what the institution was doing with its agricultural program. What the trip accomplished, however, was to allow kids to interact with inmates and realize that *the pen was no trip to the county fair*. Shane went on that trip as a sophomore, and while he had no issues, this trip helped cement the idea that being a nerdy student was a good path.

Many male post-teens who grow up in the rural culture are influenced by what they see in their communities. The formula for young men usually is one of the following:

a) Follow the path of working on their parent's farm (if they have one) with hopes of succession.
b) Go to work for a farmer in the community.
c) Support the farm community by working for the industries necessary for farmers, such as seed, fertilizer, grain handling, or fuel.
d) Go off to college with a higher than 50% chance of returning to the county for one of those mentioned above.

Shane imagined returning to the farm with at least one of his brothers and Dad. He would jokingly muse to his buddies about his future"Whitman County... farm my blues away".

McCutcheon was the bonfire of inspirational encouragement that could provide the stimulus which might alter a student's course.

McCutcheon was also the moonlighting driver education teacher. This was a way to earn additional income and public service to make Whitman County highways and bi-ways safer than wearing a flammable suit in a firefight. The boys who knew him well would tell their female classmates destined to take the driving course, who were unfamiliar with the mythical ag-teachin' creature known as McCutcheon about his tobacco habits. This graphic insight would provide angst like the marshmallow cradle. When

McCutcheon wanted to engrain something deeply into his students, he used a similar tactic as the go-jo example. To stress the importance of "staying on the road" in driver's education, he asked the question and had students chant along to enhance memorization and learning. He would say, "I need you to stay on the road. What is on the side of the road? HOLES, NAILS, GLASS, DEATH... HOLES, NAILS, GLASS, DEATH... HOLES, NAILS, GLASS, *DEATH...*" **Shane soon found that his dad and McCutcheon both used repetition as a practical learning aid.**

McCutcheon was also the advisor of the Future Farmers of America (FFA) chapter. FFA activities gave many students exposure to things beyond the seat of a tractor. More importantly, beyond the seat of a school desk. FFA included agricultural activities such as soils, livestock judging, parliamentary procedure (how to run a meeting), and public speaking. Shane eagerly got involved with them because it was an excellent substitute for building fences, cleaning hog barns, or servicing equipment...and sometimes it got you out of school. Shane was a sturdy farm hand driving a truck during wheat harvest since age six. He did this by standing on the seat of the two-ton GMC and driving the truck after an adult pulled out the manual dash throttle. The truck crawled across the field at the pace of a string of brood cows meandering across a pasture. Once the truck reached the intended location, he would shut off the key. Because of all the new FFA activities, Shane's dad Boxcar renamed it "Father Farms Alone." The good news was that Shane's middle brother had recently returned from the Army and was following the previously mentioned "path A" back to the farm. This welcome return freed Shane to engage more freely in athletics, club activities, and occasionally school.

Shane's dad liked McCutcheon, but he couldn't picture how all this family farm absenteeism due to FFA was impacting anything but his own personal increased workload. There was more progress here than could be measured. Shane, usually a reserved kid with limited oratory skills, was now doing speeches more like a standup comedy routine. Country spun masterpieces such as the "Real I.Q of Pigs" or "The Virtues of In-Door Plumbing" to a room of 40 + folks in a county FFA speech contest were truly bringing a unique personality into focus. While the content and delivery would never make the world forget JFK or MLK, his peers' organic laughter and applause only reinforced his pursuit. This six-foot tall chunk of human raw material was as naïve as a week-old weaner pig, but he was beginning to gain needed confidence.

Her name was 'Amanda.' Her two-year-old brother was challenged in saying her name, so he called her "ADAMNA," which stuck with many folks in the county. She was a cheerleader for one of the better basketball schools in Whitman County and lived about 20 miles away from Shane. Word got to Shane that she thought he was funny because she heard about the "Genius Pig FFA Speech." A mutual friend broke the ice for the two of them, and soon they were dating. She was a lovely young lady; if the county had a calendar of the "Girls of Whitman," she would be on it. All this was as new and nearly as refreshing as the adrenaline rush from a speech competition for Shane. When Shane's basketball team played the enemy team for whom Adamna was cheering, he was sure to be dialed in for an above-average performance so that Adamna's friends couldn't tease her about what a loser he was.

Nothing is as motivating as adolescent adoration. Like about a billion men before Shane, this had quite an evolutionary shape on the future and society. Shane, as you recall, was thinking about "path A" of returning to the farm. Trying to meet Adamna's expectations would end up challenging that. She was a very driven individual with parents very partial to education. She had known since age seven which college she would attend and probably had her 4-year class load charted out by age eleven. Shane realized he could not pursue a career as an "artist with a manure spreader" if he were going to continue his relationship with Adamna. At this point, if she had said she was joining the circus, Shane would have been at the tailor getting fitted for a clown suit. Shane was conflicted and went to the only place he knew to clear his head.... He went to see McCutcheon.

It was a Wednesday night, and McCutcheon returned to the shop to do lesson plans, grade papers, read the newspaper, and connect with his students from 7 to 10 p.m. three nights a week as long as there wasn't a basketball game. Shane started by telling McCutcheon he was thinking about going to college. McCutcheon, knew the value of an education and couldn't imagine Shane doing anything else. It was a long conversation by McCutcheon standards, but in 15 minutes, Shane decided he would attend college. He chose to emulate McCutcheon by getting an agricultural teaching degree and following his passion for basketball with a coaching certificate. Role models do make a difference. This would lead to options of coming back to the farm or allowing him to follow Adamna through some other uncomfortable metamorphosis.

The following year Shane was enrolled at Washington State University. Adamna was less than an hour away in her pre-planned learning, but it might have been in Greenland. Within two semesters, they had forgotten each other in a million distractions that come with higher education. And they had both become 'Cum Laude' in the extra-curricular on and off-campus frivolity.

McCutcheon always had his **exit motivation** closed-door discussion with his seniors just before graduation. Again, nothing was off limits, such as the helpful hint to college-bound first-year students, "NO NEED FOR FORNICATION... NO NEED FOR FORNICATION... NO NEED FOR FORNICATION". The discussion wandered down some paths worthy of getting the attention of a bloodthirsty attorney for a class action lawsuit or, indeed, of an overly protective mother. He would congratulate, embarrass and inspire everyone in the room.

He finished his speech with his *stemwinder* chant. "LIGHT THE FUSE ON YOUR LIFE!...LIGHT THE FUSE ON YOUR LIFE!...LIGHT THE FUSE ON YOUR LIFE!".

Shane's Learnings

On the impact that can come from others: Certain unexpected people can impact young people's lives. We can all make an impact on someone no matter what the oddity of our habits.

On how personal ownership can slow or increase progress: "So much could get done if no one cared who got the credit." If you have ever seen someone resist an idea, an initiative, or a project, they are often afraid that someone else will take credit for it. For things to happen, it is often essential to make it so that others can declare victory. In a corporate setting, one of the most critical parts of your job description that is not written is to: MAKE YOUR BOSS LOOK GOOD! Politicians are the worst example of this truism of life. Their full-time role when they get elected is to get re-elected. This results in infrequent collaboration between parties or even peers. In their artificial world, who gets credit is all that matters. If you want to get something done, restrain your ego and be surprised at how smoothly it goes. The good people will know your role without having to publicize it.

. . .

On the use of ways to drive cognitive imprinting: Repetitive learning in short bursts can stick with you for a lifetime. I still try to avoid driving in the ditch or removing the go-jo lid. To get your point across on the occasional memorable nugget, repeat it in an authoritative and out-of-character voice three times and pause to watch the effects.

On the use of laughter in everyday situations: Those who can make people laugh at themselves are endearing and appreciated by others. And sometimes, it can get you a date with one of the world's most beautiful creatures. I met my wife because of a good laugh.

On the motivation of infatuation: The influence of potential romance has changed the course of lives for generations. Since Adam and Eve and through Dark Ages, women's effect on men has profoundly impacted the world. Today women account for most of the world's non-commercial and feed store purchases. The policy has been changed, monarchies have been established or destroyed, and many of the bible's teachings were altered by the power of the female. Embrace their power, as they are so much wiser than men.

On the learning inside and out of the classroom: College rituals, as well as education in and outside of the school, can be the catalyst to unconsciously change the larva of a young person to a butterfly at a rapid pace. The only advice for the transformed is aggressively embracing every moment of it. Yep, you will be changed for the better.

. . .

On the legends and lore of hazing: Rural and scholastic rituals such as the marshmallow cradle or snipe hunting are typically a hoax designed to distract your mind into thinking they are real. The perpetrators of the event are counting on you to create the movie of doom in your head. Consider it one of life's non-cost learnings.

On Ag teacher pickups: If you are ever looking for a pickup in a used car lot, pass on the one with a couple of pounds of tobacco-steeped saliva coating the gauges and dash, and it may be advisable to avoid the brown shag carpet.

3

BOOTCH AND THE DREAMWEAVER

Shane's High School graduation class of 1976, now down to 25, hugged, toasted success, and randomly scattered, with some sense this may be the last time they see each other.

First-year College students experience some level of anxiety. Both Shane's brothers and sister did. His dad once commented, "They acted like weaned calves walkin' the fence line lookin' for their mother until they came home for Christmas break." This was another time when Dad was right. Shane had some discomfort in the first trimester of his college life. Another prominent event was that Shane noticed that after he left home, the hogs were gone. His first cynical thought was that they went off to college, but the more obvious fact was that one of their 'housekeepers' had gone to college.

The routine at college was simple. Study exhaustively and sometimes frantically during test periods to make the actual academic pain disappear. The payoff was to perform well enough to stick around to experience the extra-curricular life lessons, which were a hell of a lot more fun and would never happen around the home. Shane stimulated himself with caffeine to clear the academic hurdles, joined or started study groups, and made practice tests. These activities helped him stay in school, but he was prominently absent from the Dean's list.

So how did he get into Wazzu? Shane had done enough positive extra-curricular high school activities and was aided by a letter from his high school counselor, 'Godzilla.' He was an enormous human with enough body hair to construct a throw rug. He liked Shane and had the same interest in basketball. This recommendation would accompany Shane's 2.8-grade point average and probably was more than necessary for Shane to receive an academic slot at Washington State University.

Basketball for Shane these days typically involved an intramural game against the likes of such dynasties as the 'Allert Hall Shockers' or the Psych department's own 'Typecast Maniacs'. This was not unexpected as his 6'2" stature and his time in the 40-yard dash, which was best measured by a sundial, was not precisely what Pac-10 schools would ever be looking for in a player. He had enough gym rat contacts to be a support player on some of the more competitive intramural teams.

The first-year college *anxiety colic* of being away from home passed after the first Christmas, just as his dad Boxcar predicted. Two years flew by with many of the rituals of college life experienced at full throttle. Shane was now a college junior and constantly benefited from his many new exposures. His agriculture and education classes were needed to get his teaching certificate.

Shane was proud of one personal tactic: his self-invented '*Interpersonal Dragnet*.' The workings of this maneuver brought hundreds of new relationships. His new Rolodex of friends would often result in an extra 15 – 20 minutes to walk across the hilly campus because of the many acquaintances he would encounter.

Interpersonal Dragnet or I.D. he claimed was an antidote for communication complacency.

So, what is this *'Dragnet'* deal? You can get 3 TV channels in rural America on the black-and-white Magnavox. Some of the programs were often absent meaningful content. This meant you often watched masterpieces like **Perry Mason** or the drivel of **Petticoat Junction**. Any person in rural America knew those Petticoat Junction clowns were not how country people would want to be recognized. However, as a young adolescent male, you watched the three beautiful sisters from the Shady Rest Hotel and fantasized about taking one to the Prom.

One of the more essential rerun icons that inspired Shane was Joe Friday of the classic show **Dragnet**. Joe appeared to have sprayed heavy starch on his hair. The only thing stiffer than his hair was his battleship gray sport coat, white shirt, and of course, ALWAYS a black yardstick tie. Joe was the alpha cop who would drag along his partner Bill Gannon, who looked more like a grandfather that was along to sell vacuum cleaners.

What Shane loved about the show was that during each episode, Joe methodically interrogated a show character playing a degenerate citizen about their involvement in some inner-city mischief. Joe could discover everything he wanted to know in less than two minutes with aggressive probing questions and heavily biased dialogue.

Shane reasoned that if this system could perform for a pillar of Hollywood, he could playfully engage and befriend almost anyone with the alchemy of the Joe Friday playbook. With this approach, he could find out enough to expand his catalog of contemporaries.

Shane's pragmatic, unscientific logic was:

1. Most people are shy but don't necessarily want to be.

2. College students who are stressed and in a confusing environment still want to feel important.
3. Confidence comes from talking about a subject with which they have some expertise.
4. The subject about which folks have the most expertise is simply themselves and their environment.

Thus, the *Interpersonal Dragnet* was born.

So how do you apply it? If Shane was at a party or event, he would approach someone with a smile that made his face look like it was more than half teeth. He would then break the ice with, "Do you know who Joe Friday is?" Whether they knew Dragnet star or not, he would playfully say that in 4 to 5 questions, Joe Friday could uncover enough information about someone to transform them from total strangers to colleagues in less than ten minutes. He always asked, "Would you like to try it out?" To the participant, it smelled much like asking many random silly questions. But it was relational dogma magic in the hands of a youthful, rural pioneer adorned in railroad-style bibbed overalls.

The playlist of questions he had groomed from many unstimulating hours on a tractor seat could come out in random order depending on the connection of the participant's response. If he were even vaguely unfamiliar with the person, he would usually start with:

"What is the city (area, town, county, State, Country) that you call home best known for?" The first insight he picked up when he did this was: that they would always tell you where that was without having to pry or ask the impersonal awkward question of "Where are you from?" The participant would usually smile and drift off to their home-based mental database.

Shane often received the Chamber of Commerce gift-wrapped

answers like: "I am from Snortopia, and we were the first city to have a Waffle Barn franchise." Or "I am from Devil's Elbow, and we are the gingivitis capital of the world." This easy-access question engaged them, and participation was quick, with most of their defense mechanisms disarmed. He could also ascertain their level of pride for their hometown by the enthusiasm in their answer.

In true Joe Friday rapid-fire fashion, he would follow directly on the heels of that answer with another question.

<u>"Who is the most famous person from or that ever visited the area you are from?"</u> Shane wouldn't let them off the hook if they couldn't think of someone. He would force them to voice someone like the butcher or mayor. In Shane's hometown, McCutchen, the Ag teacher, might have gotten a vote. Unless the reason for the fame was apparent, the participant would always volunteer what made the person named famous. There is no pattern to the fame answer. However, famous people must come from somewhere. For example, "Lawrence Welk used the bathroom at our local hardware store once on a tour bus stop." The beauty of this approach is that if the person they name is famous and Shane knows who they are, there is an instant commonality between the questioner and participant.

It becomes more evident if you momentarily analyze how these two questions might benefit Shane's college connection portfolio and apply Uncle Bo's nickname system. In less time than it takes to burn a cheese sandwich, Shane had a connection with these folks on campus that most others wouldn't... and he most likely won't even know or remember their name. So, the next time he sees one of these people he questioned while walking on campus, he can address them by the name of the famous person among them. Some examples: "Hey, Lawrence Welk," or their Hometown, "Snortopia, greetings," or the central attribute of the town, "There is my man, Waffle Barn," or "Yo, Gingivitis."

Returning to the questioning approach of Interpersonal Dragnet, the next step would be to broaden the openness of the question but make it about themselves and their experiences.

"What has been the best day of your life so far?" There was, of course, much contemplation by the participant because of the depth and personal nature of the question. It would also take a bit of a back story, setup, and explanation, all adding to the growing connection. As this was shared, one of the bookends of their life is revealed. Asking about the worst day would take people to a dark place and suppress most other discussions. Best to be always positive and even better to be a bit whimsical.

Next added to the mix was "What is the best practical joke you have ever played on someone?" Shane reasoned you could tell much about someone in their answer, including: How creative are they? What do they see as the proper boundary for fun? How well they tell a story as this requires set-up and explanation.

He would add if he still had a willing participant and enough time. "You will win the lottery tomorrow; what will you do with the money this summer?" The reason for the boundary on the question is to eliminate the easy answer that they would quit college tomorrow. So the summer break parameter helps to understand travel, free time pursuits, or even charity.

Shane ended with one targeted question that got into how people see themselves.

With the sixth question, he would go for the crown. "So let's say I interviewed your best friend and asked them to tell me about you. What would they say?"

By this time, they will feel comfortable enough to share what they think of themselves by speculating through the eyes of their best friends. 'Interpersonal Dragnet' customarily ended with the other person saying, "OK, now it is my turn," and the questioning would take on a reverse approach to Shane. Mission accomplished, and an improved connection was established by two people with higher learning in common.

Human relations were the only area where Shane had a shot at being Valedictorian, and the 'Dragnet' was on the menu quite frequently. He playfully claimed he had patents and iron-clad trademark protection on it.

He saw 'Adamna' occasionally at a party or event that featured the rival schools they attended. She was engaged to a guy best classified as utterly resistant to any Dragnet Serum. Separation time and study stress healed a lot of potential bad feelings between them.

No loss, no pain ... all good.

While occupying the campus library with aimless pursuit one evening, Shane had a mid-college revelation that ***life was like a library***.

He reasoned that all the books in the library were the people you would meet. This seemed like an unusual comparison since Shane was not an avid reader. He did know that when he got hold of a book he truly enjoyed, each page exposed him to new experiences. He made a correlation when meeting others, and he applied a liberal dose of Interpersonal Dragnet to further contact. They shared chapters much more colorful than almost any novel.

Some examples of the book to Dragnet comparison: he found out that 'Cooter,' a sophomore fraternity man from Paola, Kansas, was a ping pong prodigy whose parents toured as the road crew for the legendary band 'Foghat.' And there was a young lady that proudly flaunted the moniker of 'Cereal Killer' because that is all she ever ate. She frequently fantasized about being a reptile curator in a South American zoo. Her "famous guy," her great grandfather, had established National Peanut Butter Sandwich Day to stimulate sales for their 'Smoothola peanut butter empire.'

It was amazing how many pages he could turn and what he

would find due to questions that rolled out of the mythical Interpersonal Dragnet. God protect Joe Friday and the ever-potent 'I.D.'

One of the student celebrities Shane connected with as a result of 'I.D.' was 'Fronk, the Wheat Gangsta.' He learned many developmental lessons from Fronk, whose nickname was shortened to 'F.W.G.' Fronk, like Shane, was a Washington wheat farm kid. He was a very athletic gymnast, and at every Cougar football and basketball game, pep rally, and alumni event, he would take on the persona of the school mascot, 'Butch the Cougar.'

Butch was beyond the typical gigantic-headed mascot that reminded you of an onion pulled from the ground and turned tuber up. F.W.G.'s physique was chiseled like a Division Two linebacker. His build made the costume that much more lifelike. The Mascot with a lengthy heritage was called 'Butch' after the actual live animal cougars that were taken, heavily tethered, onto the field during football games. The original live cat Butch inhabited a far too primitive and confining cage for such a majestic animal in the center of the campus. Due to the compromised life of these animals and the fear of Butch jumping into the stands to maul a drunk co-ed, wisely, it was decided that a human mascot would be utilized.

F.W.G. was the second tenant in this majestic feline likeness. Shane saw the costume at Fronk's apartment up close. He knew better than to ask to wear it. Doing so would be like a cub scout guarding the tomb of the Unknown Soldier. There are no 'posers' for Butch. Shane did notice how weathered and worn the costume looked when you got closer to it. He thought if it were alive, a trip to the dentist and a thorough review by the Animal Science department might be in order.

One of the lessons Fronk shared with Shane regarding wearing the costume was that if he wasn't smiling and excited inside the costume, 'melancholy' would ooze out of the costume's pores. Fronk claimed that exact phenomenon applied to the humans you meet every day. Fronk compressed the thought: An unenthusiastic inside will come across as a carcass. He continued, "I can tell by the volume and the length of the crowd's cheer of 'BOOOOOOOOTTTTTCHH' how well I am doing, and I adjust my inner smile based on that feedback."

The philosophy fits squarely into the enthusiasm portion of Shane's theory of the Interpersonal Dragnet questioning pattern. Shane didn't think he could phone home and tell his dad he was getting essential life lessons from a mascot with a faux skin ailment and tooth decay.

Fronk addressed how Shane's study habits were over the top "Why do you abuse yourself studying like that?" he questioned. Shane playfully replied that he was deathly afraid of having to clean out hog barns for the rest of his life, especially now that he had gotten a taste of the world off the farm. He wanted to do anything to stay in school. Even though the family hogs were gone, the smell still haunted him.

Fronk took an unusual tact by asking Shane a left-field question"Have you seen the new Chevy's?" Shane realized that Fronk was headed to 'sage philosopher mascot' mode.

Shane was a Camaro nut since they had come out more than a dozen years prior and answered, "Yes."

"Isn't that new Camaro commercial great?" asked Fronk. Shane acknowledged curiously, as he didn't know where his peer was taking him.

Fronk continued aggressively and deliberately, asking, "Do you remember the 'gear ratio' from the ad?"

Tentative as he contemplated, Shane replied, "No." Fronk then said, "Wheelbase specs?"

Same answer from Shane "No."

"Compression ratio?" "Turning radius?" "Fuel tank capacity?" Each time he didn't answer, it was no. Shane had been with him long enough to know the Ward Cleaver learning moment from ***Leave it to Beaver*** was just around the corner.

"Why didn't you get all that out of the ad?" pressed Fronk.

Shane responded, "Because it wasn't there."

"Why not?" Fronk chuckled, now wryly smiling.

Shane said, "I don't know why, but my guess is there was more important stuff they wanted to tell the potential buyer?"

"Great answer! So why are you cramming that superfluous stuff into your head while studying for a test?" Fronk continued. Shane stood there, tingling as he realized where Fronk was going"I watch you stay up all night funneling academic trash into your head." He expanded by saying his experience has been that if you jam too much stuff into a box, you have a tough time getting it out.

Fronk continued, "The same is true with your brain and all that endurance studying." Shane had watched Fronk's pre-exam ritual the evening before a test and thought he was crazy for his less-than-athletic studying decorum. While Shane and the study group attempted to imprint themselves with deep, detailed memorization, Fronk would get something to eat and a beer if he could served at a local establishment. He would then come home and locate his class notes and a textbook, thumb through them for 20-30 minutes, collapse his class notes, and announce to the room with a generous swagger that he was "headed to bed." He was nearly a 4-point student.

After recovering from the Camaro ad discussion, Shane asked him how he did the twenty-minute once-over and why?

Fronk said with the conviction of a trial lawyer, "Basically, you only have room for three things in your mind on a subject. Remember the Camaro ad? They brought you car images with people driving, smiling, and having fun, and listening to popular music. That is what they wanted you to remember."

He pointed out that students often ***overconsume*** facts beyond three critical elements on a subject just as one hits the law of diminishing returns. Fronk continued to prove a point, "You have some association with the church, so holler out the Ten Commandments for me." Shane was starting to get to the end as his mind went blank after no killing, no stealing, and no lust for thy neighbor's wife. Fronk was now full throttle and increasingly aggressive in making his point.

"Curly, Larry, and Moe, who are they?"

Shane replied that this was like third-grade math, "The 3 Stooges, of course".

Fronk was now evangelizing, "How many wise men were there?" ending that question with a dead man's pause.

Shane now answered more to defend himself, "Three."

"Yep, you notice they didn't trust such an important event to a battalion because no one would ever remember the story."

"How many Olympic medals do they give?" Same answer.

Fronk now in a triple-decker frenzy exclaimed, "**The Bee-gees, The Good, the Bad and the Ugly, Apollo 13 crew**,…if you would add another member to any of them, they are all forgotten". He continued, "How many members of *"Earth, Wind and Fire"* are there"? A long pause ensued. He finished the thought, "That's right, nobody knows, but you notice that they only have three nouns in their name."

Shane didn't want to break Fronk's conviction, but the most popular band ever, The Beatles, had four members, and people knew more about them than just about anyone in the world. Shane rationalized that by bringing up that fact, he could be entwined in some Pete Best/Ringo Starr discussion with potential to turn foul.

He stated that there is "Power in the number three."

Fronk wrapped it by saying, "That is my quantum theory on studying, and if I don't do well on a test, I can tell the world I over-studied" ... "Gotta keep it simple." Shane noticed Fronk always delivered his pearls to the commoner, *three portions at a time.*

Later that winter Shane, 'Lugnut,' 'Scooter' and 'Brother Vern' were with a group of heavily Revlon-ed girls from 'Mega Delta Whatever' sorority. Seated eight rows up in the student section, they enjoyed the great basketball action between UCLA and the Cougs who led most of the way. At one particular break in the game action, following a thunderous dunk by an awkward 7-foot Coug center known as the "Vanilla Gorilla," the crowd was going crazy. 'F.W.G' made Butch come alive on the court in a fashion that would make Marlin Perkins, the Mutual of Omaha safari guy, stay in his truck. The crowd cranked well above 90 decibels, clapped deliriously, and chanted in unison, "BBBOOOOOOOTTTTCCHHH." One of the sorority manikins screamed into Shane's ear, competing with the WSU fight song from the band, "I swear, Butch is having so much fun he looks like he is smiling out there." Shane nodded and thought to himself, 'I guarantee it.'

At a basketball game after party at 'Sumo's' apartment Shane offered the Blue-Plate Special helping of Interpersonal Dragnet to several attendees.

He met a *poli-sci* major he sarcastically called 'Reagan' because Shane knew he would hate it. This guy wanted to legalize all drugs, collect one-third of the tax money, and distribute it to the unemployed, and thought it a worthy idea to allow pets to vote. The great thing about the 'I.D.' was, as the pharmacist, Shane could shut off the 'I.D. serum' whenever he wanted. This was one of those times.

'Sumo' was a guy that Shane knew well from class projects. He got tagged with that name because of the irony in his stature. At 5 foot 4 and 125 pounds it seemed *'Uncle Bo appropriate'* to tag him with Sumo. Sumo asked Shane, "Any plans for summer internships?"

"Nah," replied Shane, "I gotta drive a combine for my dad."

Sumo filled in more detail. "The Alumni Animal Nutrition Company is coming a week from Thursday to the Butte restaurant to tell folks about their internship with their company. I know 'Mayor Zim' can get you on the attendees list if you want to go."

'Zim the Mayor' was the head of the Agricultural Education department and a great guy. He was Shane's advisor and could be considered McCutcheon Lite.

"I appreciate it, man, but my sled for the summer is a John Deere 6602 hillside combine," said Shane, even though it did seem a bit compelling for a fleeting moment.

Later that week, as he walked across campus between classes, he ran into Mayor Zim.

"Hey, Mr. Zimmer," Shane called out. (When it is the head of the department who can certainly shape a lot of your future, you call him by his proper name).

"Just the man I am looking for; I need to see you in my office at 3:00 PM today. Can you make it?" Zim said relatively formally.

"Yes sir, see you at three."

At 3:00 P.M., Shane was in the Ag Education building waiting area dressed in his frequently displayed 'rugged rural' collection. This ensemble of pinstriped railroad blue bibbed overalls accented with the ever-present WSU ball cap and closely matching t-shirt or sweatshirt, depending on the climate. His clean, shoulder-length brown hair, parted in the middle, but hidden by his hat and small **Goose Gossage** goatee mustache, eliminated him from nearly 50 % of all job opportunities. Zim was only mildly aware and fully unconcerned about Shane's appearance. Being closely engaged with college kids can make you numb. He probably would love to switch places with Shane. If not for the wardrobe, certainly for the 23-year age difference. Mr. Zimmer was known as the 'mayor' of Ag Education City because of his frequent reference to 'Ag Tomorrow Land' in his teaching curriculum.

Straight ahead, as he always was, Zim said, "Mr. Engineer (referring to Shane's bibs), I need you to do me a favor."

"Sure"

"There is a guy who is one of the head guys at Alumni Animal Nutrition Company coming to talk about their intern program next week. I need you to go and represent the Ag Education department."

Shane, for once, was silent.

The mayor continued. "It looks bad if our department doesn't have someone attend when such a high-profile outfit as Alumni comes to town." Zim realized by the puzzled looks that he would have to start selling a little. "It is an honor to be asked to attend, and it will be a fabulous experience." Then he changed bait, like trying to coerce a bass off her nest, and threw one of the most effective attractants in front of a college student. "There is a free lunch at the Butte Restaurant."

With a mischievously wry smile, Zim knew he had him, so he thought he would do a little end zone dance on Shane by saying, "Will you do it, or do you have to run a train to Spokane that day?" as another poke at Shane's wardrobe.

"I'm your man" Shane smiled as Fronk had schooled, but internally he was hiding a heavy quota of angst.

Zim gave a few more details beyond time and place: "Do you have anything to wear besides this Osh-Kosh stuff? Suit and tie?"

"I will figure something out," said Shane. In college junior speak, that meant reviewing a Little Black Book titled **From Whom Can I Borrow?**

"I will not tell you about the guys you will meet there or what to say or how to act. That will make it an even more meaningful experience." Zim continued, "I doubt they will want an ag teacher.

These corporations know there is a high possibility that ag-ed students go into the State educational school system". His tone was either to challenge Shane to go for it or to prepare him for disappointment. Shane couldn't tell. "And besides, it's your life." 'Zim' summarized, "So throw out some of that '**Dragnet Joe Friday hullabaloo**' or whatever you call it and see what happens."

Shane sat in front of 'Zim' with his mouth open, visibly paused at that last statement. He couldn't imagine how the head of the department would know about something Shane had viewed as personal, let alone referencing it so irreverently. Since he had never directly told Zim about his questioning hobby, it was a great lesson in that all people, including your friends, talk about others with both positive and harmful intent. Puzzling Shane was in what light Zim received the info? Shane soon rationalized that Zim, the Mayor wouldn't be offering the intern appearance if he viewed him as demented.

The time was approaching for the Alumni Nutrition event, which lampooned by Shane as the 'Animal Feed Beauty Contest Luncheon.' Shane made a list of what he needed to do before that event. His friend 'Chewbacca,' of a similar build to Shane, allowed him to borrow a sport coat. He was a great guy with an insatiable appetite for everything about Star Wars. The lending cost for Shane was a box of 'Storm Trooper cereal.' Coincidentally, it is one of the products made by Alumni's human food division, a fact discovered in the Alumni Nutrition background research Shane was asked to do by Zim. That was the second thing on the list. The last task was a resume. The counseling service at the college helped him put it together. The 2½ years of college coursework and farm labor at his dad's farm resembled graffiti on the big easel of his resume. The resume font from the Corona typewriter barely filled half of a page. Shane had seen more impressive grocery lists. Zim reassured him that a novel was not what they were seeking.

All the class notes and tests were completed in advance of the Alumni Feed event so Shane could skip classes for that Thursday luncheon. Enough research had been done about Alumni Feed so as not to embarrass himself. Strategic shaving highlighted the Foo Man Choo mustache. His hair length was still **militarily objectionable** but clean. Shane thought about the impression Joe Namath's appearance had made on his generation as he combed it.

With the echo of a former coach screaming about 'Lombardi time' rolling through his head Shane arrived 15 minutes early. He had only been to the Butte restaurant once previously for a formal Sorority function. He was unsure which event was most anxiety-inducing.

Hydrox cookie brown wood paneling, seasoned with second-hand smoke, covered the hallway to the banquet room—the hallway collected over twenty junior and sophomore students. Shane knew most of them from agricultural classes and graciously straightened his buddy 'Duroc's' lightly starched shirt collar from his errant necktie execution. Duroc had bright red hair, which resembled the similar red color of Shane's favorite breed of hogs. Duroc's family raised a bunch of hogs in the center of the state, which made **this nickname** fit him even better.

The doors opened to the low-ceiling banquet room with a U-shaped table and a projector centered between the two most extended table arms. There was a table outside the U design with printed material about Alumni Nutrition. The most redeeming element of a restaurant, past its prime, is the view with full-length glass windows overlooking the Palouse. Steptoe Butte looked like an irritated warble on a bull's back from this distance.

As Shane walked through the door, a barrel-chested man in his early 50s with a full head of silver hair and dressed in a much nicer sport coat than Chewbacca's, reached out and grabbed his hand. He sported an 'I just ate a banana sideways' smile that reminded him of

Fronk and the mascot discussion. What happened next was nothing short of amazing. He said, "You must be Shane?" Now it was more than a bit unnerving that this guy knew his name.

"Yes sir," now shaking his hand with a firm grip and looking him in his hazel-colored eyes as McCutcheon had taught him in the high school dark ages. He thought to himself, how did this guy know my name? Was it Zim? Did another student tell him?' He had to ask"I am curious how you knew my name?". His answer revealed the tension Shane was feeling.

"Your name tag; you are the only one without one," he replied. Shane was so wound up that he had forgotten to put it on in the hallway, and his was the only remaining name tag. Shane's mind was racing as he had officially embarrassed Zim, and lunch had yet to be served.

"Ronald Gilmour with Alumni Feed," he said in a way that would help Shane move past one of the most awkward exchanges of his entire life.

"Mr. Gilmour, it is a pleasure to meet you."

They exchanged a few other bits of discussion about Shane's college major and where he was from. The co-op with the feed mill that manufactured those great aromas in Shane's town was from an Alumni Feed dealer. Mr. Gilmour deftly moved onto the others in the room, introducing himself.

Two other younger men in suits from Alumni were also working the room. They asked many questions and developed some college connections through their small talk to make the crowd feel more relaxed. They are bright fellas with some "Dragnet" training somewhere in their careers.

A coma-inducing roast beef lunch that a college dorm couldn't dream of the offering was served after Mr. Gilmour's introductory comments.

Following lunch, Mr. Gilmour began to surgically enchant the room with his excellent command of the English language draped behind his vast but sincere smile. He talked of higher callings, personal growth and wealth, and interaction with great people and weaved it around the Alumni Animal Nutrition message. He then ran a short film with a sixteen-millimeter projector highlighting important information about Alumni and how it was working to feed the world. Lots of beautiful imagery, great music, and smiling people engaging customers. The audio that competed with the clicking of the reel-to-reel film was narrated by the canyon-echoing voice of James Arness of Gunsmoke television fame and gave insights into the history and future of the Alumni organization:

"The Galbreath family founded the Alumni Animal Nutrition empire in 1922 in Gasconade County, Missouri. W.T. Galbreath was a Professor of Nutrition emeritus at Purdue University who ventured daringly into the entrepreneurial world of animal nutrition. His vision and drive was to create products that improved the lives of farmers and consumers alike. This desire led to much innovation at the company's foundation and an impressive staff at his 4000-acre Oklahoma research farm near Broken Arrow. The Broken Arrow facility is named "Prerequisite Ranch" because it does the necessary advanced work before it arrives on the market" Prerequisite" features state-of-the-art research facilities for swine, dairy, beef cattle, and horses and as broad a companion/pet research and grain utilization experimental lab as exists today. The work of the dedicated people behind the scenes at Alumni has led to the development of some of agriculture's most storied line of products. Such as the feed starter product lineup for different species marketed under the 'Freshman' brand name or the largest selling brand of growth diets for animals, sold under the 'Syllabus' label. A proprietary record-keeping system for animal owners named 'Transcript' is today the standard by which all others are measured. The network of products and business units that are part of the Alumni Association Inc. organization is vast. Holdings include sourcing

grain and protein, human vitamins, and distribution of a full line of garden supplies. Alumni also have the nation's first and largest fully integrated barbeque supply organization, including a lineup of fresh pork and beef cuts fed Alumni diets, sauces, and equipment under the "Fred of Como" brand label. Through depressions and golden eras of agriculture, the "Mortar Board" logo of Alumni Nutrition and Alumni Holdings has been signified as the symbol of high-quality, value-added products. This innovation comes from staying close to consumers to develop leading-edge knowledge systems at the corporate, dealer, and consumer levels. Alumni Nutrition Dealers are individually selected and highly respected in their community for their profound knowledge base and willingness to help consumers and give back to the essential things in their local communities.

Alumni today is a leader in agribusiness and consumer foods. With over 5000 employees, they have a straightforward driving mission instilled from Dr. Galbreath's teaching background "learn something new every day." Alumni Nutrition employees have been challenged to be as comfortable in the coffee shop with a customer as they are integrating their knowledge-based platform with leaders of foreign countries. All great societies' success has been charted through history on two significant themes: Nutrition to strengthen their masses and Education for growth. Come join an organization that has combined the two. Alumni Nutrition and Alumni Holdings "a smart investment in your future."

As the film projector finished the movie, the collection reel sped up, and the excess film at the end flapped in rhythm. After halting the projector windup, Mr. Gilmour took center stage at the front of the table openings. His presence was similar to a ringmaster in a circus, but with a much more charismatic and commanding presence than most of the teachers Shane had experienced.

"I want to thank each of you for coming and mention to you that the opportunities that await your generation are the greatest in the history of the world." He didn't stop there. "You will experience things in your life and working career that the generation before you could never imagine." He was now working the room with the vigor of somewhere between a revival evangelist and trial attorney in the final summation. "You will endure more change; you will be exposed to more opportunity, and you will bank more prosperity (here he turned on the high-beam grin of his). if you challenge yourself to learn something new every day and have the ambition to dream," He related it to the film they had just seen and the words of the founder of Alumni, Dr. Galbreath.

The more Shane listened to this gentleman, the more interested he became in his proposal. Prosperity didn't sound bad. Being your own *'entrepreneurial self'* inside the brand strength of a significant agriculture conglomerate seemed different. And on a more personal point, it sounded like it offered experiences well beyond the end of a 'hog cleaning shovel'. Sometimes we never know where a thought comes from, but as Shane drifted along in an imaginary overload of unsuppressed success as a by-product of what he had heard from Mr. Gilmour, the song *"Dreamweaver"* from Gary Wright crept into his head. Taking a page from Uncle Bo, at that instant, Mr. Gilmour now had a nickname.

The Alumni intern experience was during the summer and Mr. Gilmour positioned it as a test drive for the participant and the company. "You can see how you like sales and our organization, and we see how you fit with what we are looking for in future employees." Shane was struggling a bit with the idea of sales being a profession, and it was like **the Dreamweaver** had sensed that and asked the room a question. "How many of you think you can sell something?" About 1/3 of the attendees raised their hand as Shane was still wrestling with the lyrics to the Gary Wright song and abstained.

"Ok," says the Dreamweaver, "How many of you have a spouse or significant other?". Nearly all the room raised their hand; Shane did too but was fudging on the significant part. "So, with your wife or significant other, have you ever convinced them to eat somewhere, see a movie, or do something you wanted to do.... even though you knew they didn't want to. Or have you talked them out of something they wanted to do?" ... The room filled with snickers, and he was smiling and exceptionally pleased with himself and, with the reaction, said, "See, you are all salespeople."

He explained that he was looking for one intern for the company's West Coast Region and would also be visiting Oregon State University and U.C. Davis. Shane's somewhat surprising, elevated interest in such an assignment took a bit of a kick in the undercarriage. It would be tough enough for him even to get a chance to interview for a role at W.S.U. let alone with two other schools in the mix. The afternoon wore on as waves of now overly eager students tried to impress with clumsy handshakes and manufactured enthusiasm. Shane thanked Mr. Gilmour and enjoyed his time with the two gentlemen he brought along with him. They had only been out of school a couple of years, but their professional approach and the fact that their suits actually looked appropriate, not borrowed, was a quick way to pick them out of the crowd.

Shane left the Alumni Feed event to go home to change attire for a big casino night to raise money for the Ag Education department. He was going to be a pit boss for the blackjack tables. He thought to himself as he left that he had already won as he had eaten a free lunch. The more immediate issue was getting that **'Dreamweaver'** song out of his head.

The casino night was a huge hit, and Shane's tables brought in nearly enough to fund the annual "Carnivore and Cobbler Festival." This was an even more significant event than most campus associations, dorms, and Greek organizations participated in. Volunteers prepared meat dishes and desserts; students and potential employers bought tickets to sample a portion of the offerings. The event was as much a mixer as a fundraiser. Featured at the festival was the traditional fare of beef, chicken, turkey, or pork, accented by ostrich and bison. The unique item was '**Finnerty Hall Gator Tail,**' sent from Florida and prepared in a sweet and tart lemon/molasses marinade. On the dessert table were gooseberry cobbler, raspberry chocolate pudding pie, and homemade sweet corn ice cream offered by the Brock and Bridle rodeo club. At casino night, a couple of students were at the Alumni lunch. Shane's buddy 'Urinal Cake' (yep, he always felt like he was getting hosed) said in his normal down-beat tone, "I will never hear from those Alumni guys, but man, do they ever have some cool stuff happening." He claimed he knew a guy whose cousin worked for them and was making "eighty-five large" per year living in the Dakotas. Like his friend, Shane surmised that he wouldn't be hearing from Alumni any time soon.

A month passed, and at the end of Zim, the Mayor's class on teaching welding dynamics, he stopped Shane and said, "I got a call from Mr. Gilmour at Alumni Feed, and he would like to interview you next week."

Shane's expressive side kicked in and bleated out, "***Ooooh, Dreamweaver, I believe we can make it through the night***" Gary Wright would have been disgusted, 'Zim' was just confused.

"Inside joke," Shane offered Zim to explain away the unusual outburst, but 'Zim' had more important things to do than to come out and play with some college junior.

"He left his number and wants you to call him in the next day or so."

"Okay, I guess I better."

"It will be a good experience to interview," said Zim and then, feeling overly generous Zim offered the Ag Education department office and phone from where he could make the call. He said, "I would do it today or tomorrow to show that you are interested."

Shane worried all night about making the call to the

Dreamweaver. Was he doing the right thing? Would he be seen as a clown? He had never been to an interview before, and what was he supposed to do? Was his teaching and basketball coaching career in jeopardy? Could he really sell anything? He didn't even want to think about the most significant hurdle ahead.

He talked to Fronk the Wheat Gangsta, who told him he needed to go for it. His logic was that the chance of regret in the future was inversely proportional to the amount of angst he felt today. Shane acted like he had heard that before or remotely understood it. Both would be considered lies. Fronk did give him some coaching on the interview. His experience in the mascot costume had taught him that you need to be yourself, as they can tell if you are faking it.

The call to the Spokane office of Mr. Gilmour was answered by his personable assistant Ms. Tempo. "Alumni Nutrition, Ronald Gilmour's office, Mary Tempo speaking."

Shane was as nervous as if he was calling for his first date and didn't even use his last name. "Hello, ah, hello, yes, this is Shane from Washington State University; Mr. Gilmour asked me to call him."

"So, you are Shane?"

"Yes, ma'am." Short answers seemed safer.

"Well, Ronald told me about the great meeting and the fine candidates he met on his trip to Wazzu. How goes everything in Pullman?"

"Go Cougs" was all he could come up with.

Ms. Tempo laughed out loud, sensing Shane's tension, and said, "That is exactly what they used to say when I went to school there."

Shane knew better than to ask **when** she attended, so he nervously said the next stupidest thing he probably could have said, "Well, I appreciate all your generation did for us to continue to be here, ma'am."

Ms. Tempo went along as not to embarrass him and almost

laughed when she said, "Yes, so many sacrifices by us pioneers." Shane pictured that she probably had been to a 20-year reunion.

She was highly professional, polite, and disarming with her quick wit. It was like having a conversation with his sister.

She made the appointment for Shane and the Dreamweaver to meet for lunch at the Butte restaurant in a week. Shane thought that because of the location's repeat nature, Dreamweaver might have a club card there.

He found out Chewbacca not only had a sports coat but also had a suit, and for a fee of two boxes of 'Storm Trooper cereal,' Shane was flirting with a spot in GQ, the Farmer's edition. In the coat pocket of the borrowed suit was a book of tickets to "Carnivore and Cobbler" with six tickets remaining. That was about the same number previously sold with their stubs stapled on the edge. He decided to leave them in the coat pocket and remind Chewbacca that they were there.

Shane got his hair shaped just enough that he wouldn't lie if anyone asked him if he got it cut. He still looked more like he was going to Woodstock than an interview. Keeping *Fronk's power-of-three* in mind, he didn't over-study for the interview. However, he prepared some questions to show interest in the role and specifics on how the summer might go.

As Shane walked into the Butte restaurant, the song **"Muskrat Love"** played elevator-style across the ceiling-mounted speakers. He thought he had no idea you could make that song more repulsive. He asked a hostess where the 'Tekoa room' was located. That was where he was to meet for the Dreamweaver encore. Shane entered quickly, surmised that Ronald Gilmour was more comfortable with an entourage. He again had two other gentlemen accompanying him that Shane imagined would be handing scalpels and running the anesthesia during the intern surgery that 'Dr. Gilmour' was about to undertake.

He met Shane with a firm handshake and appeared happy to see him as a jug of water to a dehydrated desert walker. "Shane, it is great to see you again. That suit looks good on you". Shane picked up that he might have been getting his pumpkin carved just a bit, but he wasn't offended.

"Thanks, Mr. Gilmour; it is amazing what a couple of boxes of cereal will allow you to rent." He explained his deal with Chewbacca; all three thought it was hilarious. One of the gentlemen commented that he had borrowed a suit when interviewing over 15 years ago at Oregon State. This encouraged Shane to follow Fronk's advice and lay it out like a confessional. With all the activity and his nerve generating an elevated heart rate, Shane couldn't exactly remember the names of the two guys. The one from OSU quickly became 'Bucky the Beaver' (OSU's mascot), and the other much younger man from Kansas State became 'Manhattan' because of the location of the university in Kansas. It was ok to **think** of those nicknames, just don't say them.

Shane commented on how nice Mary Tempo was on the phone. Ronald said, "She enjoyed talking to you as well."

"Hope I get to meet her someday." He realized after he said it that this was a bit presumptuous. It was evident that the Dreamweaver didn't feel any pressure.

He began the incision, "Tell me about your life before college and go back as far as you feel comfortable."

Shane talked about childhood in Whitman County, farm life, the loss of his mom, and the impressive work of his dad raising four kids without a wife. He talked about the pride of being a "C" student, which made 'Bucky the Beaver' smile. He talked about sports, driving combine, FFA, McCutcheon, and the aversion to hog odor that he had developed.

'Manhattan' jumped in with the standard bearer question, "What are your goals for yourself?" Shane said," Ag teacher, coach, and avenge a hungry planet." Sounded like a canned enough answer to a canned question.

"What is the biggest risk you ever took?" asked Bucky.

"Attending college at all," Shane said, "I thought my lot in life was to work on the farm, and I still might, but a 2.8 high school GPA doesn't instill much confidence, so I guess that would be it".

The 'Beaver' was now in a smile competition with Gilmour as he added "I was the same way. A farm kid that got enlightened". Shane thought Bucky would end his proclamation by standing with his fist in the air and yelling, "C Students unite!".

They liked Shane's work ethic, his savvy for a college kid, and his style...here is who I am with no suck-up. An hour of good conversation had passed when his turn came. He asked a few insightful questions about how Alumni operated. He also asked the three gentlemen why they were with Alumni. Their responses followed the path of working with great people who wanted to achieve; enormous potential for economic returns; and "learning something new each day." We then spent some time backtracking and talking about the intern role. Shane learned that from June 1 to August 15, a project would be assigned and that the position would pay $800/ month plus expenses.

The Dreamweaver took the conversation on an off-road adventure that Shane had not anticipated. He started by saying, "I want to tell you how impressed I am with your accomplishments. You also interview well. If I were sorting out my candidates for this role today, you would be in my top three". Shane was trying not to let his ego swell up like an engorged dog tick as he listened to Mr. Gilmour talk.

Gilmour continued, "You want to know why you are not number one on the list?" his voice playfully trailed up at the end to coincide with that ever-present smile.

"Absolutely," said Shane. There may have been less conviction on the inside than on the outside about wanting to hear the answer. Certainly, Fronk the Wheat Gangsta would not have been impressed.

Dreamweaver leaned forward in his chair, almost like a lineman getting into a 3-point stance. "First of all, I don't think you know how good you can be." Shane was trying to determine if this was a pitch, he frequently made to make people feel better about themselves or if this was a pro's honest thoughts. Shane was smart enough not to ask for clarity about his belief system.

"That is a real compliment, sir," said Shane.

Dreamweaver replied, "I REALLY want it to be a challenge versus a compliment so you can do something great with your life." All kidding aside, as a college student, that feedback will get your attention.

"Secondly," Gilmour continued, "I really don't know if you can sell something." That's when Gilmour did his *'solitary confinement'* pause on Shane. You know, the one where the person who commented now stops talking and stares at you like a piece of modern art. A well-practiced exercise at mime camp. This circumstance allows one the amount of 'rope' to make a complete fool of yourself talking with underthought verbal vomiting. Silence is one of the most underrated actions on the planet. Your inexperience shows when silence scares you, and you start to overload the air with words that you think will keep you from drowning. The other option is to say nothing and let the silence make the room more septic. Shane was in pause mode, which made him uncomfortable enough to fidget slightly, and he stuck his hand in 'Chewbacca's' suit pocket. What he re-acquired there made him decide to go on the offense.

To break the uncomfortable silence, Shane looked around at the 3 of them, smiled, and then in complete non-sequitur, said, "I noticed that all of you had some meat protein for lunch." He paused as their smiling heads nodded and said, "With a salute to the 'Fred of Como' brand of barbeque that you all sell at Alumni; I assume from that you like various types of barbeque."

Heads nodded and smiled as Shane waited for them to say "Yes."

Shane continued, "I also assume you wouldn't turn down a great dessert or the world's best homemade sweet corn ice cream from WSU's Ferdinand's Dairy." The three gentlemen were smiling even more, wondering where this was leading. Shane added, "As concerned stewards of the future of agriculture, you know the importance of supporting youth, *ESPECIALLY* in learning and education."

He added more color, "I heard your James Arness film presentation about **learning something every day**." Shane reaches into his pocket, gets Chewbacca's tickets, and says, "I would invite each of you to purchase two tickets for your wife and you to attend the WSU Carnivore and Cobbler Festival on Saturday, May 5th. The tickets are $10.00 each or $20.00 for the 2 of you. I guarantee you will be a hero at home and do something great for the scholarship program".

All three Alumni guys burst out laughing as they knew they were in a corner. They all shelled out $20.00 to get out of the jam. Shane felt he had diluted some of their apprehension about whether he could sell. He might now have a new answer to that 'most significant risk in your life' question. He hoped Chewbacca hadn't promised those tickets to someone else.

Dreamweaver gained control again for his 3rd point. "I am unsure if your summer schedule and our program work for both of us," Shane said that he understood. Gilmour went for the close. "Shane, if I asked you today if you would take the program, what would you tell me."

"In all honesty, sir, I don't know, I would have a lot to think about, but I am definitely interested," Shane replied.

"Last question is more of a technical one related to the mechanics of the job. Do you have reliable transportation?" asked Dreamweaver.

Shane had to be cautious as he explained his vehicle, "Emmitt." Farm kids drive farm vehicles, and "Emmitt" was a recycled piece of agricultural history—a thirteen-year-old, 1967 Chevrolet half-ton pickup. With the help of his brothers and a good friend, Shane had rescued it from a neighbor's field, rebuilt the drive train, repainted the body, and upholstered the bench seat. Shane had invested his hog earnings in reclaiming this chariot from the curse of oxidation. The pickup was maroon in color with a white two-tone roof. It featured rally wheels and an eight-track tape deck supported by Jensen six-by-nine coaxial speakers behind the seat. The music could knock the fleas off a dog when cranked up.

Containing enthusiasm about an old pickup was an intelligent strategy as Shane answered simply to the transportation question, "Yes, I do."

They shared appreciation for the lunch meeting and agreed to stay in touch. Shane had lived the 'learn something every day' and was starting to get into this corporate deal more than he thought he might. Now there was a more profound concern. How would Dad handle it back home?

Like most father/son relationships, Shane did not understand his father's perspective. 'Boxcar' had a quick wit but a quicker temper. This was Shane's concern, and upsetting his father by not being able to work for the family during summer break was not an attractive thought.

The more significant unsaid concern was what he might say about his son being a salesperson. Shane watched for many years as 'Boxcar' dismantled salesmen that would show up to sell him something for the farm. The family always had at least two and sometimes three farm dogs. These fifty-pound, never purebred, always "mongrel" guardians were harmless. The dogs had a proud heritage of not liking strange cars, handed down over generations. Much to Boxcar's delight, they choreographed their barks angrily in unison with hair raised on their back and bared their teeth. Most salespeople who ventured down the lane would not leave their car as the scene drew similarity to sharks circling a raft. If they were bold enough to tame the dogs with a kind hand, the cold shoulder from 'Boxcar' would typically be a worse fate. A familiar example of sales disdain was one evening after Ed had a long day of fertilizing and seeding wheat: a crop chemical salesperson cold-called on the phone. Shane answered and thought it was someone his Dad knew. When he got to the telephone, the chemical salesman never took a breath for at least 3 minutes, telling an increasingly agitated, dirt-covered, fresh-from-the-field, Boxcar about the huge increased yield and the money he would save by adding this product to his fertilizer tank. "Sounds great," Dad said. "Why don't you drink a gallon of it"? He promptly hung up.

Shane was home from college for the weekend to help the family with spring seeding. After driving the tractor until 4:30 in the afternoon, Shane stopped at the house to phone the fertilizer plant. At that moment, the same phone was ringing that the fertilizer additive salesman had been humbled on years earlier. Shane answered, thinking it may be the fertilizer company. Instead, it was the Dreamweaver. "Good afternoon, Shane," came the precise diction and smile that shone through the phone that Gilmour was famous for.

"Hello, Mr. Gilmour, this is a bit of a surprise," replied Shane, whose heart was pounding so hard it nearly knocked the accumulated dust out of his coveralls.

"I called your number at school, and when I didn't reach you, I thought I would take a chance and call your home."

"Oh, yea, I am home helping my dad with spring work," said Shane nervously.

"I hope it is going well," said Gilmour, but he had business on his mind. "You probably know why I am calling, so I will get to it." Shane's kidney was now beating in unison with his heart. "I would like to offer you the Alumni Summer internship. However, I will need to know by the end of the evening because if you are unavailable, it will be offered to a girl from Oregon State." He ended by sharing his contact number. Shane said he understood, and he would hear back from him later that night. There was only one problem, 'Boxcar' was moving some equipment and would not be back until tomorrow. Shane had shared a few of the details of the internship with his dad but never indicated there would be a chance he might get it. Right now, Shane was trying to recover from the Dreamweaver call, which had a physical impact similar to drinking 3 gallons of espresso. He was wired up.

Shane regrouped and called the fertilizer company to order the nitrogen he needed to have delivered. He left the house with a 'couple of badgers chasing each other around in his belly.' He heard clanging down in the shop 150 yards from the farmhouse. He quickened his pace, hoping that his dad had returned early. But it was Uncle Bo using a hammer and an anvil, trying to fix a bent and broken fertilizer shank that had collided with a rock. "What you up to, '8 Penny'? I thought you was out seeding?"

"I was, but I needed to call the fertilizer company."

Uncle Bo was always perceptive and a tad bit nosey, "You look like somebody done licked the chocolate off your cupcake. Somethin' up with you"?

Shane didn't have anyone else to talk to, so he unloaded a carload of confusion onto Uncle Bo's listening ears. In less than 10 minutes, the whole scenario was laid out for Uncle Bo; the internship, the opportunity, the possible disappointment of 'Boxcar,' leaving him and the crew short for summer work and combine driving. The more significant point of Shane's indecision was probably if working for these guys was what he wanted to do. Then he mentioned the deadline of tonight.

Without Shane asking, Uncle Bo said, "So what is the problem? Looks to me like you got a cart full of groceries that you don't even have to pay for. If you play it right, you might have the whole store".

Shane was now more confused than ever, "What do you mean, Uncle Bo?"

"Well, let's break 'em down here so you can get back to the fertilizer guy. You are concerned about what your dad is gonna think?"

"Yep." Said Shane.

"Well, let's take a look at his situation. If he hadn't left South Dakota when he did, do you think he would be as successful as he is today?" Uncle Bo answered for Shane, "My guess is probably not." "Do you think he asked his dad before he left?" Again, he answered, "I know for a fact he didn't. So, the last thing that I think will bother him is that." Uncle Bo continued with a bit of a summary, "I guarantee what he will want most is for you to make the decision that is right for you."

"That is helpful, thanks." Replied a more relaxed Shane. "But I am not getting the rest of the grocery store comment."

"They want you, right?" said Uncle Bo.

"It appears that way."

"You want to help during harvest, which is clouding your decision?"

"Most certainly, as I feel obligated," Shane confirmed.

"Well, that doesn't happen until around August 1. If they want you, they will let you finish early in August and work harvest," he said confidently. "All you got to lose by asking is some breath."

"Thanks, Uncle Bo, your logic is savory," replied a grateful Shane.

"Wish I had time to find out what '*savory*' means." Shane was pretty sure Uncle Bo saw it as a compliment.

Shane returned to the house after a few more minutes of reflection and dialed the number Mr. Gilmour had given him. It was early in the evening, and since it was a weekend, Shane didn't know if he would get an answer. "Hello, this is Ronald," came the familiar but more subdued greeting than Shane was used to receiving. He hypothesized that the Dreamweaver had a couple of cocktails that may lubricate the conversation if there was friction.

"Mr. Gilmour, this is Shane."

With a Cheshire cat calmness, Gilmour heaped on the smooth. "Why, Shane, I am so glad to hear from you and so soon."

"Yes sir, I should get back to seeding wheat before the fertilizer truck gets here and I will go pretty late tonight as rain is expected."

"My, that farming is hard and intense work."

Shane decided to build on that point as he gave his decision. "Yes sir, grain farming is quite labor intensive with some narrow and time-sensitive work windows." Here we go. "That is part of the reason I called this evening sir".

"Oh," he could tell he got Gilmour's attention.

"I really do like all that Alumni Nutrition has to offer in the intern program, and there is a great opportunity for both of us to understand if there is a longer range fit for each of us." The silence on the other end meant the Dreamweaver thought he might have lost the fish he was trying to reel in.

"So what are you saying Shane?" the smile had evaporated from his voice.

"I would like to accept your offer; however, I need one small concession."

"What could that be, Shane?"

"When harvest begins for our farm, I need to be able to suspend the internship for the summer. That normally means the First week in August, as long as we don't get a lot of rain. If that means I need to work weekends or whatever, I will do it, but I can't let my family down."

The silence on the other end was extended like Gilmour may be pouring himself another cocktail, or maybe the phone was disconnected. He said, "Is that all you need? I thought you would ask for a whole truckload of Storm Trooper cereal to get yourself a new wardrobe".

They both had a needed laugh of nervous relief. Appreciation was exchanged, and arrangements would be handled later.

The Dreamweaver summarized some Alumni culture "So, did you learn something new today?"

"Yes sir, I will have the whole summer to tell you about it; however, the fertilizer man is coming up the lane right now. Many thanks. Looking forward to it."

Shane's Learnings

On the use of strategic questioning to build new relationships: One personal tactic Shane was very proud of was his self-invented *'Interpersonal Dragnet.'* Interpersonal Dragnet or I.D. he would claim was an antidote for communication complacency.

On Shane's logic behind the value of questions in Interpersonal Dragnet:

1. Most people are shy but don't necessarily want to be.

2. College students who are stressed and in a confusing environment still want to feel important.
3. Confidence comes from talking about a subject they have some expertise in.
4. The subject they have the most expertise in is simply themselves and their environment.

Interpersonal Dragnet was built on the four principles above. Try out the process with the questions Shane used:

- "What is the city (area, town, county, State, Country) that you call home, best known for?"
- "Who is the most famous person from your home? Who is the most famous person to visit the area you are from?"
- "What has been the best day of your life so far?"
- "What is the best practical joke you have ever played on someone?"
- "You are going to win the lottery tomorrow. What will you do with the money when Summer arrives?"

And if the discussion is going great, ask the last one:

- "So let's say I interviewed your best friend and asked them to tell me about you. What would they say?"

<u>On the idea of finding out about others is like reading a book</u>: By asking 5 or 6 well-practiced questions of almost anyone you meet, you will be amazed at the chapters of their lives, similar to a book, that will open up to you. When you pick up a book, there is very little understanding of what is in that book unless you read it. Often there are surprises and unexpected content in that book. The same can be said for almost every person you interact with. They all have surprises and random ranges; without taking the chance to interact or ask about them, you will miss the good stuff they all have to offer.

On the value of your inner attitude: One of the lessons Fronk shared with Shane regarding wearing the costume was that if he weren't smiling and excited inside the costume, **melancholy** would ooze out of the costume's pores. Fronk claimed that exact phenomenon applied to the humans you meet every day. Fronk would compress the thought: "An unenthusiastic inside will come across as a carcass."

On the idea of focusing on critical elements when studying or bringing things to react to: "You only have room for three things in your mind on a subject." The power of 3 is an implementable rule that helps you focus on what is essential. Three things are often easier to remember than multiples and sometimes even more recallable than just one item.

On the idea of talking bad about someone else: No matter what you do or say about someone, it will get back to them …somehow. You will never make a mistake if you make it as positive as possible.

. . .

On the idea of taking a risk in your life: Traveling the road of life, success appears to gain the most traction the more chance you take.

On tips to consider during an interview: You need to be yourself as an accomplished interviewer will be able to recognize if you are not. Authenticity is unmistakable.

On the idea of asking someone close to you for advice: The support of a loving family starts with them teaching you how to work and respect others; what you do with the rest of it is up to you.

On the idea of what to do when unsure: If you have a choice when under pressure, play offense versus defense. Shane went all in *on offense* to sell the Alumni leaders with the Carnivore tickets in the pocket of Chewbacca's coat.

4

THE ODOR OF STRANGERS

The group of college students known unofficially as the 'Underground Agricultural Society' collected in a semi-circle of barstools (converted nail keg seats) that served as uncomfortable but indestructible tavern chairs. They assembled for their loosely orchestrated 4 PM Thursday refreshments. Late spring would bring a more significant than customary attendance as most felt they were past the expiration date on caring about scholarly excellence. Most were burnt out. The bar was named **'The Laboratory,'** located in Moscow, Idaho, ten miles from Pullman. There, the drinking age was 19 versus 21 in the State of Washington. **'The Lab'** served drinks in beakers like the same patrons had used for science or chemistry experiments. They had a game called **'Periodic table darts'** for food discounts, but the crowd favorite was hard-boiled eggs that the regulars affectionately referred to as Chicken Embryos. The warmer weather brought out the casual clothes, and most patrons were singing along to The Car's **"Best Friend's Girl"** as it brazenly fought out of the jukebox. To Shane, casual and formal attire was the same. It meant bibbed overalls that had been cut off just above the knee and, of course, not hemmed. They looked more like homemade lederhosen than an agricultural fashion statement. Getting him to care about fashion was a complex and wasteful endeavor.

Duroc redirected the conversation from how terrible the Mariners season was starting by saying, "Zim told me today that you are going to take the Alumni Nutrition internship for the summer. Is that right?" Shane was uneasy talking about it since many of the folks at this tribunal were active candidates at the Alumni lunch in February.

"Yes sir, I start the 1st week of June," he said as quickly as possible, hoping the subject would be averted.

The spontaneity of the celebratory toast from the group to his achievement made Shane feel he had clearance to expound. There were many personal accolades from these friends. The major exception was from one of the hard-charging young ladies majoring in Animal Science. She was known as 'Battle Cap' because she liked to mix it up, even sometimes when she didn't have to. She was an overly intense academic student who would be on developmental probation if graded on her social skills. With a half-full beaker of Rainier beer, she sat silently pondering to herself, how in the world could this court jester, Shane, be picked to do anything civilized or significant? Most others at the event had summer internships or jobs planned. There was plenty of note-sharing about what all would be doing. Shane explained that he would have a project of working with Alumni Animal Nutrition Dealers to gain their perspective on how they and Alumni Nutrition could grow the business together. He was going to get lots of training in interviewing and questioning skills. Travel would include trips to Alumni's **Prerequisite Research Farm** in Oklahoma and points all over Washington, Oregon, Idaho, and California. He would work with Alumni Salespeople and spend much time in dealerships with the owners, managers, and the dealership's salespeople who called on customers and prospects of animal owners. As the others shared their internship itineraries, it was clear Shane had the trophy, as his assignment was more organized, challenging, and engaging. The idea of clearing out drainage ditches, counting cattle in a feedlot, or assembling hay balers when they arrived from Canada didn't appeal to him like the Alumni program.

During a bathroom break between beakers and embryos, Shane was shoulder-to-shoulder in the urinal stall with a buddy. 'Tire Iron' was from the Palouse and knew Shane's family. He was also, like Shane, an Ag-Ed major. Shane's family bought tractor and truck tires from his family's tire shops that mainly catered to farmers. He had been included in the conversations about internships. However, his summer was dedicated to recapping tires in his dad's shop.

Tire Iron would routinely overextend his English diction in dramatic words and phrases. He would also deepen and elevate his voice, adding a grating tone to his exaggerated vocabulary. "Essentially, you will extract yourself from the 'Agrarian Commerce' family this summer. How did your dad assimilate with that?"

Shane rolled his eyes internally and responded, "Pops was surprisingly cool about it. There might have been a lot of scar tissue until he found out I would be back for harvest". Shane's brothers were more concerned than his dad as they didn't know how much bigger their workload would be.

Tire Iron kept up the clumsy verbal annoyance. "Rather magnanimous of him. And is there similar mutuality with Zim"? As the two of them washed their hands in the sparsely populated restroom, they focused on pictures of jars filled with brains fixed with formaldehyde. These pictorial artifacts accented the airbrushed Einstein mural on the restroom wall.

"Zim was a different story as he was concerned about whether this internship was right for me." Shane understated it a bit because he didn't want it to get back to Zim that Shane was disappointed there was not a little more enthusiasm around the whole deal. Shane rationalized that Zim and his staff prepared a target amount of high-quality, classroom-ready agriculture teachers each year. And when they lose those to corporate raiders such as Alumni Feed, it tarnishes their perceived effectiveness. Shane promised Zim that he would finish his degree, including a student teaching stint in the spring of his senior year. Besides, there was no commitment to Alumni beyond the harvest deadline of the upcoming internship.

Tire Iron had to be annoying even himself by now when he said, "Zim has always been transparent and reticent in his endeavors." Shane looked at him as he dried his hands and acted like his comments made perfect sense and hoped it would end the agony of the conversation.

Back at the table, the group ordered the 'Fahrenheit' appetizer bucket and the Bunsen burner to heat them on the table. Releasing an open flame to overserved college students to heat their food always seemed like an ill-advised risk to Shane, but this was part of the reason college kids flocked to this place.

His finals went well. Shane practiced Fronk the Wheat Gangsta's patented **Power of Three** systems of study and got his best grades ever.

It was time to transition from a hog barn laborer with a smelly wardrobe to a respected future Ag leader. Shane enlisted help from one of the girls whom he thought had good taste in selecting his appropriate business clothes and knew his budget constraints. He would be required to wear a company-issued tie designed with graduation mortar boards generously dispersed across it. Mary Tempo told Shane that it goes with everything. He decided he needed to join the human race and got about a quarter of the length cut off of his flowing mane. However, he still had longer hair than the Beatles when they arrived in America. He also eliminated the drop-down handlebars from his Foo-Man-Choo mustache. While he might not look like he belonged in a prep school boardroom, fewer people would question whether he might be homeless.

Shane went to the Alumni Animal Nutrition milling facility in late May in Spokane. He was sporting his newfound **conformity appearance** for orientation and to meet with the Dreamweaver. When you remove that much hair, you keep touching it to see if it is still there. When he met Mary Tempo by the entrance, he was giving his follicle inventory one more check. She was much younger than he had imagined (by about ten years) and even more pleasant in person. She shook Shane's hand like an exuberant lumberjack and smiled as if she had just met her idol. Shane thought it might be the water she and Gilmour drank at the milling facility. "Is this the famous Shane?" she said excited yet inquisitively.

"Yes, ma'am," blurted a slightly uptight Shane. He hoped not to say something as stupid as the last time they spoke.

"How was the trip in?" asked Mary. The softball question would hopefully allow Shane to get his feet under him and relax a bit.

"It was fine, ma'am. I had less than 50 miles to go, and I have driven by this place taking hogs to the stockyards for years".

They shared backgrounds and Coug stories. Shane found out she was a cheerleader when she attended Washington State University. She was married, and her family lived in the Spokane area. Shane was still more nervous than a calf in a slaughterhouse, but she was undoubtedly a great icebreaker. She explained, "Mr. Gilmour was running a bit late but asked that I put you in his office while you wait." He followed Mary upstairs in the feed plant to the offices. Shane was given a cup of coffee. He would never drink that at school unless it were test week. Because of Fronk's 'Power of Three' tutelage, Shane did not need mild brown stimulants.

Shane had projected how Ron Gilmour's office would look. He imagined a spacious, plush setting with top-notch furniture and a breathtaking view. He quickly learned that Alumni Nutrition would not put heaps of their assets into luxury. Gilmour's office was located on the upper level of the feed mill. There were several million dollars in noisy feed milling equipment just outside his uninsulated panel wall. Someone would have to get accustomed to the constant hum of the pellet mill and the occasional air hammer blasts that were knocking excess product out of the grain bins. That distraction, in combination with the relentless racing and 'safety honking' of warehouse forklifts, made him think that living between an airport and a firehouse would be more desirable. The office was skinned with Sienna brown paneling, similar to the Butte restaurant. Maybe that is why Gilmour was so fond of that place. The difference was that this catacomb had no windows and was twelve-foot square with an underwhelming metal desk set. It was all nestled into some seasoned long-cut green shag carpet that Elvis would have envied for the Jungle Room at Graceland. The exposed four-foot fluorescent lighting was the final asset that punctuated the moment. He displayed sailboat pictures and plaques that hung at eye height and were the room's highlight. After about 40 minutes, Mary, whose office was across the hall, stopped to see how Shane was doing and said that Mr. Gilmour had just arrived.

He entered the room like a charming, veteran-warm front. You know, the kind you are glad to see after some rough, cold weather. All Shane knew is he was delighted to be out of Gilmour's morgue of an office.

Mr. Gilmour was as smooth as cake batter that day as he greeted Shane. "My goodness Shane, I hardly recognize you with cropped hair, professional clothes, and mustache reduction. By the way, that Mortar Board tie never looked better on anyone except me." He gripped Shane's hand with that '1st and Goal at the 2-yard line' smile. He was chuckling in an ascending rhythm like a train climbing a hill. All Shane could do was go along for the ride. Man, that ride and that laugh lasted a long time. It was almost like he had won a bet on whether Shane would cut his hair.

"Yes sir" was all a nervous Shane could muster.

"How were finals for you?" asked Gilmour.

Proudly Shane reported, "Outstanding; I should finish on time next year after student teaching."

"You have to be proud," beamed Dreamweaver.

"Go Cougs," interjected Mary. Mary knew Shane, by tradition, had to respond "Go Cougs," which he did. She also reasoned it would loosen him up a bit.

"How do you like my office?" A giant pause was not because he couldn't answer but because he didn't know how not to offend. The Dreamweaver's 'chest chuckle' was even bigger and louder, with a substantial serving of sarcasm dripping off the top.

"Cozy and functional" was all Shane could muster. Ronald's laugh got even louder and more amused.

"I knew I was going to like you, and your diplomacy is engaging," Gilmour said.

Dreamweaver now kicked into corporate mode and explained that office costs would not help the customer in the least and are the last priority. He pointed out that spending several thousand dollars on office surroundings is a waste since he travels constantly. He told Shane that if he wanted to use the office during his project when he wasn't there, he was welcome to use it. Shane was hoping that didn't happen.

Shane and Mr. Gilmour spent the morning laying out his summer objectives and planning employees and customers he should spend time with. Mary was brought in to arrange details for informing those folks and his travel arrangements.

<u>His objectives were pretty simple</u>:

"Learn something new every day."

1. Gain a strong understanding of Alumni Feed dealer needs and how Alumni Nutrition can benefit from meeting those needs. (survey questions were included) A mandatory presentation was required at the end of the project.
2. Assimilate as much learning about the Alumni Sales Force roles as possible.
3. Create a wrap-up summary of your project to be presented to the Alumni Sales and Management team.
4. Have Fun and be able to tell your story at WSU next year.

When he received the list of travel locations and itinerary items from Mary, he was teetering between excitement and anxiety. He was advanced some expense money, report information, and given Alumni wear that fit the dress code. The following Monday, he was off to the 'Prerequisite Ranch' in Oklahoma for a week of training and orientation. This would be Shane's third airplane experience and his fourth time outside the State of Washington.

The day was concluded with a thank you to everyone. Dreamweaver was still amused and smiling about Shane's **cozy and functional** description of his office.

The Prerequisite Ranch was over 4000 acres and was used as an experimental station to test product performance. It was the creative innovation center for all Alumni products sold. The reason for so many acres was the need to recreate the brood cow range environments. Over three thousand acres were dedicated to Range Cattle study. There also existed a 300 sow farrow to finish swine operation, 50 head horse operation, a 100 cow-fully contained dairy, 50 acres of aquaculture research, a fishing pond for visitors, and a 10,000-layer poultry operation as well as 3,000 broilers and turkeys. The place was enormous, with over 50 Ph.D. scientists actively involved in research projects to improve overall nutrition for each species.

Thirty-one interns (in Alumni speak; they were called 'Pledges') gathered on the first evening to meet and greet one another. What an awkward event. Over thirty college students with above-average egos were sniffing each other like new coyotes that just joined the den. There was no alcohol served because most were underage, which might have been a pretty good lubricant for the gathering. The leader of the intern event was an energetic guy nearly six feet tall, had a steady burn on positive fuel, and looked good in a suit. Because he was constantly forcing the cheerful, upbeat nature of all things Alumni, he reminded Shane of a game show host. They all found out later that his nickname inside Alumni was 'Camp Director.' He had a knack for engaging the crowd with activities that would lower tension.

While in class, he wore a mortar board on his head with a gold tassel and often referred to his clipboard. The color of the tassel depicted your accomplishments in the organization. Gold was the highest, but up to 10 levels of Gold could be achieved. His hat and the premise seemed a bit hokey, but Shane reasoned that the Romans built a great society by wearing bed sheets and vegetative headgear. The pledges had white tassels hanging from their name tags to indicate they hadn't accomplished much yet. Shane was just glad to be there. He met a guy from Texas A&M that called himself 'Rim Rock.' Nicknaming yourself broke a fundamental Uncle Bo rule. So Shane had a hard time hearing about the significant accomplishments that Rim Rock had in his life. Rim Rock also worshiped the sanctity of an institutional tavern in College Station known as the Dixie Chicken. He seemed like a nice enough fellow but a bit raucous.

Many of the pledges identified with their school. There was 'Bulldog.' She was a pleasant young lady from the University of Georgia. 'Gator Boy' was a southern gentleman who reminded Shane of Atticus Finch in *To Kill a Mockingbird*" because he carried himself a bit like a lawyer. 'Hokie' from Virginia Tech was a very sharp individual who was quiet and would tend to lay in the weeds until it was time to filet someone with his dry and productive wit. Interpersonal Dragnet was flowing by the liter.

The pledges studied hard all day, learning about the company and their summer roles. But Alumni wanted to show them some fun as well. Each night they offered a unique activity to get folks involved and even more excited about the company. One night they could go to the ponds and use barbless hooks and cheese bait to catch 6-to-8-pound striped bass on almost every cast. The winner of the fishing derby was 'Cat Head,' a lady from Tennessee who, in conversation, bragged about the flaky cat-head biscuits that her mother made back home. Because of the oddity of visualizing eating a 'cat head' and since most of the crowd had never heard of this southern staple, the nickname stuck immediately. Shane, who had now picked up the name 'Coug,' caught the smallest fish, four pounds. They, of course, gave him the 'minnow man' treatment, which made the exchanges much more fraternal and added pigment to color up some of the relationships between the interns.

Another night the pledges boarded a string of pack horses and made a meandering trek to one of the back pastures. Here the group got to self-cook their steaks on a wagon train cook-out and watch star groupings so bright they looked like neon. After a cowboy poet and a country music trio performed unplugged, the group rode the trail back home in the dark.

The next night the group heard from the Vice President of Enthusiasm, who lived up to his title. This guy made Camp Director look as tranquil as a monk. He talked about starting as a pledge, like an un-sculpted chunk of raw material from a small town in Illinois to what he was doing now. He was sincere and passionate. He was building up the froth on the edges of his mouth like Shane remembered from the young boar hogs when they would smell a sow in heat. The pledges could relate to his 'from pledge to Whale' story. No intern didn't want to storm the stage like a kid after an ice cream truck by the time he ended.

The final night and crescendo were when the 'Alumni Nutrition Marching Critters' entertained the group with enthusiasm and zeal that most college marching bands wish they could emulate. Twenty-four members and retirees of the Alumni Nutrition Company marched and rocked out a choreographed four-song set. They were draped in spotless white, black, and gold marching band uniforms with an image of the golden mortar board on their chest plate with the word Alumni under it. Their hats resembled a tall black, shaggy haystack that screamed, "I am wearing a small pet llama on my head." In an odd but appropriate enthusiasm development strategy, these dedicated marching music mercenaries were paid a stipend to perform and be part of the band. They were employees with a real job the rest of the time. Across the country, nearly 100 musicians would rotate into the 24-member band. Shane knew now where the funds for Dreamweaver's office went. The rumor was that they were asked to practice about 15 hours a month. Camp Director said they do occasional corporate events but were mainly included in significant dealer events and species trade shows.

An example was that every morning they would open the floor of the National Swine Conference with a marching rendition and present the colors of the United States. At the same time, the whole hall (and all the competition) had to watch silently at attention. What a humiliating three minutes that must be to the competition. The 'Critters' always ended their performance with the fast-paced and raucous **Feed the Best, Alumni Rag.**' The trumpets and trombones battled with the percussion section to be the most significant contributor to this influential harmony in this signature number. It was quite a way to end the evening. Shane and his band of pledge mascots stayed up, talked, and joked most of the night.

The last day was the finalization and summary of the project in which the Camp Director outlined every detail. The coffee flowed that day like Niagara Falls to take the edge off their previous evening late-hour convention. The final speaker was a stemwinder speech from the Vice President of Future Success. He was a level 5 gold tassel holder that painted a picture that the world would starve without what we as interns were doing, and of course, he dared us to 'learn something new every day.' He reminded Shane a bit of George C Scott in his Patton movie role without the slapping of the soldier scene. He delivered a message that genuinely stuck with Shane more than anything he learned that week. Shane was convinced that whatever was going to happen in the future, it was in the hands of these thirty-one adolescents to make it happen. Patton was triumphing.

One line that assailed Shane's consciousness during his speech was, **"I have learned more from our Alumni Nutrition Dealers than anybody else in my whole life."**

'Futureman' paused and repeated it for thorough consumption. Then he added some color, "No matter what issue I was dealing with, business, personal, and yes professional, I always gained more practical and usable knowledge from the feed dealers than I did from internal or most external sources."

"That is why the project you are working on with them is so important, as they hold a big part of our future in their hands by what they tell you."

"You were hand-picked because we trust you with our most precious asset," he said as he walked the room strategically. "Do you think you should take this project seriously?" Silence followed, which was not acceptable. "WELL, DO YA?"

"Yes Sir," the group said in unison.

"I AM A LITTLE HARD OF HEARING"!

"YES SIR!" Shane thought for sure the slap-the-soldier stuff was next.

The speech ended with thunderous, almost submissive applause. That is when 'Patton' hollered to 'Camp Director,' "These Pledges are ready to graduate." The **'Pomp and Circumstance'** music started from a recording of the 'Critters' performing the ceremonial tune. Each Pledge walked up when their name was called to the catcalls of their nickname as they approached Camp Director to get their plaque. When Shane's name was called, the clowns yelled, "CCCCCCOOOOUUUGGGGGG."

The group was ready to move out and conquer after enough handshakes to get a callous swapping of contact information and side saddle hugs. The reality that many would never see each other again didn't register. Probably a good thing, or there would have been more hugging than departure.

Shane returned home to check the answering machine Mary Tempo gave him as a loaner unit. This was the first time such equipment had been in Shane's family house. He had to plug it into the family home phone, which offered a great deal of extracurricular communication on a party line with eight other farm families. He received a heavy ration of ribbing from his brothers about the

'Mission Impossible' machine he was required to have for this job. Every time the phone rang, one of the brothers would holler, "Mr. Phelps, should you choose to accept it," relating to Peter Grave's smoking recorder message on the TV show.

The machine's technology would start with a pre-recorded, robust lawyerly voice to announce the order of the message. "FIRST MESSAGE: *Say, Ed, this is Milly Williams, my husband Sam asked me to call and ask if you might have some bales of hay for sale. So that was why I called; it would be appreciated if you could call back. I am not sure what I am supposed to do next; I don't normally talk into these gadgets, so I gue...* BEEP. CALL ENDED"

"SECOND MESSAGE: *Hey Shane, this is Egon Whittaker with Alumni. We met at the Butte restaurant last February. Congratulations on your internship. Would you give me a call? Please meet me Monday AM at a dealership so I can give you details. Mary Tempo told me you have all our contact information, so please give me a holler this weekend.* BEEP. CALL ENDED".

That was 'Manhattan,' the young Alumni employee from Kansas State.

"THIRD MESSAGE: *Good Morning Shane. Ronald Gilmour calling. Please call Egon Whittaker as I would like you to spend next week with him and his dealers. He will have all the details. I hope you enjoyed Prerequisite Ranch and did you learn something today?* BEEP. CALL ENDED".

"YOU HAVE NO MORE CALLS."

Shane called 'Manhattan' and learned that he needed to pack for a week of surveying and bring work clothes and work boots. He was to meet Egon at 'H-D Feed,' 30 miles North of Spokane. 'H-D' was a significant dairy feed supplier with a retail feed store that had been there for many years.

On that Monday, Shane was sitting outside the locked gates of H-D's parking lot at 6:45 AM with a box of a dozen donuts he picked up from his favorite location Dirigible Donuts. 'Dirigibles' are zeppelin-shaped raised cakes that Shane and his buddies call piglets because of the way they lay in the box representing pigs nursing on a sow. He was early to the store on purpose to show his initiative. He fired up Emmitt and left home around 5:00 AM. A Hall and Oates tape in the 8-track accompanied the drive"***Abandoned Luncheonette***" percolated from the speakers as the vintage pickup gobbled Highway 195, meeting less than ten cars and twice as many grain trucks during the journey.

The sun was peeking above the skyline, which illuminated the structure of the H-D Feed buildings. Sixty-foot-tall grain bins circled the tin-covered building nestled among the taller grain structures. The Alumni Feed mortarboard logo was prominent on top of the elevator leg, poking a hole in the early morning sky. The loading dock was the apron around the front of the building, with concrete steps leading to the top of the dock. The parking lot was spotless, with groomed, compressed gravel to handle the weight of trucks. In the parking lot sat two bulk feed trucks painted white with the Alumni logo on the side of the truck. There was also a small greenhouse and flats of blooming flowers that greeted customers at the entrance to the nursery.

A dirty-white pickup truck with H-D Feed emblazoned on the side approached the parking lot's locked gate. The pickup door opened quickly because the blaring country music from the radio helped push it open. Out came a man dressed in clean denim painter pants, an Alumni Feed golf shirt, work boots, and of course, the mandatory logoed baseball cap. He opened the gates, but before returning to the pickup, he looked over and saw Shane sitting in a strange rig. This unfamiliarity of someone in a rural community can heighten curiosity. He walked toward the unknown vehicle with a purpose. Shane jumped out, and the gentlemen came to meet him. "Are you that Alumni intern, fella?"

"Yes sir, my name is Shane."

"Glad you are here. My name is Don, but everyone calls me Cap." He gave Emmitt a quick but affectionate look and couldn't help but comment. "Now, that is a sweet ride. 67?"

"Yes sir."

"Can't wait to learn more about it later. You and I gotta go make some magic happen and sell some feed". Don was in biker tavern-fighting shape for a 43-year-old guy. His 6'3" inch frame had about 30 productive pounds on Shane and made him aware that this was a guy you wouldn't want to tangle with.

In the background, Cap's farm truck radio was making Merle Haggard proud as it filled the open spots in the ozone.

"Ready for whatever!" exclaimed Shane.

"By the way, did Egon Whittaker (Manhattan) get ahold of you?"

"No sir."

"Well, his wife got a hold of me before I left the house just a few minutes ago. He was taken to the hospital for emergency surgery. He won't be joining us today, so bring your pickup in and park it around back where it can't get hit and has less chance of elevator chaff messing up your pickup's finish. We will get this all sorted out".

Emmitt was safely stored in the back of the facility next to Cap's pickup, near the fertilizer truck and large liquid feed storage tanks.

Shane entered the store through the back dock area, following the exact path that Cap had taken. He made sure not to trip and spill the Dirigible Donuts while wholly distracted by the surroundings that made up H-D. The walls were covered in rough-sawn lumber that had absorbed more than one experience, which may have something to do with their faded and oxidized hue. The store had at least a fourteen-foot-tall ceiling with what appeared to be struggling fluorescent lighting and gondolas running the length of the store.

At the front window, not far from the main front door, the rattle and 'chirping' activity of a bunch of 2-day-old baby chicks in a brooder distracted Shane. He was not a real fan of chickens. The store had posters on the wall above the merchandising shelves screaming the virtues of the Alumni Feed products. Above the main counter hung an oversized mortar board suspended as if floating. Dangling below it was sharp graphics that said, *"As an Alumni Feed Dealer, we learn something new every day from our customers. Please teach us to make us better".* The store was about 5,000 square feet and crammed with farm merchandise clear to the massive ceiling. Agriculture has many great aromas, but this location did not pass that test. It had more than a hint of farm chemicals masked by the odor from the chicken brooder.

"I see you brought some of those **cucumber donuts**. You will be a hero. Can I get you a cup of coffee to lubricate one for yourself?" asked Cap.

"No, I wouldn't want to ruin my palate when I munch on a Dirigible."

"Fair enough," said Cap, pouring himself a 32-ounce insulated mug full of Parsons Root Beer from the refrigerator. "I went to college with Bob Parsons, whose family makes this exotic root beer. They send me several cases of the stuff, and I get them a country ham or two during the year." He continued, "I have tried 12-step programs and séances to get off this stuff, but I still hammer down nearly a case a day".

Shane asked for a glass, and he could understand the addiction.

Sharing a carbonated beverage seemed a good place for Shane to dig deeper with Don. "How did you get involved in the business?" asked Shane.

"Went off to college at Cal Davis," he said. "Wanted to get away from home for a while. But after five years, I was ready to come back. I studied Ag, found a bride, and came back to learn from Dad, and now I run the place after his passing. Where do you go to school?"

"Wazzu," said Shane.

"Go Cougs," said Cap. "Man, I gotta tell you, I went to a football game or two there last year. My god, have they ever got a lot of beautiful coeds there."

Shane smiled wryly and said, "Yep, most of the Miss Americas redshirt there."

Cap let out a snorting laugh that kind of scared Shane. "Let me open up the store to get acquainted." As he walked an aggressive pattern, it was easy to see Cap's procedural familiarity.

"Do you mind if I use your phone to make a call?" asked Shane.

"Phone on my desk would be best; use line two.'"

Shane sat at the neatly organized desk and called the Dreamweaver to see if he could get more details on Egon Whittaker. He wanted to know his next steps, as Egon was to give Shane the rest of the details of his week when they were together. He doubted that was going to happen with 'Manhattan's' misfortune.

Mr. Gilmour was unavailable, but Shane left a message on the 'Mission Impossible machine' similar to the one he now had at his house.

The H-D crew started to arrive for their day of work. Most of them were confused about who Shane was until he explained and offered them a 'suckling pig' donut. Cap explained later that retail people see someone new in the store early in the morning and think it might be their replacement. However, nothing makes you more a part of the family than a 'Dirigible.'

Cap got things lined out with his crew and told Shane, "Jump in the truck. We are gonna go hold court".

Shane was obedient but ragingly curious as to what this meant.

Cap moved the buckets of milk replacer, rodenticide, and

tomato fertilizer out of the passenger's pickup seat so Shane could sit down.

Shane was dressed in darker tan dress pants and a short sleeve white dress shirt with the Alumni logo near the pocket. He wore black slip-on penny loafers with black socks. Cap, thought he looked like a Mormon on a mission but didn't say anything, figuring that Shane was instructed to dress like this. Shane was supposed to wear the Alumni necktie but conveniently left it somewhere not to be seen.

As they drove down the road waving or honking at every vehicle they passed, the radio in Cap's truck was advertising the Spokane Indians minor league baseball season. The radio then rolled into the Statler Bros., punishing the rest of the world with "*Elvira*"; thank God he had turned it down. While in transit, Cap asked many questions about Shane's background, family, college major, and intern job specifics to get caught up.

The pickup meandered slowly down Main Street as Cap looked in every shop to see if anything had changed since yesterday. Cap parked his pickup diagonally in the town square next to the other 15 pickups already in place. Cap's truck was not clean by Shane's standards but was by far the most pristine in that collection of vehicles. They walked across the street to enter the crowded "Tip-Top" Diner. Before they entered, he turned, paused, and said to Shane, "The World's Greatest Leaders are the World's Greatest Observers. Your role today is to be a Great Leader". Cap turned without Shane getting to ask what that meant and walked into the restaurant to jubilant greetings, more handshakes than a wedding reception, and a strong dose of uncreative ribbing. Cap could tell the waitress, whom he called 'Vy,' was trying to tame this circus of denim-wearing patrons, and she needed his help. Cap jumped behind the diner counter, which ran ¾ the length of the restaurant, grabbed the coffee pot, and filled the patron's empty cups. Shane found a spot at a table in the corner that made for perfect viewing. Sitting there, he thought how uncomfortable he would have been walking in there without Cap. As he looked around to take inventory of the hair in the diner... he guessed he had 1/3 of all of it. His only competition for the mustache was on 'Vy.' Strangers have a peculiar odor in small towns, and Cap was his deodorant. Shane watched him as he interacted with all the patrons. Shane quickly realized that these patrons were customers and prospects of H-D Feed. Many were dairymen who were done with their first milking of the day that had started around 3:00 am and had just finished in the last hour. Their most recent milking resulted in plenty of stray cow offal on their coveralls and the smell of their cologne, known as a teat dip. This, of course, didn't bother Cap. He was focused on asking most of them how their feed was working and if the last order was delivered correctly. He asked one particular dairyman if he had thought any more about the mineral program that he had recommended. Shane soaked it all in, still nursing the Parson's root beer Cap had given him back at the store. Cap introduced Shane as a new intern from Alumni Nutrition and Washington State who would be spending a day or so with H-D. They graciously nodded to the stranger, whom they surmised was okay because he was with Cap. One of the older dairymen was a WSU grad who explained to Shane how different things were there 30 years ago. Those comments were hardly stimulating stuff. Shane acted interested.

As it often does in rural communities, the conversation amongst the dairymen turned to high school sports. This got the attention of the entire flock in the diner as there was a significant initiative before the school board. Shane picked up that Cap was a member of that school board. That initiative was to consolidate sports programs with a neighboring school district. What just a few minutes ago seemed like a reunion of best friends turned into something beyond religion, politics, or the extraordinary

'Ford/Chevy' wars fought by all farm kids. The volume of their voices increased, mixed with the emotion behind the thought of 'joining arms' on the same field of battle with such an unworthy partner as the neighboring Freedom School District. The subject made this once-happy diner a den of controversy.

Cap listened intently and calmly but firmly told the group, "I got a problem you all need to help me with." He continued, "The fact is that the voters, which most of you are, voted down the school levy that allowed more funds to support the athletic programs here in the Garden Valley school district. Are you with me so far?"

Group acknowledgment through head nods and grumbling.

"Freedom school district is 12 miles from us, and their levy was also defeated. Still with me?"

More unorganized grumbles and blank stares.

Calmly and deliberately, Cap kept going, "Neither school district could put more than 20 kids on the football field last year, and that is a problem all of our smaller agricultural communities are going to have to face."

The crowd was silenced and somber. They knew he was right.

Anticipating the following objection, Cap leaned into it, "You know I have a son and two daughters that play sports here at Garden Valley High. Am I worried about their playing time? Of course, I am, but I have never seen competition make them improper citizens or send them to therapy. I welcome competition, and both towns' parents should too."

Vy tried to cut the tension by adding her senior citizen wisdom, "It's about the kids, you guys." Shane was unsure how much relief those treasured words added, but hearing someone else talking for Cap's sake was good.

One of the more senior constituents, who looked more like a Western movie extra than a dairyman, felt it was time to weigh in on the sports topic. Sporting his abused white straw cowboy hat, losing a battle with sediment and perspiration, his slender but weathered face was equipped with a voice that sounded like it had been fine-tuned with years of Crown Royal baths. "Cap, we have known you for a long time, and we appreciate your perspective." An overly lengthy pause was followed with, "Let me give you a little peek into how the town feels. It's a little like my favorite Red Angus bull; whether I like it or not, he will probably break loose from my pasture and have *a merger* with the neighbor's Jersey heifers down the road." This off-road discussion confused most of the diner patrons and certainly Shane.

No one felt compelled to stop him, "You see, like that calf that is coming, what everyone fears is how the merger will turn out. I, and everyone in this room, grew up proud to play for or somehow represent the Garden Valley Cobras". A long pause was designed to signal that the good stuff was finally coming, "A lamb with testicles is the most despicable and detestable mascot of all time, and that is the one that represents the Freedom High Rams. I am sorry, but my grandkids don't want to represent male sheep". A few laughs and many heads nod around the room, bobbing in rhythm with their pulls on the coffee cup.

Cap soaked it in briefly, as he had never thought about or heard about the mascot problem. He then reversed field, "You know I have heard this before. The other day, I was out at Gerald Van Terrell's dairy, and he brought up the mascot issue. He was so mad he was shaking. He looked a lot like my dog crouched over in the yard trying to pass a peach pit". A couple of dairymen in the room choked on their coffee at the image because they knew about Glenn's temper. He then continued sarcastically, "So what you are saying is the Freedom school people have been so envious of our cold-blooded reptile that crawls on the ground that they have been blocking this merger until the hooded snake was available to them, and now is the time?" The room knew how silly it was, but it was an excellent lesson for Shane about the power of emotion. It also helped drive home the meaning of his dad's statement, *'**Arguments flourish when facts are scarce.'***

Cap summarized, "There is not enough money to cover sports for boys and girls at either school. Kids want to play, and we want them to play. Neither one of the schools wants to change anything. That is not an option."

After he let that soak in, he continued, "You all elected me to represent you just like you decided not to fund the school levy, and I appreciate and respect both of those decisions."

"I only see two remedies: we put some sheep testicles on a snake, OR we bury them both with great reverence and get some agreement between both communities on a new and different mascot."

"Thank you for the input today, and now I have to make sure your feed bins are full so you can make some money to help pay for a new mascot costume." The sanity of the last 30 seconds broke the ice, and even Vy laughed and chortled along with the patrons as she made her fourth gallon of morning coffee.

Cap and Shane left the assembly to talk about the subject of the last 15 minutes. Vy was 10 dollars richer from the tip Cap had placed into her hand. This stipend might be handy when support is needed in his absence.

Shane and Cap were back in the confines of Cap's white pickup, ambling back towards the store, waving at all that passed like parade royalty.

"You did a good job in there, son." Cap acclaimed.

"Huh?" said a confused Shane, "I didn't say much."

"Weren't supposed to. Remember what I told you when you went in."

"Yes sir, leaders are observers."

"Excellent, and what did you observe?"

"I saw you pour coffee. You asked about product performance and service issues and discussed the sporting issue."

"Very good, and why did I do that"?

Shane delayed a bit to think and then responded, "Because it was important to them?"

"Man, I can see why you were picked for this internship. You are a quick little minion." Shane smiled; he liked this guy's style. Cap added additional insight, "Today that community-merger sports deal is the most pressing matter in the world to these guys. Let me let you in on a little backroom secret. I talked to one of the dairymen that are a great customer, 'Ayrshire Al Zeloski,' while I was checking his feed bin at his farm. I asked him to bring it up the next time I was in the restaurant with those guys. He was the guy in the Bumper Yield fertilizer hat".

"Huh? Why?" asked a puzzled Shane.

"Well, the boil had to get lanced on this damn thing, and if I bring it up, it is my issue! If they bring it up, it is theirs. People only want to solve their issues. Sometimes they want you to solve them for you, but they care most about their stuff."

Cap then asked Shane a philosophical question. "What would have happened in that conversation if they didn't know me pretty well?" Without giving Shane time to answer, he added a different dimension, "What if I had gone into a coffee shop in Pullman or Seattle and a similar conversation developed? How well do you think it would have gone?" A step further, "What if it would have been in a room full of ladies I didn't know? How would I have done?"

Shane stated the obvious, "Not as well."

"Probably fatal," rationalized Cap as he honked and waved at one of his customers passing the opposite direction with a stock truck full of pigs headed to the Armour Foods packing plant.

"That worked out the way it did because I know the language."

"What language?" asked Shane.

"I call it the ***Unwritten Language of Rural Living***."

Shane was confused and looked for clarity without offending, "You are going to have to unpack that one for me."

"The Navy, the urban barrio, your college dorm all have a rhythm and set of unwritten rules that successful people figure out and use to their benefit."

They were pulling into the lot at the dealership, so Cap said, "Let's table that conversation for later."

As they entered the dealership door, they were greeted by that pungent baby chick brooder. Cap was already shaking hands with the 4 or 5 customers there. He asked about kids, horses, and garden progress. He introduced Shane as the Alumni guy. Shane noticed he didn't bring forward the sporting consolidation to them. When a break was possible, one of the female counter employees they called 'Fritter' mentioned to Cap, "Ron Gilmour from Alumni Feed wants you to call him as soon as it is convenient."

Shane was nervous that he may have screwed something up and was curious why Dreamweaver was not calling him back instead of talking to Cap.

Cap and Gilmour were on the phone and practicing stand-up comedy routines on each other with some apparent success. Cap was laughing with unforced natural vigor. They wrapped up the conversation, and Cap motioned Shane over to the phone. Cap covered the mouthpiece and whispered, "Mr. Gilmour wants to talk to you."

"Shane, how is your first day going?" asked the 'Dreamweaver.'

"Learning something new every minute." reaffirmed Shane.

"I bet that is the case. Cap, whom I have known for a long time and respect, is impressed with you." That made Shane feel better, as he was still a bit nervous about the call. "Say Shane, I am sorry that

Egon Whittaker cannot be with you. He had to have an appendectomy this A.M."

"Is he all right?" asked Shane.

"Not sure yet, but doctors were not concerned about his recovery. It means that since you were scheduled to be with him this week, we have a change of plans. I have talked to Cap and asked him under the circumstances if I could impose on him to have you work in his organization this whole week."

"OK, what about the survey work?"

"There will be plenty of time for that. Given your unfamiliarity with several dealers and how they operate, I think it best for you to hang close to Cap and his group. This will get you grounded and familiar with what feed dealers think about. So if you agree, I would like you to work in his organization for the rest of this week. Call Mary Tempo, and she will get you hotel accommodations for the week".

"Whatever you would like me to do." Shane liked to be obedient.

"Ok great. I will look forward to a great progress report. Good luck and learn something new this week".

After watching the **Mascot Ambush** in the Diner, he thought to himself…Every day is a master's degree. Instead, he replied, "Yes sir."

Cap was on his third Parson's root beer and leading the orchestrated chaos of dairy feed orders, fertilizer to be spread on customers pastures, and the stream of walk-in customers searching for hugs and solutions when he signaled to Shane as he walked out of his office.

"So I understand you got a new Boss for a few days. You ok with that?"

To mimic Cap's early statement, Shane said, "Let's make some magic happen."

"All right don't worry about calling to get a hotel cuz I got an extra bedroom at the house, and the wife and kids are visiting relatives. How is your softball game? We will need some players this week."

Shane was a little uncomfortable with the speed of all this coming at him, but he did as usual when this happened. He compared what he was facing with the plight of prisoners of war and quickly thought, I can handle this!

Regarding the softball comment, Shane sarcastically offered, "They don't call me Cooperstown for nothing."

Cap laughed and gave him his first assignment. "Go over there to the work clothes department and get two pairs of jeans and work boots that fit you so we can get some work out of you."

Shane thanked him, explained that he had all that out in 'Emmitt' and thought, "What a relief to get out of these corporate clothes."

"Great, the Alumni feed truck will be here in less than 30 minutes, and I want you to help 'Boo Squared' unload it when it arrives. Let me introduce you to him."

They walked across the wood plank floor to the warehouse area attached to the showroom. The high ceiling structure in the warehouse was at least three times larger than the retail outlet. For an older wooden and darkly lit facility, the warehouse was pristine. The radio was hollering out country tunes but could not keep up with the aggressive whine of an electric motor that sounded like a vacuum. Pallets of feed, salt, alfalfa seed, water softener, pet food, shavings, mulch, potting soil, and metal fence posts stacked two to three high in nearly every cubic inch of the warehouse.

Cap yelled out, "Boo-Boo, where are you?" No response as they walked toward the vacuum noise in a determined search.

As they turned the corner around a wall of wild bird seed, they alarmed this diligent worker whose hearing was compromised by the noise emitting from the electric backpack vacuum he was wearing. He had a look of shock on his face that made one think he may have gotten caught eating all the Dirigible donuts by himself. He had a plastic feed scoop in his hand, which he playfully threw at Cap as he turned off the vacuum to let him know he didn't appreciate the surprise.

"You know, the last guy that snuck up on me like that had a statue built of him in a park somewhere."

"Sorry about that, Boo. Meet Shane, an intern with Alumni Feed. He will be with us for a few days to learn how we do stuff".

"Not if he sneaks up on me like that again." He stuck out his weathered hand that felt like a dry alligator to Shane. "Are you the Dirigible guy?"

"Yes sir."

"You might just make it, kid. If you don't mind me asking, how old are you?"

"Twenty, sir."

"Good lord, I got underwear older than that." Cap laughed, and Shane didn't know how to follow up.

"Congrats on that." Shane said deadpan as he tried to keep in step with the fun.

Cap got the two of them lined out for unloading the feed truck and told Shane to do whatever Boo-Boo told him to do. After that, Cap had some fertilizer to spread. Shane changed his clothes, which probably made Boo-Boo more comfortable. Boo-Boo, who most called 'B2,' was actually named Norman. Shane later found out that it was a name he hated. Boo-Boo came from the comparisons to the Yogi Bear cartoon's sidekick. Norman was the sidekick of Cap's father, Harry, who was a jovial giant of a man. Norman had worked for him since grade school. He was in his mid-40s and went to high school with Cap, graduating a few years earlier. Five-foot-eight inches tall and maybe pushing 170 pounds if you included the perspiration, but that is where the comparison to the much bigger Cap stopped. Shane slow-walked some modified 'Interpersonal Dragnet' with B2 as they unloaded the truck. The previous day, the forklift had blown a hydraulic line, so they had to stack feed bags on the old hand carts and wheel them into the warehouse. Shane found out Boo was divorced and had a couple of teenage boys that lived in town with his ex. He also deduced from the conversation that he absolutely loved his job. He felt he owed everything in his life to Cap's dad. Harry hired him after Boo's dad was killed in a traffic accident. Undoubtedly, he was a family member in more ways than one. Shane was amazed that, despite his diminutive stature, Boo could quickly move some bagged feed. What usually would take 20 minutes with the forklift took nearly 2 ½ hours by hand. They were both soaked in sweat, and B2 had a stronger appreciation for Shane because he dug into the task without complaint. Immediately after they were finished unloading the feed, Boo had the vacuum backpack on and was sucking excess feed and tracks left by the hand trucks off the floor. Shane wanted to compliment Boo for how clean the warehouse was and decided to ask a question that turned into a fantastic lesson.

After he shut off the vacuum, "Man, this warehouse is cleaner than any I have seen. How do you do it?"

"It all started with Harry. He would tell me that if they ever had an injury at the dealership that needed surgery, he would be extremely disappointed if the surgeon didn't pick either the bathroom or the warehouse to do the surgery. Have you seen how clean our bathrooms are?" Shane acknowledged they were great from his experience expelling root beer that morning.

"So how did he instill that desire for cleanliness in all the employees?"

"True story." (This is the start of any story in rural America, and it means there is better than a sixty percent chance it happened somewhat like what you are about to hear.) "I am on the dock working my Saturday all-day shift at the store. I see Harry about 8:30 in the morning take two wadded-up napkins out of his pocket and drop them onto the ground in the parking lot." Boo pointed out the spot in the parking lot as he described it. "I was loading customers' purchases and occasionally doing bulk load out that morning, so I was quite busy." Shane is trying to figure out where this is headed. "I had several chances to pick up those napkins and didn't think it was that important. Well, about 12:30 after lunch, our fertilizer salesman, Ken Lewis, parked his pickup on the far end of the parking lot to be sure he didn't clog up the lot in front of the loading dock. He walked toward the store, bent over, and picked up the two napkins that had been run over by vehicles for a good bit of the morning. He threw them in the trash can as he walked up the dock. Waiting just inside the door was Harry, who reached in his overall pocket, peeled off a 50-dollar bill, and handed it to him." Shane was now curious for sure. "He thanked Ken and told him that he had dropped the trash there to see what would happen. Harry never said anything else."

"What do you mean he didn't say anything? Did he bring the employees together to tell them about this?" Asked Shane.

"He didn't have to because Ken Lewis told every employee about it, and they got the message. I can't tell you how many pieces of trash we have picked up, thinking there might be a 50-dollar bill as a reward."

"Did you ever receive one?" as the little kid poured out of Shane.

"Nah, I got more than $50 out of that lesson because every time I pick up something, I get to think about old' Harry".

Shane wasn't sure if the story had a romantic impact on him or if temporary insanity had kicked in. He had an idea. He asked Boo, "What have you planned for me this afternoon?"

"Nothing that can't wait."

"Are you OK if I tackle cleaning up the chicken brooder? I noticed it needed a little attention."

"Why do you think I work out back?" laughed Boo Boo. "Let me clear that with Fritter at the counter first so no one thinks you are stealing their job."

"Yep, that would be grand larceny for sure," Shane said sarcastically.

The cleaning of the brooder was cleared with Fritter, and they positioned it with the other employees that this was like an initiation for the college kid. She gave him directions and the materials he needed. Shane pulled the chickens and ducks out and put them in a stock tank along with a heat lamp to keep them warm and from running off. He then rolled the 4-level cages that would hold a maximum of about 200 chicks at a time, fewer when they had ducks. About 75 total critters were getting acquainted in the water tank. Boo Boo had set up a pressure washer on the concrete slab for Shane to run pieces out and thoroughly clean them. It took most of the afternoon to clean it off and pull it back together. The brooder had been located near the main door and the front window. Before putting it back, he noticed the floor was a mess, and the primary front window was covered in a refrigerator size fresco of duck manure. As Shane, armed with a putty knife, a pair of rubber gloves, and a warm soapy sponge, scrubbed and scraped both areas, he thought about his buddies and their intern projects. He imagined they had a first day quite different from his.

An excellent distraction came about halfway through this squalid process. A babysitting grandmother had brought her two grandsons with her on errands. The four and six-year-old grandsons with bloodshot red hair, buckshot pattern freckles, and bib overalls rushed competitively exploring the show floor. They were contesting each other physically and verbally as they canvassed aisle after aisle. Their grandmother was a combination shepherd and part marshal. As the two turned the corner, they ran into the stock tank, which housed the baby chicks from the brooder Shane was cleaning. The chaos and clamor turned into amazement and affection as these two young men stared into the tub. The youngest ran with purpose to encourage Grandma to view this incredible site. While moments ago, the two boys were vying for feed store supremacy; they now were on the same team.

The older boy struck first. "Gramma, can we please take some of these chickens home? We will take care of them, feed them, let them watch TV, and keep them away from the cat. Please Gramma, please, please, please."

Grandma deflected like an NHL goalie providing plenty of logical wisdom to support all the reasons they should NOT take home any of these young birds. Shane was listening closely in anticipation of what might happen next.

The pint-sized bib overall gang came back at her again with more pleading and provided their logic about being able to get eggs every day. These shrewd little dudes even claimed they would eat two dozen eggs each week.

Grandma would put the death nail in this tumult with one more piece of logic, "Boys, I appreciate your enthusiasm for getting these birds, but I want you to think about the *smell*."

The boys looked at each other for a unified response. The youngest one spoke with raw clarity to Grandma's comment. "Gee Gramma, I think the chickens will get over that."

Shane, Fritter, and the rest of the staff had gathered around to witness the excitement live animals bring out in kids. They were all snickering at the response of the innocent. Shane remembered his similar age and reflected on his deceased pet duck, 'Jeeper-the-Creeper.' Maybe his willingness to commit to this brooder job was in tribute to his childhood pet duck that could crap enough to rejuvenate the Dead Sea.

At age six, Shane and his dad, Boxcar were at Coeur d' Alene Lake on the Fourth of July, walking the carnival midway, which had several children and adult rides. His dad gave Shane some money to play some of the many carnival games. These included standard stuff like "Pop the balloon with a dart and win a prize" and "Toss the Rings on the neck of the soda-pop bottles and win a stuffed animal." After a few feeble and unsuccessful attempts, Shane spied, "Throw a nickel and land it on a glass dish and win a duck." Yes. An actual live 3-day-old baby duck. Boxcar handed Shane two nickels, thinking two impotent throws would allow them to head for home only ten cents lighter. The first throw, as expected, fell well short of touching any of the eligible glass dishes. The second throw wouldn't have been repeated with all the nickels made that year at the Denver Mint. The nickel was lofted carelessly halfway to the top of the tent that covered the game. Like a NASA engineer would have planned it, the nickel flattened out, made re-entry, and landed flatly near the center of one of a dozen eligible dishes. Then it bounced once straight up and rested dormant as the carney barker running the game screamed, "Quack, Quack, Winner!" Shane was shocked, but not quite as shocked as his dad.

Shane was handed a large craft paper grocery sack with holes poked in it. Accompanying the bag was the rhythmic squeak of a baby duck. His dad had to provide permission, which he did, probably thinking that this duck was destined for an unceremonious funeral in the first three days. Shane took the duck back to the farm and watched over the next three years as it developed an array of unique habits under the tutelage of the family's three farm dogs. Since Jeeper didn't have any other duck role models, he just assumed he was a dog. He slept with the dogs in the shop and ate dog food kibble off the floor along with the dogs. He was a 'watch duck' as well. He would run down the lane lagging behind the faster dogs, aggressively meeting unfamiliar vehicles arriving at the farm.

A smile captured Shane's face as he thought about that crazy duck while he pushed the cleaned brooder reloaded with the poultry that had been vacationing in the stock tank. It was near closing time, and Cap was coming in the store's backdoor covered in dirt and potash dust from spreading dry fertilizer for a customer.

Cap belted out in a high-pitched pep rally voice, "Holy cow. You bring a box of donuts, and you clean out the brooder. I will tell Ron Gilmour we will start the adoption papers today." The comment made Shane smile like his first little league base hit. "Time for a Parson's. Any of them football donuts left?" inquired Cap.

As the last customer of the day received their feed and a hug from Fritter, Cap's queen of Customer Service, the door was locked, cash counted, and deposits prepared. The crew departed for their life beyond the store. Boo had three deliveries to make on the way home. He wasn't supposed to do that, but folks knew him well enough that he wouldn't say no.

Cap closed and locked the gates after he and Shane drove through. "Follow me to the restaurant, and I'll buy you dinner."

"Can't turn that down as long as they don't specialize in chicken," said Shane.

Shane steered 'Emmitt' down the street, following directly behind Cap. Emmitt had been christened with a light coating of feed dust from sitting in the path of progress behind the store. Shane noticed as he followed Cap down the street that all the drivers of the vehicles traveling in the opposite direction waved at Cap like they were in a homecoming parade. But they stared at Shane and Emmitt like someone who might be in town to attack their grandparents. The *'odor of strangers'* could also work visually. After a pickup of pre-order of cheeseburgers at 'Billy Club Tavern,' they twisted and turned toward the elevated bright lights of the local softball complex. Four softball fields were back-to-back, with one concession stand strategically placed behind home plate on all four fields.

Cap had stopped by his house on the way back earlier in the day and picked up his uniform, team equipment, extra stray uniform, and baseball mitt for Shane. The 'H-D Scholars' throwback uniforms had the Alumni mortar board logo below the front lettering accented by black pinstripes and baggy 1920 styling. Cap joked that these uniforms were left over when his great grandpa owned the business. Shane swore his uniform smelled like it had been stored in the bottom of the chicken brooder he cleaned earlier in the day. Cap introduced Shane to the other teammates as the 'player to be named later' and said he had to give up four bales of Peat Moss to get him. Shane thought it was clever, and the others stared at him as if he just walked off a prison bus.

Cap had assembled a team of post-high school kids and adults. The team had some capable on field talent for the game. Conversely, the team had major league expertise in postgame activities and social interaction. Cap was the oldest on the team and still one of the best hitters. The evening was a typical 'past-your-prime softball defensive struggle,' with the H-D Scholars pulling it out 21 to 20 in the last inning. Shane went 3 for 5 at the plate and scored two runs with some heads-up base running. The after-party celebration happened in the gravel-coated baseball field parking lot. Cap commented that most "hall of fame" celebration commences with an ice chest full of beer on the tailgate of one of his dairyman's kids mud-crusted pickup. Shane mingled and observed at least 3 or 4 laws being broken with underage public consumption. As the sun went down in the still of the evening, the atmospheric inactivity forced the dust in the air to convincingly fall to the ground. Shane thought this was quite an enchanting moment and could understand why these folks wanted to live in this community.

One of his new teammates, the strong-arm second baseman, called 'Choppy', the son of the owner of the dry cleaners, was swooning over Emmitt. He wanted to know all about the details of the truck. Shane was proud but cautious about sounding obnoxiously fond of his pickup truck to folks still trying to figure out how this long-haired varmint fit into the herd. He answered all the questions, popped the hood when asked, and quickly reversed field to learn as much as he could about what he was driving. It is hard to get excited about an eighteen-year-old Dodge pickup with more rust than a marooned tuna boat. The missing grill parts made it look like its teeth were falling out. But Shane let Choppy give him the lowdown on this corroding chariot like it was the "Detroit Auto Show" climax. Shane gushed about Dodge's potential and listened to Choppy fantasize about all he might do with what most people, including Shane, would consider fully depreciated.

Shane started to recognize that the more comfortable people get with you, the more accessible they become with personal information. A few alcoholic beverages seemed to quicken the pace of the sharing. A firsthand example was Choppy calling over his buddy 'Mort' to share a story with Shane that was probably not entirely ready for public consumption. Mort played first base earlier in the evening, and Shane learned that Mort's family ran the local funeral home. Mort was, of course, an affectionate abbreviation for the term mortician.

Mort drove a 67 Ford Mustang. Choppy pointed to it parked on the other side of the lot. It was painted a slightly pastel orange color. Choppy, having a little fun with Mort, commented, "We call her the Mutant. The 'S' and the 'G' chrome letters have fallen off the rear trunk moniker, so the trunk now trumpets M U _ TAN _." The Mustang had extra wide rear tires and aluminum mag wheels,

FEED YOUR LIFE

all offset by slightly oxidized paint. Shane engineered a plausible tone of infatuation for such a fine piece of American-modified sports car. His mild inebriation was enhancing his performance. Mort smiled approvingly, showing a missing tooth and the accompanying incisors in distress. His neglected group of choppers, with his slender stature and uncooperative posture, made him appear more of a prisoner of war than a first baseman.

With enthused command, Choppy grabbed the conversation back to continue the story.

"So last Saturday Mort and I had double dated with a couple of girls from Treehorn. We went to Spokane to watch that *Ferris Bueller's Day Off* movie and scored a couple of bottles of the Boones Farm. You know, vintage two weeks ago. The girls like that stuff quite a bit. We were returning from Spokane after a night of cruising Riverside after the movie."

Riverside was the name of the street in Spokane that featured Eastern Washington's most prominent young adult automobile flirting, social, and beauty exhibition. The merging of octane, car wax, perfume, and testosterone is rolling bedlam.

Shane knew we were getting to the good part because Choppy was getting more animated, and Mort started to snicker. Choppy continued, "About two AM, we decided to take the old highway with very little traffic, if any, at night. We were about five miles out of town when this dreadful grinding noise started coming from the rear wheels. Mort slowed the car and pulled the car off the completely abandoned highway. We got out to see what the issue was. After a quick inspection, we could tell the Mutan had broken an air shock hose, and now the rear fenders were grinding the extra fat rear tires. No way we are gonna make it home with this situation."

Mort weighed in with witty and adept color commentary, "We were screwed."

Choppy resumed, "We thought about all our options, from hitchhiking to walking home. None seemed possible or appropriate because of no traffic and the distance. Mort and I thought maybe if we jack up the rear bumper, we could stick a rock or something between the axle and the bottom of the car to get us back to town and to my car...no rocks to be found. We were getting nervous, and the girls' mood went from giddy to panic. Mort and I walked to the front of the car and sat on the hood, both symbolically admitting defeat. As we put our weight on the hood, we heard a creak and scrape from the back of the car. The rear end is raised. We turned and looked at each other like we just invented beer."

Shane was engaged and howling with amusement, "Don't tell me."

"Yep, the girls moved into the front seats, and Jill drove. I laid headfirst spread eagle on my stomach with my knees bent so my shins could ride on the windshield. Mort laid directly on top of me in the same direction, using that wingspan to grab the edge of the fenders to hold us on."

Mort clarified, "That was the only way that would ever happen."

Choppy grabbed the reins again to summarize through the hearty laughter the story generated. "The girls **keep her steady** at about 15 miles per hour, watching the lines on the highway's edge to guide them. It took about half an hour with a wind chill around fifty degrees on these cool evenings."

Shane was spent from laughing, frenzied at the story, and a bit dizzy from the alcohol.

It was time to leave before the local law enforcement made their rounds and tried to cover their salary with tickets for youth infractions. In the back of his mind, Shane thought it would be uncomfortable staying at Cap's house, but a night incarcerated in the county jail seemed much more problematic.

"You all right to drive?" said Cap as he grabbed a two-handed grip around the second to the last Parson's root beer of the day.

"Could drive around the world," assured Shane being careful not to slur his words.

"Ok, then follow me to the compound, and we will get you settled in." Cap continued, "You had a pretty interesting first day, didn't you?"

"Yep, learned much new stuff today," keeping with the company line of Alumni.

"Tomorrow, we will make dreams come true," said Cap.

Shane agreed and was genuinely curious to see how much root beer impacted a person like Cap the next day.

Shane's Learning

On the use of facts in meaningful conversations: "Arguments flourish when facts are scarce." The key to helping diffuse conversations that seem to be rooted in conflicting substances or agendas is to remain as calm as you can. Aggression, emotion, and animation in these situations can increase tempers to where one of the participants might blow a gasket. A pointer to help potentially neutralize these situations is to bring as much solid data (facts, not evidence, as this is not a court of law) to the discussion as possible.

On being associated with Community Leaders in Rural areas: High-quality people tend to attract high-quality people and have the most influence over the most people. If you can get community leaders on your side, they can have the most profound positive or negative impact on your business. When you are looking for employees, a shortcut source is to ask people that are of good character themselves. They often have put people through that pre-screening themselves.

On the need for a fancy office: An office does not define a person. As a successful feed dealer used to tell me, "Office décor investment is the worst there is." He would continue, "For this company to succeed, it will NOT happen in this office. Every time I step into this office, I want it to remind me."

On listening and observing: "The World's Greatest Leaders are the World's Greatest Observers, and your role today is to be a Great Leader." Cap emphasized the point of sitting back and watching versus offering insights when first meeting people and customers in his world.

On getting employees on board for company activities that create enthusiasm: The final night and crescendo were when the 'Alumni Nutrition Marching Critters' entertained the group with enthusiasm and zeal that most college marching bands wish they could emulate. Twenty-four members and retirees of the Alumni Nutrition Company marched and rocked out a choreographed four-song set.

On the value of a powerful speech: The Vice President of Future Growth made poignant comments that Shane thought were the most important of all that he learned in Intern training.

His main comments were, "I have learned more from our Alumni Nutrition Dealers than anywhere else in my whole life. No matter what issue I was dealing with, business, personal, and professional, I always gained more practical and usable knowledge at the feed dealers than I did from internal or most external sources." *Those words echo the thoughts that inspired this book.*

His speech continued: That is why the intern project you are working on with dealers is so important. You were hand-picked because we trust you with our most precious asset.

The key takeaway is that an audience will seldom remember what you say but **WILL**, *more importantly, remember how you made them feel.*

On issues that need to be solved: Cap pointed out, "If they bring it up, it is their issue. People really only want to solve their issues. Sometimes they want you to solve them for you, but they care most about their stuff."

On the meaning of prefacing something with the term "True Story" in it: This is the start of any story in rural America, and it means there is better than a sixty percent chance it maybe happened *somewhat* like what you are about to hear.

On how cleanliness became a part of the culture at H-D Feed: Boo Boo elaborated on the origination, "It all started from Harry. He would tell me that if they ever had an injury at the dealership that needed surgery, he would be extremely disappointed if the surgeon didn't pick either the bathroom or the warehouse to do the surgery. Have you seen how clean our bathrooms are?"

On reinforcing the importance of cleanliness to the rest of the organization: Harry, the owner of H-D Feed, placed the trash strategically in the parking lot and watched to see if someone would pick it up. The one that did receive a hefty financial reward of $50.00. The strategic approach was that the receiver of the money would do a better job of telling the story about the premium and the importance of cleanliness than the owner.

On Volunteering for the unwanted job will result in a job you will want: Shane went the extra mile to clean the chicken brooder. The adages "do more than you are asked" and "look to work yourself out of a job" are much more recognized and accepted practices to get ahead than insisting you are more than you may be. As a dealer explained, if you want to get ahead, you should accept and look for work others don't like. "You won't have to do them forever, and the character development will pay off for a lifetime."

On how emotions can cause a mighty detour in clear thinking: Cap had seeded the idea about the merger of the neighboring school district with the influential coffee cartel so that it would come up. The emotions about the 'mascot' surrounding the conglomeration of the teams were dragging down the ability to bring the process together. Cap presented facts that got the conversation back to a productive one. This illustration is another example of how *'Arguments flourish when facts are scarce.'*

. . .

On how many people in rural America will look at strangers in a frosty way unless they are with someone they know: While not always unfriendly, rural folks are very guarded towards those they don't know. Cap knew this would be the case for Shane when they first went to the diner. Once Cap, a leader in the community, was able to endorse this outsider and explain his intent, he was seen more as a symbol of future leadership than someone plotting to drain their savings account.

On taking an interest in others and their circumstances can significantly impact their acceptance of you: Following the 'Scholars' softball game, Shane participated in the postgame festivities and took an interest in the possessions and stories of some of the others on the team. His actions allowed him to learn how to improvise when you blow an air shock hose, but more importantly, he multiplied his approval level with those that, hours ago, would consider him a shady stranger.

5

"MOSES WEARS CARHARTT"

Shane woke up looking around the room to get his bearings and to see if that raccoon that pooped in his mouth had left a note. The rare combination of more beer than he would typically consume, Parsons Root Beer and Billy Club tavern fare, came to collect.

It was about 5:30 a.m., and the kitchen below him was alive with Spokane's KGA Country Music radio personalities spewing some coffee-prompted trivia and the noise generated by someone in the kitchen, which was somewhat foreign to its operation. The solace to all that was the heavenly smell of bacon. The guest bedroom Shane was attempting to 'rally' in was nearly the size of a two-car garage. The walls were covered from floor to ceiling with high gloss local cedar wood. The entire room was decorated with an agricultural woman's touch. Evidence of this was displayed with wheat bouquets and dairy milk bottles marked with logos of dairies that exited the industry through attrition. These used milk bottles are like a tombstone reminder of the former 'family farm' milk producers. The dense, thick smell of potpourri in the room was powerful, but the bacon aroma was progressing in overwhelming the several bowls of scented twigs. He dressed to go to the farm with Cap's team to meet some customers. Cap hinted, but it felt like he begged him not to wear the mortarboard tie. After a quick shower to knock the big chunks off, Shane was dressed and ready to be an observant tag-along.

As he walked into the storage container-sized kitchen that Cap had been stumbling around in, Cap asked the obvious question, "Get you a Parsons Root Beer?"

Shane politely declined and slugged down two glasses of orange juice to establish equilibrium from last night. However, he had no issues helping Cap work on the bacon and egg inventory.

"You have a beautiful home, Cap," remarked Shane to help break the silence.

"This was my Dad Harry's place. My wife and family moved in after he passed away. We didn't want to, but you don't want a big house like this vacant, and the rest of the family couldn't afford it."

It was a precisely groomed estate secluded in the wooded area outside of town. The house was the size of the high school gymnasium where Shane played ball back home but held much charm that might make a city girl stay glued to the country. Large cedar log columns, like the wood in Shane's guest bedroom, held up a wraparound porch big enough to drive a couple of pickups on. Cap continued, "Dad built the place to keep my mom happy. He knew the long hours of running the business could take a toll on their relationship. I am glad he did because it has come in handy more than once with my wife in similar circumstances."

Cap continued, "My dad always told me you can't flaunt your success in front of your customers in the agriculture business, or you won't have them for long; that is the reason for the seclusion of the place. We have much involvement in the community, but we always had a rule that you didn't bring that involvement here to the house. No events, fundraisers, or meetings here at home."

Shane could tell from Cap's furrowed brow and determined stare that he wanted to share or discuss something. Shane focused intently on him, hoping this approach would either get Cap to talk or he would seek the mental hemorrhoid relief that Shane thought might be Cap's real issue. "Remember I mentioned to you last night that there are unwritten rules in Rural America?" said a seemingly tranquil Cap.

"Yes sir, I do, and I wanted to ask you more about that today," responded Shane, who was still attempting to shake the potential need for a brain transfusion from his mind.

Cap slid the breakfast dishes over the tile-covered counter by the sink; he pulled out a somewhat worn, if not abused, handwritten piece of paper. At the top of this weathered artifact was scribed, as promised, *by Don Wiggins, The Unwritten Rules of Rural America*. Shane had almost forgotten that Cap's name was Don.

"Read through those while I finish the dishes, and we can discuss them."

Shane let his mind caress each of the lines. Some of these declarations would need more tutoring than others, but there was profound substance here for a guy addicted to root beer and softball.

THE UNWRITTEN RULES OF RURAL AMERICA
By Don Wiggins

1. No one will ever condemn a person for doing what you say you will do, especially if it is the right thing.

2. When you live in the real world, "counterfeits" blossom and rot quickly.

3. The work of feeding the world and your reputation as a supplier starts with two of your customer pickups parked on a dormant gravel road.

4. An expectation is one of the best things you can give to anyone you work with.

5. Always wave at who is looking out their farmhouse kitchen window, it may be the biggest thing in their day, and you can never overcome the negative impact if you don't.

6. Never belittle a man's hat or his dog, and never do anything but admire a woman's children.

7. No matter what you say about someone......it will ALWAYS get back to them; you better make your comments as positive as possible.

8. There are two universally accepted actions..... humility and hustle.

9. Never take the role of helping feed someone's family lightly, or someday you might not be able to feed your own.

10. A handwritten note of appreciation resembles a tattoo; it can stay with them forever.

11. In times of a neighbor's discomfort, those in rural America are most comfortable offering support. Be one of those folks.

Shane's mind wandered from line to line, and each message created a mental image that accompanied most of the sentences. The magnitude of these messages sent Shane down an Old Testament off-ramp of Don being 'Moses in a pair of Carhartts.' **The root beer partisan delivered the tablets to a hungry, thinking man.** Growing up with a farm background, Shane related to many of the concepts, and he couldn't wait for the dishes to be done so he could dig further with the author. Cap turned down the KGA jabber. That relief of the radio clamor may have been what Shane wanted most to support his head's reclamation.

"I share this with you because I think you are the kind of kid that can get it." Cap continued, "I see how you handled yourself with the employees and the softball derelicts last night. It is not difficult to see you as a real worthy student. You listen well, and you want to help and learn. It is a gift. I implore you not to waste it." Shane didn't know what to say, so intense silence seemed the best approach. He hunkered in for what seemed like a potentially deep conversation. "I think you can understand this because I was a slow adopter of the idea of interaction with the human race, and unlike me, I see you as someone able to benefit from my early inability to see the value of this."

Cap mused, "So I assume you are thinking…where did the list come from and why?"

"Yes." That was the only answer that would keep this conversation going.

"My dad Harry was loaded with intellectual prowess. I was a respectful but impatient young soldier, inaccurately thinking I was ready to be the General of my own business." Cap continued, "Harry knew better and challenged me with several elements to examine my readiness for more responsibility."

"He told me to come back to him with the list of things that the customers of H-D Feed wanted from us." Said more honestly,

"What is really important to your customer." Cap continued with more explanation and the apparent need to share. His testimony came across as therapy surrounding the absence of his father. "The first list I brought to him was the obvious bullet point answers of service, quality, innovation, results, reasonable prices …blah, blah, blah. Harry was brief in his response but patient as a teacher. He unenthusiastically said it was a start but hoped that any of the employees would answer similarly."

Cap said, "For four years or longer, we would visit the subject multiple times yearly. Each time he would encourage my progress until finally, one afternoon between fertilizer and seed season, he called me into his office to discuss this seemingly lifelong assignment." Cap was more animated and more reflective with each chapter of the story.

With emotion in his voice, Cap continued and pointed out that Harry was not testing him on this list but wanted to get him to think more deeply and personally about his customers and the surrounding community. He discussed a phrase Harry would tell him often. "A rich man was one that if he had a flat tire anywhere in the county, someone would pick him up to assist him faster than his wife could make a loaf of bread," Cap said that statement was the key to unlocking his desire to learn. He concluded that he would have to study customers more closely or be stranded along the road like unwanted refuse.

Shane was fascinated by the list and wanted to know how it influenced what they would be doing today.

Cap closed the dishwasher, "It affects what I do every day. If I don't know my customer and what the 'sacred to the unimportant' issues are to them, they will spend time looking for someone that does."

Shane circled back to yesterday's conversation. "You mentioned that the unwritten rules are everywhere, and you hinted they might have a little similarity."

Cap explained that this was not high science…Harry would use the example of baseball. Some of the unwritten rules include the hard slide on the double play, the knockdown pitch following a home run, you never show up the umpire, and you don't want to make the first or the third out in an inning at third base. "None of those things are word for word in the baseball rule book but most managers and great players understand and comply with them as the RIGHT way to play the game."

Shane asked, "So did Harry have a list?"

Cap stared out the window in a less engaged and distant trance, and Shane thought maybe he wished Harry was there to answer that question. "He did." Cap expanded, "He refined it multiple times."

Shane imagined Cap would get the list out of a climatically controlled safe like the Constitution.

"He had scrubbed it, added to it, and updated it when he felt it necessary, but he was always leaning into the idea of simplicity for the list. He got the rules of the world he dealt with down to three simple everyday words." Now Shane's interest was elevated for sure.

Cap was ready to move toward today's tasks and used a cliffhanger moment to cut it off and set up some motivation for Shane to digest for the next few days. "I will tell you at the end of your scheduled stay, but I am going to ask you to guess what the three words are by trying to come up with something that should be on your list." Shane was mentally tangled up like a baby goat in a tumbleweed. Cap added, "You see, you should have your list of beliefs about whatever you are doing from being a student, dentist, father, or an agricultural giant with one feed store." Before they headed out, Cap replaced the list under the glass on his desk in his office.

They left to open the store. No need for donuts this time. After Cap slugged a Parsons Root Beer and Shane went to bless his flock at the cleanest brooder in the Pacific Northwest, things were in harmony. Now it was off to the diner to hold more court. It was nearly the same crowd as yesterday, with a couple of new agricultural coffee groupies that looked at Shane as though he might be there to rob the place. The topic consuming the airwaves this day was about some wild ass pranksters who caught a gunny sack of catfish and threw the whole darn thing over the fence into the community pool. The lifeguards spent most of the day trying to scoop the fish out with nets. One of the dairyman's daughters was a lifeguard and was amplifying the crime to require capital punishment for these fish-flinging joyriders. Vy was pouring coffee, Cap was servicing his customers with attention, and Shane was now a more comfortable charter club member of the 'Tip Top coffee cartel' because of being with Don. It was time to go. After 19 minutes, they were leaving the diner in a better place and not one word about high school sports mergers and mascots. Cap seemed to be thankful for the diversion of the catfish release.

With root beer in hand and Waylon Jennings on the AM radio, Cap guided their journey. The deliberate drone of the song '**Luckenbach, Texas**' split the silence in the cab of Cap's truck. Shane felt about half himself due to last night's post-softball gala. He was never gonna let it show. The silence provided much-undisclosed evidence about how he felt. He thought back to Fronk. His voice told Shane that if he weren't smiling on the inside of the Butch mascot, everyone would know on the outside. To combat his septic condition, Shane channeled some 'inner Butch' and went back to talk about the document Cap had made for his dad around the rural America rules. "Cap, there were a couple of the rules of rural

America that I may not understand how you would want me to. Can I ask you about them?"

"Fire away," Cap replied with an encouraging but slightly defensive gaze.

"In your document, the importance of the conversation between two guys in pickups on a dormant gravel road is something I may not understand as well as I should. Can you elaborate?"

"You probably have some experience with sororities and their members," stated Cap in a tone that resembled a question.

Shane came out to play with a wry smile and said, "I was never a house mother, but yes, I have familiarity."

"Like sorority sisters, farmers coexist with one another, while they are sometimes competitive or jealous. However, when they find a neighbor, a confidant who farms in the same region, they share like connected sorority sisters after a mixer." Cap continued, "I will bet you didn't know that the sorority sisters talked about you or whomever they dated. They talk about their date's scent and every detail of your interaction with a seasoned hint of fantasy, conspiracy, and jealousy about their experience. I know this because I married one of them and have had a windfall of illustrations to overhear, decipher and interpret in their conversations for years."

Shane showed acknowledgment as Cap added sage advice ."The men in those pickups parked on the road are like sorority sisters; this is their time to share experiences. They sometimes inflate success but are there for one another by listening and talking about common interests, and maybe, more importantly, they share what worked."

"My staff and I can tell a farmer six times or more about a new feed supplement that would help their herd performance or a new way to apply crop nutrients. This validated expertise will be information meaninglessly stuck in their head like a rural mailman stuck in a snow drift."

"BUT," Cap's voice elevated, and a playful smile appeared. "If one of their buddies parked in an F-250 tells them about it while parked on the straight stretch of a gravel road, the evidence of their two-person symposium takes on a honeymoon night appeal. And they will want whatever it is their confidant told them about, and right away."

"So, how does this affect you and your business?" Shane asked.

"If you recognize that this happens, and it does, you try to do your best to get with the **bell cow farmer** and educate him as well as you can."

"Bell cow farmer?" said Shane looking for clarity.

"You have seen a group of cows in a pasture walking in a line towards a barn or shed?"

"Yes sir."

Cap accelerated to move his truck past a slow-moving tractor and hay wagon in his lane on a straight stretch of road. He honked, waved, and continued, "Well, there is always one that leads where the rest of the cows tend to go. The Swiss dairymen recognized this and put a bell on the boss cow to tell the farmer where the herd was and for that cow to tell the others where they were going. Farmers, coffee shop dwellers, and sorority girls have this same thing happening." He paused and smiled to say, "There is always a bell cow."

Cap continued, "Interestingly, there are a lot of them that WANT to be the bell cow; but the unwritten rule of farmers is that the title of **bell cow** is earned from other farmers and not proclaimed by the more aggressive or noisy farmers." Cap returned to paraphrase his document, "Counterfeits have an odor."

"Makes sense, but what does this have to do with the pickup guys and feeding the world?" asked an even more curious Shane.

Cap hypothesized that the bell cow farmers were the most likely to get stopped on the road because of their success, and other farmers, like other people, are attracted to success. This led him to try to add more to Shane's inquiry. "That is a great question. I mentioned their sharing successes. If my staff and I convince the bell cow leader to use it first, he will get many others to use it for me." Cap brought it closer to home, "We send about ten key farmers per year to the Alumni Feed Prerequisite Ranch to see what is going on and see the latest technology that has an impact on animals. These guys come back like attendees of the last supper, and my phone will light up for weeks. Folks that didn't attend the trip will call wanting to know about this new mineral package or cattle block that they heard would help their yield. The adaptation of winning product technology will drive their success and help feed the world."

The fog was lifting for Shane, or maybe his head was finally getting traction after yesterday's consumptive abuse.

Cap had another vital point to make. "The other thing to be sure of is when they talk about you or your business in your absence (and don't kid yourself they talk about you), it is as positive to get them to be neutral as possible. I tell my staff to go beyond the required service level because if they don't, they will be the focus of almost every intimate conversation in a coffee shop or roadside occurrence in this county." He then firmly proclaimed, "I love farmers, but they tend to spend an inordinate amount of time on the troubles they have. Said another way...don't make yourself the source of their troubles."

Shane added color from his experience growing up with his Dad, Boxcar. "Yes sir. Too wet or too dry to plant, the government's interfering, fertilizer man didn't clean the nozzles on the spreader ...there is a 'Nostradamus meets Eor the Donkey' tone to most of my dad's conversations."

"You are familiar. A farmer can get their head in a hole, and the last thing you want to do to someone stuck in a well is pour water on them."

The pickup turned onto the long gravel driveway with groomed ditches leading to a dairy farm the size of a middle school campus. At the end of the driveway was an unusual and quirky homemade mailbox featuring a full-size Holstein dairy cow with its butt toward the road. The tail lifted for the mailman to deliver that day's offering in the cow's rear cavity. With some seasoned sarcasm but no disrespect, Cap noted, "Gerritt sometimes has too much time on his hands, and he is one hell of a welder." "Eclectic" was a resourceful way for Shane to acknowledge.

Cap's pickup crept along on the groomed lane like it was constipated. Cap explained that the best way to lose a customer is to hit a customer's dog or family member in the driveway. The slow crawl allowed Cap to explain that Gerritt Von Weederharry was a third-generation dairyman called "Dutch." He owned and milked 250 Holsteins twice per day. Dutch was a valued customer of Cap and his dad for nearly 35 years. As a legacy, Dutch had two sons Cap suspected would attempt to take over the dairy operation.

He explained that the genetic duo shared a wild streak to make them a *project* for most ordained ministers. Cap's voice indicated that the boys concerned him a bit. Cap expected Gerritt and the boys to be milking cows when they arrived.

Five buildings surrounded by concrete driveways were positioned like a cul-de-sac. The color scheme was all white and very clean. A prominent cupola on each building proudly sported a Holstein cow weathervane. Elevated on a berm two football fields away was a sprawling ranch-style house about half the size of Cap's, with towering oaks and lilac trees framing its setting. The house was tan brick, suggesting the person that oversaw the dairy was probably not in charge of the house. Cap confirmed that

Dutch's wife was the governing body of most everything not related to milking cows or what she referred to as 'that embarrassing mailbox.'

The pickup rolled to a stop. Cap jumped out and wrangled a four-gallon case of iodine-based teat dip from the back of the pickup. He and Shane walked a couple of hundred feet to the source of the noise and commotion they heard...the milking shed. The ruckus blaring at rock concert decibels out of this building was a combination of mechanical chaos and the same KGA radio disc jockey that Shane's head quarreled with upon waking. The clamoring symphony of straining motors, air compressors, and pumps, and the bellows of content cows, as they walked and banged into gates, created an audio brawl. Shane could feel the reverberating sounds pulsate up into his shins.

At the center of this commotion is a dairyman performing five jobs at once in the milking parlor pit. He was moving cows, washing them down, applying udder treatment, placing milking machine teat cups, and yelling. Constantly yelling. The scene reminded Shane of the scene from **The Wizard of Oz** where the professor behind the curtain was frantically pulling multiple levers on his devices while bellowing. This Dairyman of Oz dressed in rubber pants and boots hollered at cows to move into their milking chutes, even though they had done this routinely thousands of times. Shane wasn't sure which was more habitual, the cow's milk march to the barn or this dairyman's hollering.

Before they got to the building, Cap stopped and raised his voice to compete with the melee, "**Have you spent much time talking with a Dutch dairyman?**"

Shane shouted back the answer to the question. Cap didn't have to ask, "**No.**"

"**You might notice a slightly broken dialect.**" As they approached the milking shed entry, Shane saw an aggressive worker *wrassling* with a large, long two-inch thick rubber water hose that looked like a fireman's favorite ally. Oblivious that anyone was within a mile of the dairy barn, he hosed down the decks with a high volume of water while the next group of cows entered.

Having his back to his visitors, the dairyman had no way of knowing they were there. Cap hollered to get attention, *"HELLO EASY."* Cap later explained to Shane that sneaking up on a farmer will result in you getting whatever is in their hand thrown at you in surprise or alarm. After the second holler, they stepped into the milk shed, where the dairyman was ultimately task focused. He was unaware of intruders due to the blanketing noise. As in an infantry firefight, the dairyman spooked, wheeled around in defense mode, and with that massive hose pumping 20 gallons a minute, covered Cap and Shane from head to toe with high-volume pressurized water. You NEVER sneak up on a busy dairyman. Cap dropped the teat dip he was carrying, and after a chance to overcome paralysis-by-surprise, the two older participants laughed like eight-year-olds at a waterpark.

In broken Dutch-English, hysterically laughing and trying to holler simultaneously, the dairyman said, **"Damn Cap, I taut you dun knew betta den dat!"** He was almost sweating because he laughed so hard that the cows turned their heads to get a visual, much like high school boys at a wet t-shirt contest.

"My God, Gerritt, you are a frickin' assassin!" screamed a laughing Cap as he grabbed some of the paper towels used on the cow's udders. He handed a fistful of towels to Shane, who was so wet he looked like a newborn calf blanketed in afterbirth. Shane stood like he was impaled, his arms stretched out and mouth open with more surprise than when he got hired for the internship.

"This is Shane. He is CEO of Alumni Feed," barked Cap in a feeble attempt to embarrass his friend in his fraternity of customers.

Straining to get above the booming KGA radio hyper-babble, Gerritt hollered with his deep voice and clumsy Dutch-coated tongue, "**So when da lawsuit is over, dis is da young fella that vill be ownin' ma dairy?**"

After some relief from the paper towels, Shane played along, screaming his retort, "**Nah, just sign a lifetime contract to buy nothing but Alumni Nutrition products, and we are even!**"

"**No wunda he is da CEO,**" Gerritt played along.

Gerritt turned down the radio to relieve the situation and went back to milking the herd. "**Where are your boys? I thought they would be helping you milk?**" asked Cap.

"**Dey vents to pick up some of da heifers ova at da Van de Graafs, Ve don't gunna get much frum dose gizes yestaday eeder,**" he said almost lamentingly.

Shane was starting to sort through the cadence of Gerritt's vowel indiscretions.

He continued, "**Dey vent a-fishin late da nigh before ova to Calhoun's Pond. Dey vernt wort a hole lotta hoot da nex day.**"

Cap decided to dig a little. "**So when is the fish fry?**"

"**Ha, dem boyz mus be terriba bad fisherman,**" said Gerritt shaking his head in disgust. "**Didn brot nuttin' back.**" He finished with, "**I don't evva rememba a time I wasn't catch somethin at Calhoun's in da summatime, dat place is like fishin in a full bucket.**"

Cap and Shane glanced at each other like they had insider information about what might have happened to those fish. The glance also came with the common understanding that further pursuit of evidence to support the boy's inability to fish would not end in a good place for anyone.

The catfish in the community pool case was closed.

Gerritt shared herd performance issues with Cap at elevated volume, which only extenuated the jagged communication. As Gerritt rhythmically milked the herd, Shane watched the unfamiliar motions. His shirt was drying slowly, but he anticipated a good chance of 'swamp ass' for most of the day as he was soaked clear through his underwear.

Cap and Gerritt determined Shane would spend the day at the dairy doing whatever Gerritt needed. Gerritt smiled and chortled like an amused serial killer with his next victim.

As he walked to the truck, Cap leaned over to Shane so only he could hear and said, "You need an interpreter?"

"Nope, you never know when this experience could help me diffuse escalated international tension with Denmark."

Cap loved Shane's smart-ass, almost cocky demeanor. Shane didn't want to accuse him of going home to get dry clothes, but he knew that was where he was headed.

Shane's Dairy education was expeditious. He was learning to milk alongside Gerritt, move cows between groups, clean the feed bunks, remove silage clumps, and tarp newly arrived hay. Gerritt's wife fed them like offensive linemen at the training table. She left for town to get more groceries, as they were probably running low after the spread of homemade bread, smoked meats, freshly made potato salad, and chili. The volume of food and heavy exercise was a textbook prescription to fix the excesses of yesterday. All this amusement is a typical day in the life of a dairy owner whose routine begins at 3:30 a.m. EVERY DAY.

At lunch, Shane tried to comprehend the mysterious and surprising diversity of his summer experiences. In the past two weeks, 80% of what he had been exposed to was all new to him, including this morning. He knew it was time to get to his summer assignment.

While they talked and built rapport, Shane grabbed the conversation and asked Gerritt if he could ask him questions about H-D Feed, Cap, and Alumni. Gerritt thought he was about to be sold something and said in broken Dutch-English, "I knowz I 'yam good lookin, but still a purty tuff customa." His smile exposed a couple of broken teeth and a small noticeable smear of mayonnaise on his right cheek, accentuating where his razor missed whiskers. The question begged, "When did a dairyman shower and shave with these chain gang-like work hours?" God, these guys work hard.

Returning to his purpose. There was no reason to negotiate about looks or toughness.

"So, how long have you been with Cap and H-D as a customer?"

"He and hiz daddy Harry haz been like da family to us for nearly turty-plus year," he said with a prideful response.

"What got you started with them?"

"A number of tings, but da main reason is dey local people that has ben always done right by me and da community." He added a bit more detail "If you be askin Cap, he thinks deez cows be his, and he makes sure I gots what I need to be scessful."

"What do you mean by *his* cows?"

"If me and me boyz don't be havin success, Cap don't has no customa. Once youz a customa he done a'dopts dem almos likes you wud a kid ors a stray dog." He wryly inserted, "Someday I'z almos wish he would adopt dem boys of mine." Shane smiled and tried to avoid additional conversation that revealed his suspicions of who might be responsible for the local swim team practicing amongst a school of catfish.

Shane changed direction. "So he cares about you and your herd?" to prompt more discussion.

"He cares bout dat, my kids, my wife, and our place in da whole dairy industry and inz ours community. A guy like Cap and his daddy befo' him realize dat we iz a mirrur on him and his bidness."

"You have other suppliers that call on you, correct?"

"Dey used to almost live at da end of my driveway and took turns drivin in to tell me how dey was gonna be changin my life with what dey be sellin," he mused. "But dat slowed down dramatically cause I would have dis simila talkin with dem by tellin dem that I be doubtin that I would eva leave Cap and H-D." In a softer moment, he said, "I am not being fair to da udder salesperson as they havin a family to feed and theyz needin to spend therz time where they can beez doin themsseves more good; howevas, I do be keepin darr card in case of da big emergency."

"What if they can save you money?" Shane probed.

"Dare is da cost of learnin if I can truss them as much as I do Cap. I dun be runnin a big barn opration and vorrying about how my cows is a milkin or rebreedin is vun of the biggest 'costs' I be havin."

"You mentioned Trust. How do you measure or put a value on that?"

"I can tell you and the mose impotant ingredient in dat Alumni feed youz all be sellin is da truss I has for Cap and his groop of wurkers."

The conversation continued the same path for nearly 30 minutes as Gerritt pointed to numerous recollections of how Cap's company and family built the trust that he felt was irreplaceable. When Gerritt's calf herd had a run of a deadly disease that killed over half of his replacement heifers, Cap called a college buddy veterinarian who drove from southern Idaho just to diagnose and present a solution. He also found 30 heifer calves in Montana that would help Gerritt rebuild his herd. Cap and his dad Harry, served as pallbearers at Gerritt's dad's funeral, even though they had a ten-year family reunion in Utah they were to attend. Though the language hurdle could give an English teacher hives, Shane was beginning to understand. The success H-D Feed enjoyed was not just due to the nutrition supplied, the service, or the herd performance; it was deeply rooted in customers' trust in their operation.

Gerritt wrapped up the conversation leaving Shane with a partially finished story. He encouraged him to ask Cap about it. With his fragmented prose, "Ask Cap to be toldin youz bout the hundred and twunty gallon man, dat will pichter it perfeck fors you." Gerritt leaned back almost perpendicular to the floor in an overstuffed leather recliner, appearing to be lounging on the torso of a well-fed, precisely groomed, hibernating bear.

As he got comfortable and stretched out on the chair, he proclaimed with the most precise English of the day, "I takes me a nap for bout an hour and den start da milkin all over. If Cap comes back, tellz him thanks for lettin we wurk wit da CEO far pot of da day."

"Enjoyed it a lot, and thanks," responded Shane, knowing that his words were probably not penetrating the early onset of Gerritt's R.E.M. sleep.

In less time than a beer commercial, Gerritt's aggressive, erratic snorting noise alternated from an idling eight-horsepower two-cycle straight pipe chainsaw to the same saw, full throttle hammering down an old growth snag. Shane thought it best to slip out to the yard and wait under a shade tree. He questioned the decision as houseflies the size of fighter jets harassed him. The smell from the manure pit was nothing like the potpourri in Cap's guest room. A border collie with a collar and name tag that read 'Felony' came to show his affection. Shane thought Gerritt's boys, who had a couple of legal scrapes, may have named him. These mild inconveniences were more pleasant than being in the thunderous wind tunnel Gerritt created in his living room.

A short time later, Cap crept the pickup (at the pace of a box turtle in a determined trot) up to the shop area. He dropped off some milk replacer, a box of stove bolts, four custom-made hydraulic hoses, and three bags of charcoal briquettes.

Shane walked toward the truck as Felony tried to herd him with instinctive moves.

"Let me guess, nap time?" Cap said with a hint of sarcasm and jealousy.

"Yes sir."

"You ready to hit it?" said Cap

"Learned a ton today," Shane proclaimed. "But you may need to help me with the autopsy on some of it."

As they rolled out the lane, Shane took a picture of the dairy-cow-butt mailbox with his disposable Kodak. "Might be able to use that one in my presentation at the end of the summer."

Cap was inquisitive, "Presentation?"

In filling in the gaps, Shane said, "Yes, Alumni requires me to share my insights from the summer."

"What was the learning today?" Asked Cap.

Shane had a full cookie jar. "Never sneak up on an unsuspecting, keenly focused Dutch dairyman with a hearing problem while he has a flame thrower, live hand grenade, or a deck cleaning hose in his hands." They looked at each other and laughed with enough vigor to make driving dangerous.

"I swear he was going to knock me down with that cussed stream of water" Cap was giggling and thinking how funny it would be to have it on film.

Shane focused on Cap's question. "I learned how important you and your organization are to Gerritt and the others in the community." He shared several stories, kind words, and benefits Gerritt experienced from dealing with H-D Feed, especially Cap and Harry. Cap's demeanor went from prank-induced amusement to solemn, misty-eyed pride.

Cap said, "Let me give you another learning as the pickup ate up asphalt. Secondhand compliments are the best you will EVER GET." He continued, "Those comments are the ones you want the guys in the pickups on the road to share with one another."

Shane thought back to his own dad sharing comments and bragging about him and his family members in the coffee shop with his buddies. He was lamenting that his brothers, his sister, and he would never hear those exact words from Boxcar. Cap's emphasis on the value of Shane's dad's covert praise was helping him salvage some good out of something he never truly understood.

Shane pursued a more important topic as they eased the pickup back towards town, keeping the discussion progressing with his best Dutch dairymen impersonation. "I'z's was told to ax you'z bout da hundra twunty gallun man."

Cap burst out laughing with enough force to stress the windshield gaskets in the truck. Part of Cap's amusement came from the subject matter, but Shane selfishly took credit for most of the laughter due to his spot-on channeling of Gerritt's dialect.

As they drove into the outskirts of town, Cap slowed his pickup to a gait similar to that he had going up Gerritt's Lane. He looked to his left and pointed to a small 'tank farm' of fuel and oil tanks. The weeds had grown up around the base of the tanks as tall as a teenage boy and just as spindly. The once all-white tanks suffered the fury of the Pacific Northwest winters resulting in a free-form patina of blotched rust and missing paint. "That is the monument in memorial to the 120-gallon man," Cap commented, and his body language revealed he had no joy in chronicling the rest of the story.

In disclosure mode, Cap built the foundation of the story. "The fuel and oil delivery business is tough, with lots of competition for a common commodity needed by nearly all farmers." He explained that H-D considered adding the service to their business and determined it to be more of a distraction than an asset to a focused company.

"T.J. Coleman lived in the area for several years and ran a welding supply company, well-drilling, and a pressure washing service. T.J. was a hard-working guy with the respect of many folks in the community and, for the most part, was a good citizen."

Cap shared how Trojan Oil Company came to town looking for a distributor of fuel, oil, propane, and engine additive components. They approached H-D Feed, the hardware store group, a barn painting company, and two cooperatives in the county with successful fuel businesses. None seemed interested in representing the Trojan Oil Company. The ability to be successful was even more daunting due to the already-established competition. Only intimate family members knew that T.J. Coleman had recently come into a sizable inheritance. Community leaders, including the barber, reverend, and a couple of bell cow farmers, recommended T.J. as a petroleum distributor prospect. He and Trojan found each other. After some business planning and in-depth interviews, Trojan decided T.J. in the fuel business was a good mutual fit. Their efforts created the oil tank facility, now the symbolic tombstone Cap pointed out.

Cap added personal color to the story, "T.J. was aggressive, started with great fanfare, and gained quite a bit of market share. I bought fuel from him, and many of my customers bought home heating and farm fuel from his fledgling operation."

The Middle East cartel's control of oil tightened fuel supplies and reduced farm incomes. That caught T.J. and Trojan Oil Company in a questionable cash flow position. The objective evidence of this domino effect came to the forefront with the rest of Cap's story.

"Another example of the two guys in the pickups on the gravel road comes up again. Vern Summers is a legacy community member who runs one of the larger swine operations in our area. I have served him with feed, farrowing crates, and feed bins for years and found him to be of impeccable character. One day he came into the store, which rarely happened, as we delivered most of his feed and supplies. I knew he wanted to talk."

Shane and Cap arrived at H-D Feed world headquarters and sat in the parking lot as Cap continued the story. "Vern says to me, I had T.J. out to deliver some bulk gasoline, heating oil, and diesel fuel last week. He delivered 120 gallons of each." Cap didn't think anything of it as he had T.J. deliver similar products...but to keep the conversation going, Cap asked," Was the service good?" Cap knew T.J. could sometimes get distracted by all his other business activities and commitments. Cap also sensed Vern had something festering on his mind, and Cap wanted to help lance that boil.

"It was flawless, except...I only have 100-gallon tanks."

Cap continued between pulls of root beer, inferring that a sick feeling had come over him as he wanted to run away from Vern and dig through his own records. "Sure enough, I found at least three, maybe four invoices in the last year that were potential overcharges."

Cap lamented, "You know my business has made mistakes. I try to get them cleaned up and get everyone affected to tell me **they are satisfied that we took care of it face-to-face.**"

"Why face-to-face?" asked Shane for clarity.

"Two reasons. 1) Because it is the right thing to do, and you can use the mistake to show how they are in good hands by how you fix it. 2) Because the customer is going to tell someone else. It is inevitable. The opportunity to talk about how you fixed the problem gives them something more beneficial to talk about than what they might make up on their own." He continued, "There are many wonderful things about small towns. However, the process that community members use to handle an incident like T. J's is not one of them."

"What do you mean?"

"Many small-town people are not comfortable with conflict. Few folks are. Their approach is to avoid dealing with it head-on but tell neighbors, or that guy in the middle of the road with the pickup, about whatever issue they had."

Cap concluded by explaining that T.J. was finished in the fuel business after seven or eight months. He had become the 120-gallon man.

"Why do you think it happened, Cap? Why didn't anybody tell him?" Shane was curious.

Cap opened a fresh Parsons Root beer. "You take any finance classes at Wazzu?"

"Yes sir."

"In the area of financial instruments, **trusts** are handled by someone called a ***fiduciary***. The administrators of those trusts must be of unshaken fidelity and relentless truth." He asked Shane, "T.J., in his business, the H-D team, and even Alumni Feed, what is the most important element to success?"

Shane's mind was racing as he took a generic approach and said, "Customers?" trailing up in tone because he really was guessing.

Cap replied, "Close and certainly a part of it. However, the most important element is the **trust of the customer**. I am the ***fiduciary*** of my customer's trust; as the fiduciary, it is no one else's responsibility but mine to ensure that trust stays intact. It certainly is not the customer's responsibility, and it was not my responsibility to confront him about the three or four invoices. I quit buying from him just like many others. I would have surely told him if he had come to me to find out why. T.J. not showing up to discuss it told me everything I needed to know. Or, to put it another way, T.J.

didn't understand the fiduciary concept and lost his license to practice."

Shane looked out the windshield, slightly drained from the learning exercise. He weighed in with an unusual affirmation. "You know it is interesting that what you said about trust is nearly the same thing Gerritt said about two hours ago." With a grin, he added, "Of course, you had a few less misplaced vowels in your description."

As Cap was taking a pull on his root beer at that moment, the humor reversed the flow, and he blew root beer all over the windshield.

They laughed uncontrollably as Shane slipped out the passenger door and said, "That's what you get for leaving me at Gerritt's dairy with wet clothes."

Shane's Learnings

On how to act in front of others in the agriculture Industry: You shouldn't flaunt your success in front of your customers in the agriculture business, or you won't have either for very long. Said another way by one of the country's best feed dealers, "Your customers prefer you to be humble."

On "The Unwritten Rules of Rural America" and how every business needs to look at their marketplace and business environment to define their own set of "Unwritten Rules." See below the check marked list of Cap's Unwritten Rules and some commentary on each:

✓ No one will ever condemn a person for doing what you say you will do, especially if it is the right thing.

Doing the right thing with adverse outcomes is always easier than doing the opposite. Unwinding the wrong approach usually is more expensive. You don't have a friend or customer that wants you to do the wrong thing. If you do, run from both.

✓ When you live in the real world, "counterfeits" blossom and rot quickly.

The tighter the community, the more acute the character investigation. As someone new gets added to the herd, they are best to bring little attention to themselves and learn as much about others as possible. People are hungry to be recognized as significant. Feed that appetite if you want to be accepted into a new group.

✓ The work of feeding the world and your reputation as a supplier starts with two of your customer pickups parked on a dormant gravel road.

People talk about you every day. You can't change that, and you can't control what they say. Your actions, your performance, and how you treat people and situations correctly is the only offense you have to ensure the narrative between others potentially benefits you. Sometimes gaining neutrality where they don't say anything negative about you is a significant win.

✓ An expectation is one of the best things you can give to anyone.

An employee has desires to work beyond their W-2. Being included in decisions and the quality of the work environment usually score higher than pay with store employees. Successful bosses and entrepreneurs share the vision of where an organization or movement is going. Providing a goal and an expectation of what work you want to be accomplished is difficult work. The boss gets what the boss wants. Sharing the vision of what needs to be done and simply getting out of the way of the bright employees will allow both to thrive.

✓ Always wave at whoever is looking out their farmhouse kitchen window, it may be the biggest thing in their day, and you can never overcome the negative impact if you don't.

Waving at an oncoming car or pickup in rural America is a familiar ritual. As someone approaches a vehicle, giving a variety of greetings from the index finger windshield wiper movement to the "Hey, I am fly fishing here" full-arm campaign. In rural America, if you don't wave, you are thought to be a) Annoyed at someone in the other vehicle, b) Are not *local,* and as a result, have a much higher propensity to be a hardened criminal. or c) Have never had to answer? "I saw you the other day, you didn't wave. Are we OK?" Extend this thinking to the lady looking out the kitchen window in her house.

✓ Never belittle a man's hat or his dog, and never do anything but admire a woman's children.

Men seldom accessorize. When they break through this uncomfortable threshold, their headgear is the last area they want someone to question. This personal billboard often tells a proud story in the form of a ball cap. Tread lightly on challenging this personality extension. The most important and coveted act in a woman's life is the creation of human capital. Nothing but reverence toward a child is like graffiti on an altar. Never '*diss*' her kids.

✓ No matter what you say about someone…it will ALWAYS get back to them, so you better make your comments as positive as possible.

The routine in rural America is this. Assume that when you are saying something about someone, you are talking directly to them because, *eventually,* you are.

✓ There are two universally accepted actions……humility and hustle.

The most remembered and memorialized baseball players are those with the best stats. Ego can be a big part of the drive to increase those stats…more than occasionally; their success has driven them to be absent of humility. The most beloved baseball players have the most drive, hustle, enthusiasm, and limited chest pounding. In business, as in baseball, you pay attention to the success someone has, but you covet the hardworking underdog.

✓ Never take the role of helping feed someone's family lightly, or someday you might not be able to feed your own.

Whatever the business you are in, if your innovation and enthusiasm wane, your customers will be the first to recognize it. They may not tell you, but their perception of your decline will be first noticed when you don't treat them as the most critical element of your success.

✓ A handwritten note of appreciation resembles a tattoo; it can endure forever.

Like a song, certain sounds will bring your senses back to an earlier time in life. The music stimulates a fond or unpleasant memory whereby you visualize where you were, what you were doing, and even the smell. You retain those memories. People hang on to important legal papers, wills, trusts, and stock certificates. They put them into secure places like a safe or a bank deposit box. The greeting card industry is a 20-billion-dollar industry. People also save personalized complimentary handwritten notes at a much higher level than any other communication. Whether from first love, a teacher, parent, boss, spouse, or customer, you tend to keep them. It may not be the note itself, but the thought that someone took the time to share their appreciation can leave a lifetime impression. I recently purchased a lawn mower from a feed dealer, and two weeks later, I received a handwritten thank you note for buying that lawn mower from their dealership. I didn't keep the note, but when it comes time to recommend to someone where to buy a mower, where do you think I will send them? By the way, I would not have remembered or commented on a text message. Three minutes of your life can change someone else's. An exercise I would challenge you to execute is to send a note to a loved one, a former teacher, a good customer, or somebody you appreciate. See what reaction you get.

✓ In times of a neighbor's discomfort, those in rural America are most comfortable offering support. Be one of those folks.

Helping someone in times of trouble provides more reward than your investment. Engagement in your community will be recognized.

. . .

On Finding and using Bell Cows in your industry: A worthy objective is to spend time making these community and industry leaders your advocates. Remember, those key influencers can sell more for you than you and your entire team. The practice of hanging out with great people and customers has a magnetic effect on other customers they influence.

On the idea of having a written list for your belief system: This may seem a simple and unproductive exercise, but constantly re-evaluating what your customer believes can profoundly impact what you recognize as important and necessary to thrive in your industry. It would be best to have your beliefs about whatever you are doing, from being a student, dentist, father, or an agricultural giant with one feed store.

On the critical and essential need for customer trust: the customer's TRUST is the most valuable asset you can attain. YOU are the fiduciary of that trust. If you break a customer's trust, you can spend a lifetime getting it back. If a single customer loses confidence, it is a safe bet that your trust level in the community you are serving is in a more tarnished position. The tarnish on your reputation is like ice accumulating on the front of an airplane wing. If it grows, it makes the plane less navigable and efficient, and you lose control, thus making it much harder to fly and potentially crash. The 120-gallon man found his fate without really knowing what was coming.

. . .

On secondhand compliments: Second-hand compliments are the best you will EVER GET. If you hear something nice about someone else, your duty to humanity is to let the person or people complimented know. Those compliments have so many benefits. 1) They make the person talked about feel validated. 2) It builds the relationship between you and the person you told this compliment to. 3) It builds a better relationship between the person who initially gave the compliment and the person who complimented. With all the unproductive bile thrown at each other over a disagreement about *whatever* ridiculous topic, this is a joyful way to make the world better.

On a small business owner, dealing with mistakes face-to-face: Businesses make mistakes and have controllable and occasionally uncontrollable issues. The best remedy is to seek those affected and connect closely with them to find a resolution. Why? 1) Because it is the right thing to do. You can use the mistake to show they are in good hands by how you fix it. 2) They are going to tell someone else. It is inevitable. Speaking about how your organization satisfied the problem gives them something more beneficial to talk about than what they might make up on their own. There are a lot of fulfilling things about small towns. However, the process that community members use to handle an incident like the 120-gallon man is not one of them. Many small-town citizens are not comfortable with conflict. Few folks are. Their patented approach is to not deal with it head-on but to tell neighbors or that guy in the middle of the road with the pickup about whatever issue they had. That is why you must be on offense to rectify the problem.

. . .

On what you should regard as success: Success comes in many forms. Money is a way to put a number or quantity on some elements of success. There are several ways to calibrate or define some levels of success. There are halls of distinction, and there are many measures of what others think of you that can make up for success. You may need to decide what success would mean to you. Cap's Dad, Harry, had an interesting way of measuring success "A rich man is one who, if he had a flat tire anywhere in the county, someone would assist him faster than his wife could make a loaf of bread."

On solving mysteries, you have no business solving: No one had seen anyone throw the catfish into the city pool. Although some connective tissue led to the culprits being a couple of brothers who were sons of one of H-D Feed's customers, there was no first-hand evidence of their involvement. Those fish could have been dropped from an airplane or placed there by a disgruntled former lifeguard. There are over 46 million anglers in the United States. Any of them could have done it. Free the Van Weederharry Brothers!

On sneaking up on someone: Never sneak up on anyone—especially not an unsuspecting dairyman in a milking parlor with a high-pressure hose.

On learning a second language: Dutch, the Dairyman may be a challenging place to start.

6

THREE LITTLE WORDS FOR THE BELL COW

The weeklong visit at H-D Feed was nearly over. Shane, as required, stayed on through Saturday to work the retail store's busiest day. He was dead tired as he rolled into H-D World headquarters. A significant reason for his fatigue was that he had become a bit of a celebrity in town. He worked full days all week, meeting various livestock producers and riding with a salesperson or Cap daily. In the evening, after checking his Mission Impossible answering machine, it was a bit of a different story. Wednesday night, he had played another softball game for Cap's team. He scored three hits and 0 runs, but the H-D Scholars were victorious again. He participated in the postgame parking lot fermented beverage ritual and used the 'Interpersonal Dragnet' on several teammates. He tempered the replay of the number of beverages he had consumed versus earlier in the week. On Thursday, things took a bit of a Twilight Zone turn on him, and as usual, he went with the flow.

One of Cap's dairy customer's wives had met Shane while he was at her farm weighing calves for an animal feeding trial with the dairy specialist, Andy, from H-D Feed. She was charming and uniquely attractive for being twice Shane's age. She was unusually interested in what the men were doing and hung around attentively. In addition, she was rather flirtatious with Shane. He thought it might be one of those 'he is a cute intern thing', similar to how we treat puppies. Bernice jumped right in, weighing calves; however, she was no colleague of silence. She kept talking, asking questions about Shane and flirting to the point that Andy pulled the plug by saying, "We have enough data, Bernice. I will return in a week to weigh the next group. Thanks for the help."

When they got back to the H-D truck, Andy decided to have a little fun with the intern. "So what kind of pheromone are you wearin' there, Ringo?"

Shane was embarrassed but knew playing naïve had worked well for him so far, so he continued, "Not sure what you are asking," said Shane. That was a fib. Shane and Andy both knew to leave it alone.

That same day they met Cap at the diner for lunch, and now the formerly precautious patrons were hollering out Shane's name as he entered. Shane went over to each patron to shake hands and say hello. Less than a week ago, they thought he might be here to steal their cars, but now they would loan theirs to him. Small towns, you gotta love em.

Cap had been at the store tending to product orders and met at the restaurant to get caught up on business with Andy. After Andy left for the restroom, Cap had a proposition for Shane. "I received an unusual phone call from one of my customer's wives this morning, Bernice Lindell." Shane tried to appear solid, you know, 'golfer calm'. However, his internal temperature elevated substantially to near combustion. Shane was worried about something she might have misinterpreted or, God knows, have even perceived that Shane would be interested in her. The implication of anything going through his racing mind could mean eleven days of the shortest internship ever in agriculture. All he could think of was how glad he was that Andy had been there. As his mind zoomed, he thought having an eyewitness to what happened might be the most fortunate thing to occur all summer.

Cap continued, "She called with a strange but potentially beneficial opportunity for you."

Shane was nearly in cardiac arrest, and his head was pounding from the concern about what he might say next.

"Now, you don't have to do this, and I don't think it will hurt my business in any way if you say no." Shane was feeling some relief but still may need a defibrillator.

"Bernice has a daughter Diane, who is home from college. She is a senior at Eastern Michigan, and she is a knockout. She is not dating anyone right now, and Bernice wanted to know if you would like to meet her and go out with her Friday night."

As overwhelming relief re-entered his body, it made him hard of hearing.

"Would you repeat that, please?" said Shane.

Cap obliged and provided additional context. The family had season passes to an oval track modified stock car race in Spokane. The family couldn't go, and she wanted to know if Shane would take their daughter. Shane was so relieved that he said, "Of course, if it helps you, I am your mercenary intern."

Andy returned from the bathroom, oblivious to the conversation Cap just had with Shane. Andy wanted to share "The Chronicles of Bernice" and her interest in H-D Feed's intern teen idol.

Andy, with a hint of jealousy, was pouring syrup on the event and expanding the story's scope like it was now a feature on the evening tabloid news. Shane, who had collected himself from the news he had gotten from Cap, said, "It appears I might have been getting interviewed for my intentions, and I guess I passed." Shane walked away with his chest puffed out on his way to the bathroom, leaving Andy and Cap to live out their fantasies.

So back to Saturday morning, Shane was at the store on the retail floor packing out feed, loading hay, and sweeping the dock between orders. Cap had given 'Boo-Boo the warehouseman' a rare day off because Shane could cover for him. Shane had already consumed 3 cups of coffee, completing his allotment for the year. No matter how much 'inner Butch' Fronk would want him to spread on his toast that morning, he did not look good.

Cap had been out with a dairyman checking his bulk tanks and supplies when Mother Nature brought a breached Holstein calf to this dairy farm. No one was around, and the dairyman was milking, so Cap got his calf puller from his truck. He secured the legs, reversed the calf in the birth canal, and safely brought a new heifer calf into the world. Cap stepped proudly into the front door of H-D Feed, covered in dried birthing fluid, dirt, and blood. Knowing Cap, Shane thought he might wear these clothes as a badge of honor for the rest of the day.

Shane passed him, wheeling some bags of chick starter on a hand cart out to the front dock. The elderly lady who had ordered the feed tried to tip him, but he wouldn't take it. "All part of what we do here at H-D Feed, ma'am."

Cap waved at Shane and invited him over to the corner of the warehouse. Cap began with the high school locker room stuff right away. "So, in case you are wondering why I look like this, I pulled a calf this morning. That is the reason I look the way I do. What is your excuse? Were you in a similar predicament last night?"

Shane shot back, "One thing I will put in my intern report is that old men seem to want to live vicariously through their intern."

They both laughed like a couple of frat brothers.

"Ok. Did you have a good time? I didn't want to wake you this morning to find out." Cap was more curious than ever, even though he knew Shane's comments about 'vicarious living' was correct.

"We did have a fine time. The races were fun, and that Jan Sneva could drive. Also, dating a woman old enough to buy beer legally is great. I can confidently tell you that the 'fiduciary trust' of H-D Feed at Lindell Farms is in proud standing. I wrote the family a thank you note this morning on your stationary, and it is going out in today's mail pickup."

"You are good there, Heffner. Will you go out again?" Cap is nearly panting.

"Not sure. She is a very nice girl, and you said it well. She is gorgeous."

"So what is the problem?"

"Well, she certainly has a couple of her mother's traits. She is aggressive and likes to have a good time. But she for sure flunked mime college because that girl talks so much, she would give a woodpecker a headache."

Cap belly-laughed until he soiled himself a little, but as messed up as his clothes were, no one would notice. Shane went off to load up some peat moss and sweet feed. As he walked away, he said, "Go home and clean yourself. You have a house to clean; your family is coming home today."

As he watched Shane take care of customers, Cap was amazed at how much he liked this kid and how well he fit into their organization.

During a break, Shane checked in with a phone call to Dreamweaver. His next week was all organized, and they caught up on almost all of Shane's learnings for the week. He left out the dating discussion. Both commented on what a great guy Cap was, and Shane ended the conversation with how glad he was he could spend his first week with H-D Feed.

After the phone call, Shane sat in Cap's office chair and fell dead asleep for what might have been 10 to 15 minutes. He woke up and realized what had happened. He ran to the dock to get to work. As he passed the front counter, Fritter got her intern ribbing in, "Siesta, there, lover boy?" Shane turned as red as a freshly painted barn and blew a kiss as he went out to load hay.

Cap returned around three o'clock to help with the four o'clock hour as he knew everyone would be coming to get their supplies for the rest of the weekend. He closed at five PM and was not open on Sundays. The business was brisk, and Shane was glad he got that brief semi-discreet nap earlier in the day as he loaded several tons of product that afternoon.

As they closed for the day, Cap said, "Come back to my office. I want to talk to you"

Shane was a little curious as to what he might want.

Sitting opposite Cap's desk, he could still hear KGA country radio over the show floor in the background. Patsy Cline was enhancing the day.

"Did you have fun here this week, and did you learn something?"

"Secondhand compliments are the best you ever get. So, my boss, Mr. Gilmour, I was talking about what a great organization you have and what a great teacher you are. Many thanks for your hospitality and your patience," Shane replied.

"You are welcome here anytime, and I hope you come back so I can hire you," Cap said with a handshake.

"Well, that is about the nicest thing anyone could say." And as usual, Shane threw in the following unexpected comment. "When I marry that Lindell girl, I might be your customer."

Cap laughed, collected himself with a serious tone, and pitched back a zinger, "Which one, Diane or her mom Bernice?" As a good feed dealer would do, he never stopped selling, "Whichever one it is, we sell a full selection of ear protection." Shane nearly blew a snot bubble with his laughter.

"There are two pieces of unfinished business you and I have." With a guy like Cap, that does spike your curiosity.

Cap got back into a serious demeanor. "First, here is your H-D Scholars Baseball jersey. We didn't have any place to retire the number, so we thought you might want to wear it around campus."

Shane was sincerely excited, "That will go perfectly with my bib overalls. Many thanks, Cap."

Then Cap sat back in his leather desk chair, arms crossed, and asked, "Have you figured it out yet?"

Shane was as confused as a raccoon with a Rubik's cube.

"Uh…I am sure there is a lot I don't have figured out. Can you help me a little?"

Cap responded, "The three words that Harry got his written rules down to. Remember, I told you that at the commencement ceremony this week that I was going to ask you what you thought those words might be." Shane vaguely remembered but had not considered formulating a real answer to what Cap thought was important. He blurted out with a high voice rising on the last word so that Cap would understand he was guessing, "Service for all?".

Cap took control of the lesson. "My Dad, Harry, was a student of people and life. He loved to hang out with astute and interesting leaders. He would ask clergymen, other ag leaders, and college professors, but never politicians, for obvious reasons, what the real meaning of success in life was." He continued, "They would always have many communications about philosophy and life discoveries."

"Harry happened to be having a multiple cocktail dinner with one of the key leaders at Alumni Feed, who he greatly admired. As Dad called him, he and 'Old Blue' would compare business experiences each time they got together. On this occasion, he asked 'Blue' what he saw as the real keys to a successful business career."

Cap was now subconsciously personifying his dad, and Shane could see a glimmer of a different tone of voice and accent in his speech.

My dad said that Blue pondered for about as long as it would take to get someone uncomfortable, and then he delivered his answer. Blue would say he had met people from all over the world from many different cultures, occupations, and dialects. But he thought three words crystallized the question he asked no matter where he was or the situation. Shane watched as Cap stood and pointed to an eight by 10-inch ornately decorated wooden frame that majestically displayed a piece of needlepoint. The white canvas greatly contrasted the dark brown hand-stitched calligraphic letters that read: '**Thee, Before Me**.'

Shane blurted out, "Power of three," before he could catch himself. He then had to explain that it referred to his buddy 'Fronk, the Wheat Gangsta,' who theorized on the beauty of the world order that has things in groups of three related to one's ability to recall hits.

Cap liked the reference and said, "Maybe that's why it has so easily stuck with me all these years." He expanded, "Dad would say this became his one size fits all manual on handling customers, family, employees, and even suppliers."

Shane questioned, "I understand that giving more of yourself and putting others first will yield more rewards, but why would you say, suppliers? Shouldn't they give you more?"

Cap responded, "You are right. The job of the supplier is to provide us with products or services. However, if all one does is take from them, it will eventually catch up. Let me give you an example. How would they react if I called the Alumni feed order and billing department to tell them they shipped me ten bags of product I didn't pay for? "

"Maybe surprised, probably thankful, certainly not negative for pointing out the mistake," Shane replied.

"What if at the start of fertilizer season, we send the order ladies at our fertilizer supplier a cake that says H-D appreciates you? What if we invite all our key suppliers for breakfast and a local course golf scramble once a year? That is the stuff Harry did, and we carry on because it is the right thing to do."

"What if I help them by sitting on a feedback panel at a convention or even calling one of those suppliers to tell them they are doing a good job of helping me grow my business?"

"I think they would love it," said Shane.

"Exactly. And the next time I have an emergency surrounding feed, fertilizer, or shavings, such as a shortage of product or negative change coming that could affect my business, whom do you think they will call first among all their customers?"

"I assume it would be you," said the inexperienced Shane.

"I would hope so. They don't need to, but even the folks in large corporate organizations have their favorites if you think about it. They are all humans and have the same likes and dislikes in customers that I do in my business. People lazily miss this point with suppliers. I try to limit my suppliers to the point where I am significant to them. If they lost me, it would have some impact. Due to this, there is a better chance that I will be treated with additional respect. Merge that with the idea of giving them support back, and that partnership is potent" Cap was animated about the concept.

"Makes sense. You mentioned employees. Can you elaborate?"

"We have a prime example right here at H-D Feed in Boo-Boo. We are not trying to get a Nobel Peace Prize for human engineering, but if it weren't for my dad giving attention and guidance to Boo-Boo, he would have ended up in a bad place. Employees appreciate salary but crave acknowledgment that they are doing a good job and want to know how to do even better. That is why I get them to all the Alumni Feed training courses I can. Paying consistent attention to employees is not hard work, but it is hard to do, especially when so many things come at you, as we do in our small business. I remind myself that investing 3 to 4 minutes a week with an employee deters them from going down the street to apply at a competitor, trucking company, or supermarket. In summary, I want to build leaders at every level in my organization, and giving some of me is part of the solution to making that happen. Sometimes that can be as simple as appropriately placed humor."

An unusual rattling noise was coming from the front of the store, and that caused the two of them to stop the conversation and check it out.

A customer was shaking the locked front door. Cap moved quickly, opened the door, and graciously invited one of the dairyman's wives in to pick up some rubber boots, calf medicine, dog food, and a dozen eggs from the cooler. Cap carried her eggs as they walked to her car and explained that the register was already closed, but he would write it down so she could pay the next time she was there. The customer was thrilled and hugged Cap after he put the dog food into the back of her pickup.

Seeing this as a great exit point, Shane told Cap, "Thanks for everything, including that last example in thee, before me."

Cap shook his hand and said, "The employment offer is always open."

Shane had shined up Emmitt for his date with Diane the night before, so he was headed back home to see his family for the night. He thought about stopping to say goodbye to Diane but didn't have a tourniquet in case his ears started bleeding from her relentless dialogue.

Three Dog Night was oozing out of the Jensen speakers as he crept Emmitt through town. It was a warm evening, and he had the windows down, smelling local dairies offal and the first cutting alfalfa from the fields in the distance. Just out of the city limits coming towards him was one of his softball teammates, 'Oyster,' as Cap called him, an outstanding center fielder, pulled to the side of the road, stopped his truck, and got out to stop Shane. It was a Saturday night, so there was limited traffic. 'Oyster' chatted for nearly 20 minutes about everything going on in town over the weekend, including his knowledge of Shane's date with Diane Lindell, the water hose incident with Gerritt, and his theory on how the catfish ended up in the city pool. The speed of communication in a small town is relentless.

Shane thought about where he was currently, and a wry smile crept upon him. Shane was talking to another peer in the middle of an almost abandoned road. Shane had become a 'Bell Cow.'

What a difference a week can make in small-town America.

Shane's Learnings

On how to build leadership within your organization: Paying consistent attention to employees is not hard work, but it is hard to do. Especially when you have so many things coming at you as we do in our small business, I remind myself that investing 3 to 4 minutes a week with an employee deters them from going down the street to apply at a competitor, trucking company, or supermarket. Cap said I want to build leaders at every level in my organization; giving some of me is part of the solution to making that happen. Sometimes that can be as simple as a bit of appropriately placed humor.

. . .

On what to recognize in highly stressed situations: When overwhelming relief starts to do its re-entry into your body, it sometimes makes you hard of hearing. Breathe, take a moment, and ask for a repeat of what was said.

On the universal lessons in the world for handling customers: 3 words crystallize the best way to handle any customer situation, no matter where he was or what the situation was…'*Thee, Before Me.*' Harry said this became his one-size-fits-all manual on how to deal with customers, family, employees, and even suppliers.

On the idea of applying *Thee, Before Me* to suppliers: Shane questioned, "I understand that giving more of yourself and putting others first will yield more rewards, but why would you say, suppliers? Shouldn't they give you more?" Cap responded, "You are right. The job of the supplier is to provide you with products or services. However, if all you do is take from them, it will eventually catch up to you. Even large corporate organizations have their favorites. They are all humans and have the same likes and dislikes in customers that I do in my business. People lazily miss this point with suppliers. I try to limit my suppliers to where I am significant to them. If they lost me, it would cause some degree of negativity. There is a better chance that I will be treated with additional respect due to this fact. Merge that with the idea of giving them support back, and that partnership is potent"

On the area of praise: Secondhand compliments are the best you ever get.

. . .

On going the extra mile for a customer when you don't have to: A customer was shaking the front door of the store that Cap had locked when this conversation started. Cap moved quickly, opened the door, and graciously invited in one of the dairyman's wives. She had come to pick up some rubber boots, calf medicine, dog food, and a dozen eggs. As Cap walked her to her car, carrying her eggs, he explained that the register was already closed, but he would write it down, and she could pay it the next time she was in. The customer was thrilled and hugged Cap after he lifted the dog food into the back of her pickup. Shane did the same thing cleaning the chicken brooder earlier in the week.

On one key learning for interns: "Old men seem to want to live vicariously through their intern".

7

"HOW ABOUT SOME COBBLER WITH THAT MAGPIE?"

Shane was christened by the crew at H-D Feed. Following the inaugural assignment with Cap and H-D he worked the second week riding along with two different Alumni salespeople. Their travels allowed Shane to meet with multiple dealers across Southern Idaho. He had great interviews with dealers who shared ideas of how Alumni could help all dealers do a better job of marketing their expertise and knowledge to prospects. He had several discussions with his boss. The Lindell girl he had taken to the stock car races left a message of 200 words per minute with gusts up to 280 on his Mission Impossible home-based answering machine. That call turned his brothers loose with merciless teasing and 'tail biting'. Of course, Shane shot back at the two bachelors, reminding them that at least someone was calling and leaving him a message. Jealousy can drive abhorrent behavior, even in rural America.

Shane finished up his week with a drive from Lewiston, Idaho after working the Co-op retail floor and having a lady chew him out because he brought the wrong bag of dog food to her car. He retrieved the accurate brand quickly and, on the way back to the car, he grabbed a bag of dog treats to negotiate détente. Shane offered to pay for the treats, but the manager thought it was a great idea and said he would instruct employees to do the same in the future.

Shane was eager to see his family and specifically, their washing machine on his Sunday off. He pulled into the comfort of his Whitman County hometown around 8 p.m. Saturday.

Saturday night 'on the Palouse' could never be confused with Mardi Gras. Nevertheless, before he went to the farm, Shane stopped in town at the local landmark restaurant the Grain Bin Grill for a bite to eat. Optimistically he hoped to connect with people he had known for most of his life. The surreal thing about these relationships is that you could pick up approximately where you left off in just a few sentences. Much like missing a soap opera, if you miss six months of episodes, you can principally be all caught up in a few minutes.

The Grain Bin Grill, commonly called the "GBG", was the only restaurant open this time of night. As he entered, he was welcomed with at least fifteen minutes of steady hellos and backslaps. Most of these patrons, Shane hadn't seen in a couple of years. Not a lot had changed in the place. This local eatery is loaded with homegrown flavor. Vintage farm equipment advertising adorned the walls, iron tractor seats and autographed hats of local farmers hung directly from the ceiling. All this personalized ambience has a light coat of oil and varying layers of dust. This form of food-born patina was generated from the thousands of meals that had been served there combined with the inadequate ventilation system that struggled to keep the café's air purified. Shane got nostalgic seeing the personalized ceramic coffee cups that had the names of farmers and frequent patron painted on them by Rebecca, the restaurant owner's daughter. Shane and Rebecca dated for a short time in high school. He hadn't seen her since she went off to Stanford. After a quick search Shane saw his dad's signed John Deere hat and his cup with, **Boxcar** on it prominently displayed next to the pie safe.

The jukebox offered a steady supply of Glen Campbell with *"Galveston"* and *"Try a Little Kindness"* mingled amongst the patron's discussions. This single-focused music portfolio more than likely signaled that John 'Magpie' Wilkins was in the restaurant somewhere. Magpie just loved to dominate the jukebox in his booth with his remote playlist. His musical love affair was mainly with Glen Campbell. Each booth in the restaurant had a chrome box featuring a rounded windshield that provided a view to music choices by flipping through metal book pages inside each bubble. Once you made a choice, you punched in a number which was networked to the main juke box and eventually your choice would play. Joe Warrens, the restauranteur was no idiot. He had the jukebox supplier out of Spokane put a heavy dosage of 'Glen' on the jukebox. Like a bass to a minnow, this would draw Mr. Wilkins to the GBG with great frequency. Shane saw all 300 pounds of Magpie sitting solo in a corner booth, smoking a cigar, with a stack of jukebox quarters in front of him. His physique was punishing every stitch in his Carhartt denim painter's pants. His Wrangler shirt was a heavily starched white western style that was thankfully a couple of sizes too large. John had flowing black wavy hair that was styled with what appeared to be a quart of 10 W-30 motor oil. His locks were always clean and had color and flow that would make a beautician drool. However, he evidently just felt the additional lubricant made a statement. The misfortune of the oil was that it also left an irregular and distinctive stain on his taco-shaped straw cowboy hat. His deep tan really illuminated in contrast to his white shirt. John's voice was not particularly deep but is tone had been altered by years of cigars and truck stop cuisine. His nick name

'Magpie', which never bothered him because he had a fleet of grain trucks painted black and white. He and his company, Bigfoot Grain, transported grain all over the Pacific Northwest but Whitman County remained his home base. The graphics on the side of the trucks were tastefully done with a friendly Sasquatch the centerpiece of his logo.

As Shane escaped his adoring fans to use the restroom, he walked by Magpie's table and was bit alarmed to hear him say, "Hey there son. Aren't you Boxcar's kid?"

"Yes Mr. Wilkins, Shane is my name." As they shook hands, Shane noted the manhole cover size of John's hands and was sure he was a hell of a nose tackle at one point in his life.

John released the grip and sat back in the booth. "I see you were on a bathroom mission, when you get through please stop back, I would like to talk with you."

Shane's mind was wondering about all the things this 'round bale-sized' entrepreneur, may want to talk to discuss. After he relieved himself of the 80 miles of driving from Lewiston, he was headed back for this mystery conversation.

"Sit down young man," said John with an elevated voice to get above the noise offered by Glen Campbell.

"Thank you, sir."

"Call me John."

"Yes sir."

"So, I saw your dad in here the other day. We had coffee and he was telling me what you were up to this summer. Man, he is proud of you and the decision you made this summer," said John with a five-inch cigar partially hiding his smile.

Shane didn't know what to say but was thinking about the second-hand compliment theory being very real. He replied, "Thanks, I am not sure I would have ever heard that."

"He sat right where you are sitting and we got to talking about it. He also said you had been workin' with Cap and the group at H-D Feed."

Shane could feel the nervousness dissipate as his cheeks elevated revealing some resemblance of his trademark smile as he thought about his time at H-D.

"How do you know Cap?" a curious Shane wanted to keep the conversation moving.

"I can share a great deal about H-D and most of the Alumni Feed dealers in the Pacific Northwest, as we haul grain, feed or supplies to nearly all of them."

John was a gentleman and realized he had interrupted Shane's real purpose for coming to the restaurant. He hollered to Annette who always waited on him at the Grain Bin, "Annette, bring my new friend here a menu and put his meal on my tab."

Shane was surprised yet thankful and ordered the pork chop, applesauce and hash brown special. While this order was prepared, John was ready to hold court.

"When I first got started nearly 25 years ago Harry, Cap's dad, gave me a two load advance on hauling feed to him because he liked what I had done in my first few runs when I was driving the loads myself." John got very reflective as he talked about his beginning. "I have some favorite customers, and H-D is on that list because they know what a partnership is all about. I tried to adopt a lot of their business practices into mine and I will say it has worked."

"Have you seen Harry's embroidery that Cap keeps in his office?" Shane asked.

John lowered his chin exposing additional jowl and looked side saddle at Shane with a glance of surprise that Shane knew about this. "Would love for you to come ride in one of our trucks. On the dash on each of the trucks I own, it reads the same three words… **Thee, before me."**

"I can see how it relates to someone that deals with retail customers and farmers, but how does that apply to a trucking firm?" Shane was curious.

"I think it is almost the same with our customers, like your dad. I try to build into the driver's head that they especially need to apply the concept to the other drivers on the road. One of the biggest costs we have is insurance. However, the biggest weight I have on my mind is personal injury to a citizen or driver. The whole notion of **thee before me**, is like having a driving instructor in the cab."

That last statement seemed overkill to Shane. During dinner, Magpie said that the statement may not have miraculous impact on the drivers, but if nothing else, it just made him feel better that they would think about it. Shane also figured out that John appeared to be asking a lot of questions about him. It almost seemed like he was interviewing Shane. Truth is, he was. A good businessman in the agricultural field will look for talent wherever they can find it. Instinctively Shane was honored but he heard his basketball coach instructing him to 'lean in'. The premise of leaning in was similar to going on the offense. Shane wanted to really know how John Wilkins built such a successful business. So, it was time to lean in.

"Mr. Wilkins, I appreciate your questions about my internship, and I want to thank you for dinner."

"You are welcome son."

"I hope you don't mind if I ask a couple of questions about your business, but more importantly your success," said Shane. He was now a fierce power forward and on the offense.

John smiled and said confidently, "You can ask about anything but my logbooks," he winked like a winning lawyer.

Shane waded in, "Every time I see one of your black and white Bigfoot Grain trucks going down the road, I wonder how you achieved such success?"

With Glen Campbell crooning *"Wichita Lineman"* in the background and Annette bringing homemade peach cobbler made with flour from Whitman County wheat for the two of them, John began sharing the story of his trucking firm.

He spoke about discovering the need for the service while scooping out the back corners of delivery grain trucks at a cooperative grain elevator. There were never enough trucks available, and farmers were having to wait days to ship out their grain. He said that getting good talent involved in the operations and having safe passionate drivers was so important. The key to keeping them employed versus getting their own truck was to create a sense of ownership. He had done this with profit sharing on a per truck basis. John talked about hard work; treating people right; and handling mistakes quickly. Then he doubled back on his own offense.

"Young man, it sounds like you want to be successful," John said as he relit his cigar.

"Yes sir, I think a lot of people want that."

"I think what people wants and their willingness to do what it takes for success are canyons apart. I overheard a feed dealer in Modesto, California talking to a less-than-productive employee who wanted to be manager of the store say… The only place that success comes before work is in the dictionary." Shane was double-checking his alphabet and smiled as he appreciated the synthesis.

"Son, I want to ask you the same two difficult questions that a great fertilizer dealer in central Oregon asked me over 25 years ago when I asked him the same question." Magpie stopped for additional effect. John leaned forward for the first time and asked Shane in a slightly lowered but deliberate voice, "Number one; how hard do you dream, son?"

After a pause nearly long enough to make him think his cobbler might go moldy, Shane was abruptly not on offense. "Uh, I am not sure what you are asking."

"Well, do you dream often? Do you dream in color? Do you dream vividly? Do you dream in issue solving? Do your dreams scare you?" he was asking in a teaching manner, not in judgement.

"I do dream sir, but I gotta be honest, I am not sure of the importance of it. Can you give me a bit more of an explanation?" asked Shane.

"It is elementary when you think about it. What would the world look like if no one had any dreams? My guess is that we would all be closer to cavemen than the good looking, high functioning intellects we are today." The smile that accompanied this wisdom made a pitching wedge-sized divot dimple show up on Magpie's cheek.

"Let me give you some examples of things that have happened as a direct result of someone's dreams. The sewing machine came from someone who was a tailor dreaming of a better way to sew clothes. Insulin as a treatment for diabetes came from a dream that a scientist had. The song "Yesterday" by the Beatles, and arguably the most performed song in history, came to Paul McCartney in a dream. Einstein and Thomas Edison were strong beneficiaries of dreams; and both talked about the benefits of napping." Since 1969, Magpie said he had taken a nap every day and always had a pocket-sized note pad with him so he could write down anything of significance from the sleep break.

John said, "Show me a successful businessperson, clergyman, athlete or cheerleader, and I will bet they dream more than the average person."

"I get the impact but there has got to be more to it than just dreaming about it;" said Shane in a coaxing way to see if he could get more information.

"A great point. No matter how much or how hard I dream it,

FEED YOUR LIFE

there is a good chance I won't be a racehorse jockey," John reaffirmed as he lovingly patted his girth. He pointed out that they had to have the skills and some ability to do any of those things, but those dreams helped make the good even better.

John leaned in some more as he looked at Shane and said, "An equally important question I will ask is, number two; what is it that you love doing?"

You thought the last pause was long. Shane stared with a blank face because he didn't know the answer to that question.

"When did you know that you loved trucking?" inquired Shane.

"I used to line up my trucks in the sandbox as if I had a fleet and I would haul sand around and make believe it was different stuff that I was hauling. I could play for hours. That got me interested. **The ride** got me addicted. My Uncle Roscoe had a two-ton cab over truck that he used to haul hay to local dairymen. The very first time I rode in that Ford C-600, I was in love sitting up high in that cabover bobtail, viewing the whole road, bouncing along, listening to the whine of the transmission. The ride was heaven." Magpie was mildly out of breath and oozed perspiration because of the emotion this flashback was bringing to him.

Shane was doing a lot of reflection as John talked about his real love of hauling things in a truck. It might explain John's two failed marriages.

"I get the idea that you are a little uncomfortable right now," said John with an empathetic tone.

Shane pushed back his horse mane length hair by running his fingers through it as he looked down at the remnants of his cobbler. "Maybe more than a little uncomfortable. I mean, here I am nearly twenty years old, and I don't have something that I can identify as that which I would really love to do."

"Good," said John. Shane was thinking that now is when he

kidnaps me, throws me in a cab over truck and changes my life with long-haul addiction.

John repeated, "That uncertainty is REAL GOOD! You know why I say that?"

"No sir, I don't."

"For two reasons: One, if you are not uncomfortable, you are not growing. Nearly every day I have varying and ample amount of what I call restlessness. Tackling issues keeps me uncomfortable and it forces me to germinate new ideas and have personal growth. Two, you recognize the importance and usefulness of being able to look at an array of things that might be interesting to you. And by the way, you are young enough to find all kinds of loves."

Shane felt better and was kind of excited about what this discussion could mean for his internship and his future. Magpie had one more example.

"So few people in this world ever figure out what they are passionate about and actually fulfill that passion. I went to high school with a graduating class of twenty-three at Buckshaw High School. One of my classmates, Craig Jesse, went to Washington State University and then on to law school at Seattle University. He loved playing football, but what he wanted to do more than anything was to coach high school football at Buckshaw High School."

John continued, "The head football coaching job at Buckshaw came open paying eight hundred dollars per *year!* He had finished law school, and after four months of studying he passed the bar. He received three job offers in the Seattle area with distinguished law firms but rejected them all. He relocated back to Buckshaw and moved into a borrowed airstream trailer that was attached to the high school agriculture shop building. He took a contract job cutting and wrapping meat in Buckshaw to help make ends meet. There was little need for a trial lawyer in Buckshaw, Washington.

The first two years were rough, but the football team had four wins and four losses the third year. The fourth year, there were two young men that transferred to town from the Oregon coast with their parents. They both could run faster than a dirt bike. Craig and his players put it all together that season and went to the Kingdome in Seattle to play for the State Championship. The Buckshaw Reapers and Craig Jesse were state champions. He took a job with a law firm in Yakima, Washington, and left the Buckshaw program right after the championship game. Three months after he moved to Yakima, he learned he had contracted leukemia. He was dead before Buckshaw started their next year."

Shane had heard a little about this, but he never knew the details the way John did. "What an incredibly sad story."

"You know, a lot of people would look at it that way. I have a different perspective. While it is an atrocity, I would also say Craig was one of the few."

"One of the few?" Shane was brimming with hyper-curiosity.

"The few that actually achieve perfection at exactly what they loved and always dreamed about."

Shane felt secure enough with what they had shared to follow with a bit of a zinger for John, "Are you one of the few?"

John giggled a little and said, "In some ways, yes. But as you can tell, I am far from the perfection that Craig achieved by taking an underdog all the way to the championship."

"Passion is one of the key diversifiers that sets one person apart from another. Craig had a passion for something that few could see themselves being enthused about. Buckshaw had little historical football achievement to build on and paid below welfare wages. Craig was working two jobs and living in an aluminum tube, but he saw it through to the end."

"What an amazing story." Shane was beginning to share in John's affection for the story.

"You know, there are a lot of your Alumni Feed dealers that have similar passion and love for what they do. That ingredient, passion, is the major difference between a place to buy feed and a place to have an experience. Passion makes all the difference. I think you will see that as you meet more of the dealers." John asked, "Who are you seeing next?"

"Caldwell Grain in Moses Lake next week."

"You will see passion, diversity and some true characters there- like you have never witnessed. They are one of my favorites for sure."

Annette came to get Magpie to pay her so she could go home. Their lengthy conversation had continued while the place drained of other patrons. He tipped her about the same amount as he paid for the meal. Magpie looked at Shane, who was amazed by the amount of the tip, and said, "Booth rental." Shane smiled and thanked Mr. Wilkins excessively. Shane took his business card. He would send him a thank you note.

"I am not sure I have the ability to re-pay you for the Master's course you gave me this evening." John smiled like he just received a new Kenworth.

The payphone near the bathroom in the hallway rang multiple times. Annette left to answer it and after an exchange, came to get John. John meandered down the hallway like a brood cow on the mature dirt path to the watering tank.

The conversation took about ten minutes. Shane felt it necessary to hang around to repeat the thanks and say good night. Shane overheard John say, "I might have a solution, let me ask." John walked back and said to Shane, "When are you headed to Moses Lake?"

Shane confirmed he was leaving tomorrow night; to which John asked, "Got room for me to ride along?"

"It would be an honor to take you."

John looked a little relieved, "What time we leavin'?"

"Six p.m. work for you?"

"Can you pick me up at my shop? I will fill you in with the details on the way."

"See you then."

John went back to the phone to tell whoever he was talking to that he would take care of it and he would acquire the truck early Monday morning.

Shane's Learnings

On Secondhand compliments: As discussed in earlier chapters, they are still the most valuable you can get. Relish them and pass them along as we discussed earlier.

On the premise of 'leaning in': It is like going on the offense in basketball. This can include taking the lead on questions or action vs. laying back. In snow skiing, if you lean back versus leaning forward over the tops of your skis, you will be more likely to lose control and be a much less effective skier. Similarly, if you wait to act and let others to take the lead in areas such as conversation, asking a question, or donating time and effort to charity, you will not be as effective as you would if you lean into it. Leaning in gives you more control.

On the power of dreaming: Show me a successful businessperson, clergyman, athlete, or cheerleader, and I will bet they dream more than the average person. Keeping a note pad by your bed is a great way to capture whispers that can change your life. Provide yourself with adequate time to reflect. Dream hard.

On the intense power of Passion: Passion is one of the key diversifiers that sets one person apart from another. Doing what you love to do versus having a job or career is one of the world's most freeing exercises. The often-used phrase of ***do what you love, and the money will follow*** is not always true. But loving what you do is like a multiplication factor to your potential success. If you look at many of the more accomplished businesspeople in your community or in the world, they often say, "I would have done this or that no matter what income it generated."…. They love it.

On the liberating privilege of being uncomfortable: If you are not ***uncomfortable***, you are not growing. The reason most frequently given as to why people don't do certain things is that they feel uncomfortable because they don't have a lot of experience in that area. That dilemma reminds me of a basketball coach who once told me, "I would play you more if you had more experience." The only way to grow is to 'GET COMFORTABLE BEING UNCOMFORTABLE'. Leaning in, being a bit scared or intimidated raises your awareness of the possible. That apprehension is fuel for your personal growth.

On the splendor of someone achieving their dreams: "There are few people that actually achieve perfection at what they had always dreamed about."…No matter how insignificant it may seem to you, it may be the most important thing in the world to them…Help them celebrate their success.

. . .

On Work Ethic: The only place where success comes before work is in the dictionary. That is self-explanatory when you think about it. There are no shortcuts to success. Search out any entrepreneurs and they will emphasize this as an important ingredient in the recipe of their success.

On what to put on the jukebox in a restaurant: If one of the biggest spenders with a vast appetite likes Glen Campbell, you put on a large catalog of Glen to keep them coming in.

8

CONNIE MACK GOES TO EPHRATA

Shane spent the scorching summer Sunday with his brothers and Boxcar loading up hay before a coming storm. The alfalfa-grass-hay mix was processed into seventy-five-pound two-string bales earlier in the week. The mobile bale factory was a New Holland 68 baler powered by a purring Wisconsin, two-cylinder gasoline engine. The baler motor groaned with each bale like a first calf heifer passing a newborn. Bales randomly fell out of the back of the baler and were laid in the field to cure. Shane's Dad, Boxcar, turtled the 1953 GMC truck by driving at idle, in low gear between the rows of bales. Shane's brothers were shirtless, with hay chaff sticking to their sweatiness. They picked up the bales one by one, rushed them to the fourteen-foot metal truck bed, and lifted them to the height of the dresser in their room. Shane was tasked with stacking the load in a crosstie pattern to build stability for the unpredictable terrain on the slow trip to the barn. These green, dried, leafy bales were unloaded and stacked safely in the dry barn. They would use this hay over the winter to feed the only cows Boxcar still owned. The day was hot and uncharacteristically humid. KGA radio reported an inch of rain to fall on Monday, but the storm would start that afternoon. Wet hay cannot enter any barn, or it will mold and become a potential fire hazard. The crew was making a load an hour and had started at 5:30 that morning. There was a good chance they would get most of the bales in before Shane had to leave for Moses Lake.

The crew grabbed a sandwich in the truck between loads and backed the last load into a tractor shed undercover just as the thunderstorm and rain began to unleash. Shane packed clothes for the week, showered, and met Magpie at 6 o'clock as planned for the two-and-a-half-hour drive to Moses Lake.

John's dispatcher's call to him last night at the restaurant delivered terrible news for him. One of his most consistent drivers, 'Pipe Arms Albert' had a grueling kidney stone incident and was in the hospital in Ephrata. That is where the truckload of potatoes was when Albert got sidelined trying to pee out some rocks. Shane would take John 25 miles from his hotel to the loaded truck.

Shane's 67 Chevy pickup, Emmitt, led their crusade west on Interstate 90. John was very complimentary of Shane's rig even though there were no Glen Campbell tunes to accompany the journey. Kenny Loggins made an acceptable, but not wholly satisfying, replacement for Glen.

The rain passed quickly, and it was humid as a double shift at a dry cleaner. Shane propped open the side wing windows on Emmitt to get some ventilation moving through the cab. John may have showered earlier in the day, but it was wearing off appreciably. Emmitt's steering was pulling to the right a bit. After some thought, Shane realized that three hundred additional pounds on the passenger's side generated uneven stress on the suspension. He quickly calculated that his half-ton pickup was nearly halfway to its load capacity.

Magpie and Shane covered several random subjects, from high

school sports to working around an open State Patrol weigh station with an overweight load on your truck; to using "Fred of Como's" barbeque sauce on brisket. Magpie was 'leaning in to' most of the non sequitur conversation. Shane was quietly most grateful that John hadn't lit up one of his pungent cigars in his truck.

As they saw the sun setting over Sprague Lake on I-90, Shane asked John how a leader manages a large organization like his.

"Well, it is hard." John was starting to open up. "It's hard to keep up employee morale; hard to keep up with the numbers on how things are going; hard to prospect for new customers; hard to fix issues; and hard to keep up with regulations." He continued, "Hiring the best people you can and getting rid of the ones that can't make it. Those are a few of the most critical tasks."

"Getting rid of the ones that can't make it. That sounds harsh. I am not sure I could fire anyone," said Shane.

"I used to think so as well. But over time, my rational thinking replaced emotion. When I first started, I thought, how can I save this person or fix them? But really, I didn't want to deal with it. I have to be honest. I had a real problem letting someone go." His voice dropped off like he was ashamed of this approach.

"What changed your mind?"

"I was talking to one of my best customers and confidant, Ronny Kerbs, the owner of Yakima Feed. We were comparing notes, and he said he also had a REALLY tough time firing someone at one time. When he had to do it, he said he would grimace about the pain and setback he was causing that individual. He got to the point where he would fire them on a Monday. He would get stinking drunk on Sunday, so he had a bad hangover when he let someone go. The thought was he might be feeling even worse than they did." John was channeling his friend.

"Sounds like an unusually resourceful use of hooch," said Shane.

"Ronny had a revelation about the unsavory process, which, thankfully, he passed on to me." Magpie was smiling, and that pothole-sized dimple came out to play.

John said, "Ronny is a huge baseball fan. He loves the Seattle Mariners and all of major league baseball. The revelation came to Ron, the leader of Yakima Feed, when a major league manager got fired in early September. The fall of the year is when most underperforming managers get axed. Ron thought about the guy, General Manager or President of the team, who had to fire the team manager. He imagined how terribly distraught, or even drunk; the GM must have been." John continued, "Later that day, he heard an interview with the GM who fired the MLB manager, He remembered him saying... While no one likes firing someone, in this case, it was necessary to salvage the team. When players and teams aren't winning, no one is happy, including fans, owners, players, and the manager. No one is satisfied!"

John later added that nearly all major league baseball history had been fired. The only one he could recall that wasn't was Connie Mack, who lasted 53 years with the Philadelphia A's. He had a losing record as the manager, his only pass was that he owned the team.

John continued, "Ronny got to thinking about all the folks he had fired. He kept an eye on most of them with morbid curiosity post-firing from Yakima Feed. He found that in nearly every case, the fired employee had more success elsewhere than they had achieved with his organization. Some even flourished. He took solace in his realization that while it was uncomfortable, he was metaphorically doing them a favor by setting them free."

When he bought the business, Ronny experienced a performance issue with a long-time employee he inherited from his dad. He also happened to be Ron's cousin, Pat. Pat liked to sit in the side window of the store in the office, watching the world go by, supporting his caffeine and nicotine addiction. Ron said the office began to resemble a hookah lounge.

Magpie had delivered a load of feed and was there with Ron during the Pat dilemma, so he asked him, "Don't you really think you put your business at risk by letting him go?" Ron's answer surprised him but made him think. Ron said, "Nah, the bigger risk to the business was if I let him stay."

Pat would go to the front counter when he saw a customer coming, but he was in his window perch the rest of the time. The store was suffering. Ron tried multiple times to alter Pat's behavior. He made sure it was no surprise when he took him to lunch and said, "Pat, you are not a very happy guy. I would say you hate everything about your day at Yakima Feed." Pat was calm and agreed. Ron continued, "I will give you four weeks off with pay to find your happiness in another career because life is too short for you to be this unhappy." He used the GM's approach: "You want your teammates to win; they want you to be happy... Good luck in your search and let me know how I can help."

"How did it turn out for Pat?" Asked Shane.

"Two weeks later, Pat started a job selling coffee and supplies to restaurant chains. Two years later, he was the top salesperson in the company and had quit smoking," said John enthusiastically. "The most interesting detail was that Pat came into the store and thanked Ronny for the wake-up call."

John summarized. "I have had to fire many drivers in my firm since then. Getting my mind right about their happiness, or lack of it as it related to their performance, was one of the biggest lessons I have learned. That process makes firing a better event for everyone, especially me."

As Shane and Magpie passed through Ritzville, Shane asked John about other aspects of running his business. "So when you think about important positions in your company, the truck drivers are a given. Who else is critical?"

"Two critical roles come to mind. The first is the dispatcher, who is a little like an air traffic controller. They help get drivers married up under freight and make key arrangements. They are the most essential to the driver's success. The second most important to me is my financial person. I couldn't operate without her."

"How do you mean?" Shane was looking to pass the next 60 miles with some learning from the Buddha wearing a cowboy hat.

"I mentioned that the air traffic controller is vital to the drivers. Well, I am flying a plane, and it is the whole company. To fly that plane, I need gauges that reflect what is going on with the business, such as: what my costs are so I know how to charge for services, how much cash is in the bank (or fuel) is in the plane; what it costs to run each route; what are the financial returns per trip; and most importantly, am I getting paid? My financial leader provides me with all that in a way I can quickly understand. This enables me to adapt the plane based on her reports or gauges. I want the best financial person I can hire in my corner every minute."

Shane had only been exposed to these ideas briefly in a textbook, so this discussion was interesting and tactical. "That sounds like a hard position to fill," added Shane

"You know what is difficult is getting someone in that role that understands what is important to me in my business. It is a little like sports referees and umpires. They are experts and know the exact details about their respective sports. Ask a baseball umpire to referee a hockey game or judge an equestrian event. They will have difficulty understanding what is important and what would be considered good or bad performance. A person can have financial skills, but applying them to a specific industry is where the difference in excellence comes in."

"How do you get them to know the business to help you the

most?" Asked Shane as he cranked down the driver-side window to breathe some additional mid-June air. Magpie's body odor was now a little ripe, and his overdose of High Karate was wearing off.

"As a first step, I try to find someone with experience in transportation. And I always require they take a trip or two per year with the drivers. The closer they get to the customer, the more opportunity they have to learn. It also goes along with the philosophy that you need to build leaders at all levels of the company".

"Ok, I have heard that twice in two weeks. What do you mean, and how do you do it?" Shane asked while changing the tape deck with a free hand to Merle Haggard. Magpie gave a thumbs up.

"Involve your crew in all parts of the business and share all you can. My drivers get all the company details about loaded miles, costs, and the resulting gross margins. I want them to be conscious that they are running their truck as a business. I make them aware of the profits they make. They know nearly everything about the company except how much money I make and how many calories I consume daily."

"Is there a danger in that you make them better and enable them to leave and compete with you?" asked Shane.

"It has happened a couple of times. One has done well, and we compete fairly, and the other wanted his old job back in a year. There is enough work out there for everybody, and I think competition makes you better."

As Shane herded Emmitt across central Washington's low-lying valleys, the summer-born bugs hit the pickup's windshield like the German Blitzkrieg hit France. John kept adding to his business philosophy recipe.

"Fundamentally, employees love to be involved in the business. I pull groups of them off the road in shifts at least once a year to share the business position and ask them how we can improve it. In my opinion, that keeps them with me as much as the salary"

As they pulled into Ephrata, John asked when he could pay Shane back with a ride in one of his pride-of-the-Bigfoot trucks. Shane told him he would enjoy that but doubted it would be the addictive revelation Magpie experienced.

"Let me buy you dinner. The truck stop at the edge of town has a chicken fried steak that will give you wedding genitalia."

That image would be stuck in Shane's head for a little longer than he wanted. He politely refused and told John, "We are even," and thanked him for the great discussion about how he runs his business. This internship was like a whole season of learning by watching the '**Kung Fu**' TV show.

Shane watched John parade proudly, but slowly, toward the white and black cab over Kenworth grain truck with the Sasquatch logo on the side, peering back at him. Shane waited until the Bigfoot truck was fired up and rolling before he left for his hotel in Moses Lake.

As he entered to check in to the Basin Hotel, he met a man in his mid-thirties wearing an Alumni Feed tennis shirt. He looked to be in distance runner shape and sported a tan that Coppertone could use in an advertisement. His Wranglers were pressed and starched, covering his polished Roper boots to the top of their heels. He approached Shane with a smile resembling a few of the high beams that he quarreled with this evening driving to Ephrata. His hair was almost stitched in place, best described as 'sandy faultless.'

He looked Shane's way and ventured a guess," You must be Shane?"

"Yes sir."

"Monty Chenoweth, territory manager for Alumni. Mr. Gilmour told me you would be in this evening. Nice to finally meet you."

"You as well, Mr. Chenoweth."

"Please call me Monty or 'Choppers' as most of the folks give me a hard time about my teeth," he said with no reluctance or vanity.

After Shane checked in, they met in the spacious lobby area of the Basin Hotel, "home of the endless coffee bar." Shane thought it sounded a lot more majestic than it was.

Monty caught up on the details about Shane; his intern activities, where he was from, Wazzu, family, farming, and of course, Emmitt.

Monty shared his background. He was from Ellensburg. He was a Montana State graduate and had been an intern for a turf company, but later after an aggressive campaign by the Dreamweaver. Chose the Alumni Feed career.

Monty spent the next few minutes preparing Shane for the week ahead. He said he wanted to meet with him before his time at Caldwell Grain to gather some background, offer a forewarning, and share some ground rules.

Caldwell's is looking for a salesperson to replace their livestock feed salesman. Don't be surprised if they let him go this week if Randy, the General Manager, finds the right salesperson. What made him soil himself a bit was that Shane was to sit in on the interviews and hiring of the candidate.

Another warning to Shane was about the unconventional interaction of the Caldwell Brothers with customers, salespeople, each other, and probably with Shane himself. He described it as a combination of a 'Greek Week campus reunion' and a field trip to a comedy club.

"I just want you to be aware that some stuff could come at you in doses and recipes you may not be used to. I also want you to realize that they aren't bad guys, and when they give it to you, they are looking for you to give it right back to them. The good news for you is they are both Wazzu grads and boosters, so that they won't be too hard on someone from their collegiate bloodlines."

Shane was on high alert with this news and combined with his earlier trip to the endless coffee bar; he thought he might not sleep all night.

The uncertainty of tomorrow was quickly overcome by the physical toll of handling eight loads of hay to and into the barn and a hundred fifty miles of driving.

Shane's Learnings

On your most important task as a business leader: "Hiring the best people you can get and getting rid of the ones that can't make it are critical tasks."

On firing someone: No one likes firing someone. In the case of the major league team, it was necessary to salvage the team. When players and teams aren't winning, no one is happy, including fans, owners, players, and the manager. No one is satisfied! IF THEY ARE UNHAPPY, IT IS MOST LIKELY BECAUSE THEY ARE NOT SUCCESSFUL. IF THEY ARE NOT HAPPY OR SUCCESSFUL, THEY NEED TO GO. You must be concerned most about the individual and provide structured coaching. When the decision is made to move on, one benefit you often don't plan for is that you will get the rest of the team's attention. Often, they will weigh in after you let that person go to tell you that you made the right decision and probably delayed this decision because of your hang-ups about letting someone go.

. . .

On making the decision to remove someone: "Do you put your business at risk by letting someone go? Many times, the bigger risk to the business was if I let them stay."

On the recovery experienced by those terminated: If you look historically, those employees that have experienced job finality have often found more success following termination. While it was uncomfortable, removing them from their role may have done them a favor by setting them free to find something they could be happy doing.

On the elements necessary for running a larger organization: Your financial leader provides you with the information you can quickly understand. This information can adapt to the plane you are flying, 'your business,' to what the reports or gauges tell you. You want the best financial person you can hire in your corner every minute. The key to real success with your financial department is getting them to understand the unique elements of your business, industry, and especially customers.

On building leaders at every level: Fundamentally, employees love to be involved in the business. Share business positions and issues. Ask employees about opportunities to improve the overall business. History in almost any business shows that keeping employees engaged and feeling important can be more critical than salary level.

. . .

On the legend of Connie Mack: Most of the managers in major league baseball history have been fired. The most resilient was Connie Mack, who lasted 53 years as the manager of the Philadelphia A's. He had a losing record as the manager but owned the team. Pretty rare if someone doesn't get fired.

9

THE DAY THAT ART APPRECIATION CLASS CAME IN HANDY

Shane arose early, found a Dirigible Donuts franchise store, and bought a dozen zeppelins for his trip to Caldwell's Grain. He figured it worked once at H-D Feed; why not again? He arrived back at the Basin Hotel, where Monty was getting his attitude elevated at the **endless coffee bar.** The coffee bar was a zealous marketer's exaggeration. It consisted of three or four urns of brunette-colored fluid that would etch the bottom out of a Styrofoam cup if left overnight.

Monty shared much more about his family of four, his background, and his love for the feed business. The territory he covered for Alumni Feed, as he called it, **the Beast**, stretched from the Canadian border as far east as Othello, Washington, as far west as Snoqualmie Pass, and as far south as Ellensburg. It was nearly twenty thousand square miles. He worked with twenty-five Alumni Feed dealers and had achieved his sales quota success in six of the last eight years. He was a pro and a bit of a perfectionist, tipped off by how he dressed and how he constantly projected what might happen next. He showed Shane the dealer bulletin he had put together announcing the monthly deals Alumni Feed offered. Also included were the standings of each dealer in terms of their success or lack of it versus last year. He claimed that publishing statistics for all his dealers was an excellent motivator to keep them growing. He put much time into creating it and printed it on heavy gold paper so it would not get lost on a dealer's desk. Shane noticed Caldwell's was number eleven on the growth list. Monty said Caldwell's has always been in the top 2 or 3 of all dealers in growth, but their salesperson, Ernie O' Keefe, was having a rough couple of years, and it was starting to show. This was vital evidence of the need to explore and hire new blood in the sales role.

As they finished breakfast, Monty suggested they leave Shane's pickup at the hotel and ride together for the day. Monty was told to arrive at Caldwell's after 8:30 as the brothers had a meeting with a pet food salesperson. Shane had his icebreaker Dirigible donuts in tow as they started for the store.

Moses Lake, Washington's topography, could be characterized as somewhere between Saudi Arabia's foothills and that stretch of tundra just forty miles outside Hell. It consists of slightly rolling sand hills with occasional rock outcroppings. These forgotten acres were removed from earth's extinction list by the glorious nourishment of water delivered mercifully by the Grand Coulee Dam irrigation project. Franklin Roosevelt's **New Deal** concrete monument and reservoir resuscitated one of the world's sickest landscapes into an agricultural powerhouse. It was fortunate to hold a sagebrush and prairie grass stand without irrigation. The holy water from the Columbia River is pumped over a hundred miles through canals to be used by farmers all over central Washington to produce amazing corn, alfalfa, potato, beet, and grape yields.

This combination of agricultural commodities and available

water made Moses Lake an excellent place for dairy, a feedlot, and a growing swine market. Caldwell's worked to capitalize on this animal agriculture.

Moses Lake is named for the large lake formed in the deep potholes in the earth that are filled with water from Coulee. It offers plentiful duck hunting, fishing, water sports, and water-front living. It is also wide open and relatively flat, as Monty said with a splash of sarcasm that he watched his turtle run away for three years. With the open landscape, he also mentioned that there is a pretty girl behind every tree. There is certainly no national forest here.

The wide-open space around the Caldwell operation made it stick out like a cathedral in a sandbox. The hundred-and-fifty-foot grain elevator leg, surrounded by at least fifteen metal grain bins half as tall, made for an impressive sight. The business had been around since the early 50s, but the new complex was built in the last ten years, adding a fertilizer mixing and spreading component, a feed retail, and a garden store. The feed and farm store were connected to a warehouse that Shane thought might contain blimps as it was nearly as long as two football fields. The warehouse's walls were at least 30 feet tall, and the pitched roof made it look even more monumental. This was a serious operation. On top of the elevator leg was a metal sign the size of a small garage door with the Alumni Feed logo. Shane commented, "Kind of gives me the chills."

Monty smiled and internally giggled at the notion, remembering when he was an intern not long ago.

Randy told Monty to meet in the office at the feed store as that was where his other meeting was. They arrived, and Monty took the lead, walking in first. Shane looked around a store with walls wrapped in tongue and groove pine varnished to a golden color.

Over thirty beautiful deer and elk mounts accented the walls above the shelving and the sales counter. Shane was told that Randy lived to hunt. The power aisle from the front door to the cash register was populated with Alumni Feed branded companion animal product line called Teacher's Pet, a pallet of garden hoses, some patio furniture samples, and several barbeques. It was a fantastic store with a great work clothes area and a pet section.

Monty introduced Shane to the three ladies that worked the floor. The offering of donuts at the altar was a hit as Shane set them down on the counter. However, the elder of the group of ladies declined and said, "Those Zeppelin donuts are a gateway drug for me."

One of the ladies broke the ice in a way Shane never expected by saying, "Man, are they gonna have some fun with you and that hair." And like the chorus of a song, the other girls giggled in perfect harmony as if in on a joke.

Wilma, one of the three ladies, told Monty that Randy was meeting with one of the Fetch and Glow Pet Food Company salespeople and that he was none too happy with him.

Monty didn't say a derogatory word about the competitor. Still, he told Shane later that he didn't care for this salesperson because he tended to oversell and put down other products and companies needlessly to try to get ahead. Monty commented, "That always makes you look like the guy with the shovel behind the horses at a parade."

The door to the office was open, and most of the conversation between Randy and the Fetch and Glow sales guy was oozing out the door. Shane found himself strategically filtering the music in the background from the local country station to pick up some of the conversation coming out of the office.

The salesman was not getting the best of the conversation when it took a turn he probably didn't expect. The salesman asked, "Did you try the new cat food sample I left for your cat?"

The response was in the form of a question with an elevated volume and tone. "Can you tell me why it is?" That nebulous question was followed by a pause seemingly long enough to allow someone to eat a movie-sized bag of cockleburs.

That put the salesperson back on his heels, and he said, "Not sure what you are asking."

The more dominant voice repeated, even louder this time, "Can you tell me why it is?"

The response was more of the same "I am not sure what you are looking for."

More silence, which Shane imagined, was accompanied by body language that matched the voice tone of contention.

The stronger voice sounded even more determined as it delivered to a crescendo, "I just want to know if you can tell me why it is… that an animal… that will lick its own ass… won't eat your cat food?"

Monty and Shane heard it clearly and covered their mouths in unison to not have their bug-eyed laughter interrupt such a deserving moment. Monty retreated and waved Shane outside to the dock just outside the store.

In a hushed voice, Monty said, "Well, you just got a taste of the aggressive treatment I warned you about. Just know you are going to get some of that yourself."

The pet food salesman passed the Alumni boys about that time as they returned from the front dock. Monty said, "Hello." The competitor grunted as he headed for his Chevy Vega hatchback loaded with bags of dog food and samples. Shane was sure that the pet food baking in the heat generated by the sun that day would make the interior of that Vega smell like a rendering plant.

As they returned to the store and walked toward the counter, a six-foot, clean-shaven, bald man wearing grey painter's pants and a short sleeve camouflage shirt with **Caldwell Feed** monogrammed on the pocket approached them. He entered from the office where he had just field-dressed the pet food salesman and sent him high-tailin-it. He strode into the retail store like a lumberjack entering a tavern. It was Randy.

Without introduction, the bald, shaven man was on offense, "Well, if it isn't my favorite Ken doll, and who do you have with you here, Aphrodite, the goddess of hair?" Shane was almost as shocked as when the water hit Cap and him at the dairy.

"Randy, I would like you to meet Shane; he is our intern for the summer."

"Nice to meet you, son; come on over here by the till and take out $5.00 bucks and go get you a haircut."

"Thank you for the offer, sir; you have an impressive business here," replied Shane trying to move off the subject.

"You know, I am not sure the Beatles did us any favors by bringing that mop top look here because it certainly isn't doing much for you."

The silence was winning, and it was uncomfortable.

Randy continued like a predator that tasted blood, "You know the lord made a few perfect heads, and the rest he put hair on them." Randy took a drink of his coffee like it was a reward for such deep brilliance while simultaneously rubbing his free hand across his hairless dome.

Remembering what Monty said about pushing back, Shane decided to spar a round. Even days later, He was still unsure what possessed him to say it, but he calmly delivered, "Well, where I come from, we have a rule." Shane paused for effect, then returned his retort. "We never shingle an empty barn."

Randy spat coffee and started laughing in rhythm with the three retail counter ladies. He hooted and screamed.... "Son, you are hired." Monty was smiling like he always was, and Randy was slapping Shane's back like he was a grade school running buddy he hadn't seen in thirty days.

"Where you from, son?"

"The Palouse country, Whitman County," Shane responded.

In an elevated nasal tone that mocked high society, "Oh yes, the Tuscany of Washington. I loved it over there when I was in Pullman. Great school and great hunting. Are you attending school there?"

"Go, Cougs." Monty had told Shane that Randy was in the Butch the Cougar Athletic Club.

"Damn, Choppers, you sure know how to pick 'em." Monty smiled aggressively, representing his nickname with consistency. Randy had to take one more shot, "I still think I could take our sheep shears out of the display case and change your whole world."

"Monty said you were generous. Again, much appreciated," Shane responded politely.

"Ok fellas, we got some work to do. Who brought the donuts?" Randy was curious.

"Shane did," Monty affirmed.

"Didn't you tell him I am diabetic and I will go into shock with a couple of these?" Randy grabbed one and started mauling it like a starving coyote. Looking directly at Shane, he engulfed it like an elephant swallowing a bunch of bananas. Then he rolled his eyes back into his head and buckled his knees slightly like he was headed for a coma. He stopped about two-thirds of the way to the floor. Predictably, he straightened up with a prankster smile and bulging eyes and, in an elevated voice, said, "I bet you thought I was serious about that there for a second."

Shane wisely reacted like he thought he was going to prison, and this was a hall-of-fame-worthy prank. Actually, he saw the punchline coming before it was delivered, but he need not rob Randy of his fun.

Randy gave Shane a quick tour of the plant and property. They ended up near Randy's office out in the warehouse. The office was built near the roof's peak at one end of the warehouse. This height and the addition of windows on all walls gave it a control tower feel. The one drawback to this location was the nearly fifty steps that led from the floor to the entrance door of the office. Thank goodness for the twin handrails. Randy stopped at the bottom of the stairs and turned to see that Monty and Shane were right with him. He then turned and ran up the stairs at a brisk gait that was almost a jog all the way to the top. Monty was right behind him, and Shane joined the workout. When Randy reached the top, he turned to see Monty right behind him, and Shane was four steps behind him. "Not bad," said Randy. He then entered his office, about 1200 square feet, with peripheral visuals of the operation that the Sears Tower might only rival.

Shane had no idea what Randy's approval of the stair climb meant.

While the office view was generous on illumination of the entire operation, it had several unique features. Golden gloss varnished tongue and groove walls matched the main retail store décor. The grooved varnished white wood pattern, with random dark knots strategically arranged by nature, held many magnificent head mounts of Mule and Whitetail deer. Hanging on one wall above the copier was a pickup door off of a 1950s Chevy truck. The door was white and accented with rust and oxidation: the word **CALDWELL's** and the phone number of *JA3-5400*. Prefixes like *Jackson* were used until the late 60s when they went to three digits like '523'. Aged Alumni Feed paraphernalia randomly adorned the walls as well.

Another unique piece silently dangled and meticulously rotated from the ten-foot ceiling caught Shane's eye. It was a mobile that looked like it was made in a high school art class. The construction featured three thin mild steel welding rods strategically connected by a heavy gauge fishing line. It levitated and aimlessly rotated about eight feet above the floor. What made it unique was the Caldwell Feed Logo. It was carved white wood, about 2 inches square, and it hung prominently in the center of this mechanical art piece. The two rods hanging off the central upper rod held four wooden carvings of the letter E. The *Es* were all different fonts but strategically arranged to not interfere with the seamless movement of the other letters as they rotated around the Caldwell logo above them. Shane hoped to get more detail on this later.

A corkboard the size of a picnic tabletop, strategically hung between 2 offices, displayed a random but treasured collection of pictures Shane thought were customers. Most photos were of people in work gear and ball caps, with their families, in the field, on a tractor, or with their livestock. There were over 200 photos with stick pins holding them in place within this honored collection. Above all the pictures at the top was a professionally painted sign that read 'Our Teachers.' Below the photographs in a similar font was another sign that said, **'Learn Something New from them every day'** with the Alumni Feed Logo centered below it. Shane let his eyes wander across all these Kodacolor prints thinking there were hundreds of unique stories on this corkboard.

"What an amazing office, Mr. Caldwell."

"Let me introduce you to my brother Duffy, the controller and finance genius." Duffy came out of the adjacent office that overlooked the warehouse. His hair was in a ponytail three times as long as Shane's, ending near the middle of his back. Duffy sported a beard with his round-lensed, wire-rim glasses accented his slightly chubby face. It was a safe bet he hadn't run up those stairs as aggressively or as often as Randy. Duffy's hair was turning grey, hinting to Shane that he was probably the older brother and, by Shane's guess, early fifties, with Randy in his late forties.

Randy continued, "Yep, my brother 'Flattop' knows more about what is going on with this place than the good Lord knows about my indiscretions."

Duffy looked at Shane and his hair and said, "I am sure my brother was very complimentary of your mane there, son."

Shane, figuring he had an ally in Duffy, continued the earlier stand-up-for-yourself narrative. "Duffy, I am sure you know better than anybody that jealousy brings out a great man's benevolence."

"Holy buckets! Where did this kid come from? That is good." Monty filled Duffy with the same intern stuff Randy had gotten earlier.

Shane commented on all the graphs Duffy had posted on the community bulletin board. "That's my dashboard," Duffy inserted. He walked Shane through the ratios and how Randy and he use them to operate the business. Shane brought up Magpie, how he drove him over last night, and his comments about how revolutionary Caldwell Feed was.

Duffy said, "I love that guy. He didn't try to eat you, did he?" That generated a great laugh because it was such an unexpected comment. "When he unloads here, he comes up, and we compare notes. That guy taught me a lot about running our trucks."

Shane pointed to the 4 E rotating mobile and nodded toward it. "Alexander Calder?"

Calder was an American sculptor known for his famous mobile sculptures.

"How the heck do you know anything about him?" inquired Duffy.

"That's easy. The highest volume of co-eds at WSU walks the halls of Art Appreciation 204. If you must get a humanity credit, ensure the scenery is good. A couple of pieces of it rubbed off."

Jokingly he said, "For your sake, don't ever tell my brother that you picked up a spec of that."

Shane winked and nodded.

He was getting back to the mobile's purpose. Duffy said he put it up as a symbol of his belief that there are 4 Es to every business. The four Es he briefly explained were:

Execution: He explained it was the blocking and tackling of the everyday business. It includes the selection of talent, products, and services and how to market and sell your organization. Policies, procedures, beliefs, and strategies surrounding the customer are also in this E.

Economics: Duffy told Shane this is the score-keeping arm that must be in place to keep the business operating. He referred to the charts on the wall referenced earlier as guidance for selling, pricing, and expense allocation decisions.

Enthusiasm: The passion and motivation with which you operate your business will often come through in how your customers and prospects view you. Duffy claimed that your willingness to show enthusiasm would provide the best return your business can get.

Ego: Every person has an ego. Some are more suppressed than others. While some ego is a good thing, especially in a salesperson, like alcohol, sometimes more than a little can get you into big trouble. Duffy was emphatic that your customers won't appreciate you **spiking the ball** when you win or are successful. Being successful and being humble is often a polarizing combination.

Duffy summarized by saying all 4 four pieces are important but, by far, the more critical piece was leadership. "In the absence of leadership, stupidity normally fills the vacuum created. As owner/leader, Randy and I are responsible for keeping the stupid out."

Shane felt Duffy's passion as he said, "I get the premise, but why

FEED YOUR LIFE

the mobile?" Meanwhile, Randy and Choppers were making plans for their morning appointment.

"It is always about balance," explained Duffy. He continued, "If you are overly enthusiastic about your business, you sometimes lag on smart economic decisions, such as not issuing accounts receivable to bad accounts to increase your business."

Shane was looking for deeper meaning, "The way you talk about the four of them, it seems the first two are very task-driven, and the other two are the emotional side of the business."

"Yep, the second two certainly are the most visible components to your customer, and they often need more fine-tuning." He went on, "The example of that would be my brother."

Duffy surveyed Shane with a potently sarcastic tone, "So, do you think he is more task or emotion?"

Shane was confident it was the latter.

Duffy continued, "I love him to death, and he has done many good things for Caldwell's. I know I couldn't run the business without him." He seemed reluctant to say it, but he did anyway, "However, my brother Randy has never shown evidence of having a self-esteem problem. In most cases, when it comes to his personality, I think some folks would like him to show a little less product."

"How so?" quizzed Shane.

"We have had opportunities for mergers or acquisitions that showed promise to help our business. Randy brought too much ego to the equation and keenly angered the other participants." Duffy concluded, "So as a result, we have learned, and Randy admits, that I need to be present as a *tail gunner* in those kinds of transactions."

Duffy said, "The most obvious piece of this is the Caldwell logo which represents our leadership, or **keepin the stupid out** that I referred to at the center of the balanced mobile. If we do things as we should, they will remain balanced and in the center of the four E components."

Randy interrupted the discussion and nodded toward the mobile. "So, is Brother Zeus bringing you to speed on harmonic convergence?"

Shane showed his appreciation, "I think I learned more valuable stuff in the last ten minutes than I did in a whole semester of Business Management at Wazzu."

Duffy smiled proudly but looked at the floor to not show that he was glowing at the compliment.

"Ok, here is the deal." Everyone could see that Randy was ready to shift gears. "I have asked Ernie to be here at ten this morning. Here is what I am thinking. I want a fresh set of eyes on him. Monty, are you OK if we send boy genius out to ride with Ernie for the day while you and I go play bribe the banker? I have screened the candidates and lined up interviews for the potential salespeople for tomorrow."

Shane felt a bit queasy about giving input on someone and their career when he needed to gain experience. He then recalled Magpie's words about being uncomfortable and its growth path. Monty reassured Shane that he realized he didn't have experience in the selling process but still felt it would be a good experience for him. The main thing would be to see how Ernie operates and compare and contrast him with what he observed while riding with Cap and the other salespeople in southern Idaho.

Randy shared the rest of the plan for the week and said he hoped Shane would join him for the interviews on Tuesday. Monty thought this would be a good idea as well. Mr. Gilmour wanted Shane to have as many experiences as possible. Duffy sarcastically said he would return to "Saving all of agriculture through asset-based accounting."

Monty and Randy had a meeting planned with their 'Ag lender,' who wanted to discuss adding the bulk feed system to the mill to increase productivity. Before they left, Randy pronounced in a satirical tone that his fundamental objective before his expiration date was to take down at least two of the world's significant lenders by accumulating their assets via loans.

On cue came a relatively slow, rhythmic, almost shuffling, stair climb that could be heard ascending toward the office. Through the office door walked a denim-covered, five-foot-eight-inch male chassis carrying an extra twenty pounds. His short black hair and baseball cap no doubt appealed to Randy. Ernie arrived in Randy's office after he filled his pickup with bags of pig starter and barbed-wired to learn that the 'mop-top intern' would be riding with him for the day.

Watching his body language, it did not appear Ernie adored mentoring a college kid. Risking the relationship he had with his customers by hauling around this suckling infant was not what Ernie had in mind when he got up this morning. This attitude was especially curious to Monty because Ernie was in the same situation as Shane less than ten years ago. Randy gave Ernie special instructions to take Shane to current customers and prospects.

After both groups descended from the mountain-high perch of Randy's control tower office, the two groups split up.

Shane and Ernie were saddled up in the company pickup loaded with product, and Monty was riding with Randy in his Silverado, headed toward the bank. As they pulled away out the gate of the feed store, Shane noticed the personalized license on Randy's truck said **FUL RUT**. That seemed to say a lot. The 'rutting process' in male deer was when their breeding instincts and testosterone peaked. Randy has no shortage of the latter.

Shane worked diligently to get Ernie to talk. On the first delivery, Shane jumped in to help unload the barbed wire at the cattle operation. Ernie's resistance began to dissipate directly to Shane's willingness to break into a sweat.

They got through the watered-down 'Interpersonal Dragnet' with each other. Shane learned Ernie was never married, lived near Warden on his family's homestead, and had a few cattle to keep the marginal land grazed.

Shane started to get to the core. He asked him a comprehensive question, "What do you like about sales?"

As he drove, Ernie was in reasonably deep reflection about that question. He stared straight ahead in a glazed state and proclaimed in a hushed utterance, "Not as much as I used to."

Breaking the long uncomfortable silence, a tumbleweed from the fruited loins of Moses Lake's landscape, transported by the familiar 30-knot wind, collided directly with the grill of Ernie's pickup. It was a welcome distraction as Shane was unsure where to go following that response.

"I don't know why I said that," lamented Ernie. "I like my job, but the grinding of the customer and the sameness of what I do tends to wear on a person."

"What grinding are you referring to?" Shane was therapeutically creating his tumbleweed.

"The customer is always right, but the constant rhetoric about the cost of everything they buy from me can wear thin."

Shane saw this firsthand while visiting the Bacon Brothers hog-finishing operation. Ernie had to tell the manager that their grinding and mixing fees had gone up $1.50 per ton (a quarter percent increase). In response to the price increase, the manager recited a phone number and said it was for Wiggins Milling. He gave Ernie the ultimatum to fix it by the end of the week. Rather than accept the customer's demand, Ernie explained that Caldwell's grinding and mixing included magnets to protect against stray metals in the manufacturing process. They also use an all-natural additive that protects against **enzymatic browning reactions.** The customer stood there looking at Ernie as if he had let off a series of irate flatulence fueled by cocktail onions and chili. Shane imagined the conversation going on in the hog farmer's head, if it were public, would not be screaming about the planet's fear of the oncoming distress caused by **enzymatic browning reaction.**

He repeated Wiggin's number emphatically, "The end of the week."

After a few minutes to gather himself, they delivered the pig starter in their truck to EVB swine operations and gave an invoice to Eric, the owner, who got upset about the price, even though it had dropped forty-five cents per bag. Ernie was right about one thing. He told Shane on the trip that, often, most farmers don't really know the cost of many elements of their operations. If they change, most of the time, they assume they go up.

At the next stop, a dairyman rejected his proposal to buy milk tank sanitizer because it was thirty cents per case higher than his current provider. Ernie went into a very technical explanation about an **isomatic chlorinate complex** being a benefit that would make up for the slight increase in cost. The dairyman looked at the two of them. Shane thought the dairyman felt like he was a seventh grader in a first-semester college honors chemistry course. The more Ernie talked, the more distant the prospect became. The weekly milk pickup arrived, and the dairyman needed to speak to the driver. The interruption mercifully relieved everyone.

The waitress at the Milroy Diner in Warden was the only person that didn't seem to get under Ernie's skin that early afternoon. Ordering dessert and leaving a five-dollar tip can have that kind of impact. Ernie said he had been working up the courage to ask the waitress for a date for nearly three months. Shane took note.

The afternoon offered a lot of the same activities they experienced that morning. Several miles were driven, with a high percentage of those miles in silence. Activities included knocking on customer bulk tanks to see how full they were and counting bags in feed rooms to replace those the operation had fed. They occasionally ran into customers who seemed to work with diligence to avoid having meaningful conversations with Ernie. Other than some disjointed and clumsy conversation with Ernie, the day's constant was his absence of a smile.

They stopped for a restroom break and gas near Othello. As they left the station with a bounty of petrol, soda, and jerky, their travels were briefly interrupted by an oncoming eighteen-wheel truck. This was no regular truck but a completely reconditioned, vintage 1950s Mack truck hauling a load of cleaned baker potatoes. The black pearl paint, chrome wheels, gleaming mirrors, and spotless trailer significantly contrasted the bland matte-skinned potatoes it was hauling. The signature defiant bulldog chrome ornament was on the squatty hood. It looked like a muscle-bound sled dog pulling the entire load by himself.

Shane looked over at Ernie to see his eyes locked on this beautiful truck like the captivating opening action scenes of a James Bond movie or a Sports Illustrated swimsuit issue. Ernie's smile was nearly as blinding as the chrome in the sunlight. He stared straight ahead and stated, "That one is a little older than the one my Grampa had. I sure miss driving that old girl."

Ernie went on talking nearly whimsically for the next twenty miles about the feelings he had hauling lentils from Spokane to Portland in the classic Mack truck with his grandfather. What a contrast from most of the rest of the day.

The sales mission thankfully wrapped up after a feedlot call.

Ernie dropped Shane back at the hotel, and Shane thanked him for the day. He thought he would be less worn out if he had himself hauled twenty truckloads of hay. Talking to Ernie was hard work.

FEED YOUR LIFE

Getting Ernie to converse was like coercing a bull calf into tap dancing.

Before Ernie drove off, Shane asked him for his personal information. He got a business card. The thank you note was obvious, but Shane had another thought that might help many folks.

As Shane sat in the endless coffee bar trying to sort the problematic and disconnected conversations of the day, Monty entered and looked like he got the part in a dentist's photo shoot.

With a lottery winner's smile, Monty asked, "How was your day, young man?"

"As always, being part of a learning experience was a blessing."

"What did you learn?"

Shane explained that the day had more awkward interactions and overly complicated discussions than usual. Only a little was sold, but deliveries were made. Contact with customers was limited, but he reinforced that it may have been a blessing. "Yep, I know who you were with," said Monty in a confirming way. Shane added he learned the phone number of Wiggins Milling and Randy or someone needed to get ahold of the Bacon Brothers or Moses Lake would be lost to a deep fog of *enzymatic browning reaction.* Monty momentarily lost his smile as Shane explained the details of that exchange.

Monty reinforced that Randy would want similar details on his day with Ernie.

Shane gave a simple diagnosis that came from the conversations he had with 'Magpie.' "He is not happy and not winning," remarked Shane.

"Good observation," said Monty. "Let's go to dinner, and I can share what we will be doing tomorrow morning with Caldwell's interview approach." The following comment pegged the curiosity meter for Shane. "You will meet 'The Herd Bull' tomorrow in the interview process." Monty laughed a couple of octaves higher than usual as he ended that comment like he had the inside track on something unique or sinister. Shane thought that whatever it was, it couldn't be more challenging than riding a day with Ernie.

Shane agreed to the dinner idea after he took care of a task or two.

Shane checked messages using a pay phone to call the 'Mission Impossible' answering machine. One of his brothers had called the home number and thought he would leave a prank call. He had lowered his voice and said, **FIRST MESSAGE**: *"This is Bill Wilhelm from Lewiston, 'Ideeho' and my daughter Tammy is with child. The boys at the Co-op said there was a long-haired intern college boy that might know something about that."* BEEP. CALL ENDED. The call's content was nonsense, but the execution was admirable until he got to the end of the message, and Shane could hear his other brother snickering in the background. Call deleted.

SECOND MESSAGE: *"Hello, Shane; this is Ron Gilmour; I wanted to let you know that next week, we have you set up for the Tri-Cities, Washington, with another salesperson Riley Opums. The following week you will be in Bend, Oregon. In 3 weeks, you are scheduled to be in Central California. Mary Tempo has arranged your flight to the San Francisco Bay area. I also had heard that Monty set it up for you to sit in on interviews that week. As always, I hope you learn something new today."* BEEP. CALL ENDED.

Monty chose an eclectic local dinner location. The Pothole Diner was a converted filling station that had been highly recommended, but he hadn't been there yet. In the former auto work bay, the oil change lift was now sporting varnished tabletop planks that served as the bar. Vibrant colors and fake pastel flowers hanging everywhere accented the previously grime-coated surfaces. The servers were dressed more like Haight-Asbury holdovers and did not resemble servers in any other central Washington diner. The place was packed, and the music library ranged from the Doors and

Talking Heads to Elvis Costello, providing the cadence for patrons who were willing to be bold. Shane and Monty faced each other in a booth adorned with two bench seats from an old school bus.

Over a plate of **Aunt Melinda's Aphrodisiac Fish and Chips**, Monty laid out Randy's playbook for the interview process the next day.

Shane loved to make fun of the obvious. "This fish is delicious, but it may be a bit misrepresented on the menu. I doubt I will be able to 'elevate the table with my loins' on my side. How bout you?" corked Shane.

Monty was caught in mid-bite, and the randomness of Shane's revelation snuck up on him like a cheerleader passing gas.

'Unexpected laughter submission' (ULS) is the condition where the reaction to something humorous can overpower normal behavior with effects ranging from head-turning restaurant outbursts to loss of various bodily fluids. It was the former for Monty.

Their attractive, young, blonde server came over to see if Monty was all right. He was still in the grasp of laughter's stronghold. He was coughing and gasping for breath.... smiling but unable to talk.

The concerned young waitress looked at Shane and asked, "Is he okay?"

Shane wrinkled his nose and sarcastically stated, "I think he is okay. I think he might have first-date jitters." Due to this latest wisecrack, the waitress smiled, laughed, and walked off as Choppers went into stage two (ULS). Shane munched on the fried cod, looking on deadpanned but internally admiring his handy work.

Following minutes of un-choreographed recovery, Monty proclaimed, "You prankster goof, you nearly made me blow tartar sauce out my nose." They both had a male-bonding laugh.

Monty wandered toward the restroom to reset. The 'flower

power' server returned, sat down next to Shane, and started on a free style 'Interpersonal Dragnet' on Shane. "You look familiar to me," she stated.

"Do you go to Wazzu?" she asked.

"Go Cougs."

"Go Vandals." Which, of course, was the University of Idaho. Wazzu's next-door neighbor.

In the brief time between customers and Monty's booth re-entry, she talked about three ways they might have seen each other, and they agreed it was probably the 'Corner Club Bar' in Moscow Shane didn't care; he just thought she was cute. After she asked what he was in Moses Lake for, he explained that he was temporarily working with the Caldwell Farm store this week. She knew where that was and that her dad went there frequently. The U of Idaho waitress smiled and was off to other hungry patrons.

Monty returned with a suspended appetite and just stared at Shane with his recurrent smile as he watched him finish the last of his French fries.

Moments before they got up to pay their bill and leave, the Idaho waitress left her other customers and hopped over to Shane's table with a purpose and a smile that would rival Chopper's. She slapped a folded note down on the table. It had a smiley face, and the name Karla displayed. She looked at Shane and said, "Call me." Her number was concealed inside the fold.

Monty, who had not seen the most recent interactions between these two new acquaintances, became nearly paralyzed as he viewed her surprising actions.

As he got up from the table with Monty still dazed, Shane stuck the note in his pocket and reassessed, saying, "I might have underestimated the romantic power of those fish and chips," as he casually walked away.

He could hear Monty returning to his distinctive and engaged laugh.

Shane's Learnings

On the gift of providing an expectation: Giving people a quota/expectation and reminding them of their actions against the target is a great motivator. Keeping score is not evil and can drive much valuable behavior.

On degrading your competition: Saying a derogatory word about your competitor will NEVER help your sales process. It is best to leave 'mudslinging' to bricklayers and tile-setters.

On trying to solve a simple problem with more complexity: Adding complexity to someone seeking simplicity in their lives is a way to end your selling process. An in-depth scenario of the actual value of simplicity is coming up in a future chapter. Enzymatic browning reaction did not help Ernie solve his problem.

On the value of trust in the selling process: Overcoming customers price objections becomes much easier when they trust you and think you have their best interest in mind. Building trust is a cornerstone to selling success. Great brands and an excellent personal record of fulfilling expectations are two tools to build that trust.

. . .

On pricing objections: Often, the buyer doesn't know the actual price they are paying. They have been conditioned to object to whatever price is offered in hopes of a reduction. Facts are helpful to both you as the salesperson and to the buyer to understand what they are paying.

On the action of pushing back against mind games: When someone wants to test you with mind games, they often try to see if you will provide responsive resistance. If resistance is offered deftly, it will usually be mutually beneficial. Occasionally the mind gamer wants to know if you will push back.

On the 4 E's involved in all businesses: There are four Es to describe the broad segments/characteristics/tactics of different businesses:

√ **Execution:** This is the nuts and bolts of everyday business and includes: The selection of products and services and how you decide to market and sell your organization. Policies, procedures, beliefs, and strategies should surround the customer.

√ **Economics:** This is the score-keeping arm that has to be in place to keep the business operating. Economics guides your decisions in selling, charging for it, and expense allocations. The successful accomplishment of economic milestones will provide a platform for further investment.

√ **Enthusiasm:** The passion and motivation with which you operate your business will often come through in how your customers and prospects view you. No enthusiasm eventually leads to no customers. Passion is the fuel that provides altitude for your business. Your willingness to show spirit will provide one of the best returns your business can get. Overdo it, and it can drag you under like a riptide.

✓ **Ego:** Every person has an ego. Some are more suppressed than others. While some ego is a good thing, especially in a salesperson, like alcohol, "sometimes more than a little can get you into big trouble." Ego, when uncontrolled, has killed multiple deals. Customers also don't want to see people celebrate when they win.

On keeping the four Es in balance: The key to making businesses flourish is ensuring the four E's stay in balance. The feed dealer that taught me about the four E's reinforced that the *ratio* of these elements was the most crucial element. *Tasks*: (Execution and Economics) versus *Emotion:* (Enthusiasm and Ego) is a difficult balance that needs to be maintained to help businesses flow.

On the desperate need for leadership in your business: "In the absence of leadership, stupidity normally fills the vacuum created. As owner/leader, you are responsible for keeping the stupid out." This requires you to know the drivers of the business's success and the employees that make a difference in taking care of the customers. Sometimes that knowledge is the customer needs and best practices of some of your key employees, and sometimes it is knowing how many grandkids a customer has.

. . .

On aphrodisiac fish and chips: As Shane learned at the Pothole Diner, never disregard the subliminal messaging on the gastronomy holy grail...the diner's menu.

On U.L.S.: *Unexpected Laughter Submission* (U.L.S.) is the condition where the reaction to something humorous can overpower normal behavior with effects ranging from head-turning restaurant outbursts to loss of various bodily fluids.

10

SURGERY WITH A BACKHOE

Monty recovered from 'the great Pothole diner incident' with only mild cleanup needed. Before hitting the rack, he explained the game plan for tomorrow's interviews in the hotel lobby. There would be team interviews with prospects rotating between Randy, Duffy, and a guy named Herd Bull. Shane would sit in with Randy for sure. Shane was not to go with Randy to the bottom of the steps when Randy met with the prospects. There seemed to be a great mystique surrounding these steps. Shane would drive to the store by himself as Monty met at 6:30 with Randy and Duffy.

The sunrise over the unique landscape of Moses Lake was a Chamber of Commerce marketing opportunity. Long orange and yellow sunrise light patterns bounced off the sagebrush in contrast to the midday sun, which didn't hide the imperfections as the morning light did—a second day of donuts seemed appropriate. Those cucumber-shaped cakes jiggled along in the seat next to Shane as the short wheelbase on 'Emmitt' put a little bounce to the ride. It was either that or the 80 decibels of Credence Clearwater escorting the ride.

The parade of relentless interrogation began for Shane around 7:30 AM, or the minute he entered the door of the Caldwell retail store.

"There better be some of those magical fish and chips in that box under your arm!" Randy was in attack mode due to his early morning conversation with Monty regarding the previous night's dinner excursion to the Pothole diner.

Shane offered donuts to the ladies working the front counter and acted like he didn't hear Randy. They were very appreciative.

Randy jealously continued his pursuit of more of the details of Shane's encounter with the waitress. "How is it that a guy who looks more like her sister than a potential suitor could get a cute young co-ed to give her number to a stranger?" Monty looked over Randy's shoulder with a nearly permanent smile as if he was next to open his present on Christmas morning.

"Isn't it obvious?" asked Shane with timing that would answer the notion before Randy could get another verbal crotch kick in. "It is the Hai Karate aftershave, the Bag Balm ointment I used on my complexion, and the dandelion fabric softener I used on my boxer shorts."

Ruby, the oldest of the 'trio of hens' as Randy called them, worked behind the counter, started snorting and cackling as the two other ladies joined in.

She decided to share some of her wisdom with Shane loud enough that all could hear. "Son, you are handling this ribbing really well, but let me tell you a little secret." She continued, "In my 60-plus years, I have found this to be true; **Men insult each other and don't really mean it, and women complement one another and don't really mean it either.**" The room, including Randy, erupted in laughing approval of this sage adage. Then Ruby unexpectedly slapped down a note with her name and phone number written and hollered, "Call me!"

Shane knew he had been set up. He smiled and giggled with approval.

Randy asked, "How much Bag Balm did we have on the shelf?" Laughter blossomed.

Gratefully, a positive shift away from the orchestrated target practice on the intern came in the form of a customer. An older cattle operator entered the store in bibbed overalls cradling a plastic spit cup like it was made of crystal. He walked to the counter looking for pasture fertilizer and 200 metal T-fence posts. Shane found out later that everyone called him Dingo because of having one blue eye and one brownish green eye. Shane was impressed with his coveralls as they reminded him of the freedom he had in his college wardrobe. These coveralls were being put to the test as their load limit was more like 230 pounds than his actual 250.

Ruby decided to pull this long-time customer and friend's chain as she had just done to Shane. "So Dingo, you still headlining the male dance review at the strip club in Othello?"

He winked and smiled. "I only work happy hour, but come by and get a corn dog and some merlot."

After fake laughing at the corndog comment, Randy asked Dingo how his operation was going and if he had secured his fall cattle minerals needs. He ended the discussion like he usually would. "What is the deer population looking like out your way?" This conversation took at least ten minutes, and the enthusiastic interest in this subject completely overtook these two men's thoughts. Deer hunting, like some other hobbies of passion, has a smothering prioritization effect on some folks. Randy was the club leader in Passion for Deer. They broke their conversation with Randy getting the commitment to supply those cattle minerals. Dingo blew a kiss to Ruby and jokingly said, "Come watch me work that pole." Shane's mental taste buds were vigorously rejecting that image. He processed the thought that 'male night-club dancer' and 'clown car rider' was probably two professions that Dingo might be excluded from.

After Shane helped Dingo lift the T-posts onto his truck, he entered the store to find a pacing and impatient Randy. Monty said he would be like this on what he viewed as an important day. He was also anxious to learn how it went with Ernie.

"So, a good day with Ernie yesterday?" Randy wanted to know and move on quickly.

"I have found that when you don't have much experience, you can learn a lot from just about anyone. So yes, I learned a lot." Shane could mentally hear his dad disapproving of this heavy, nonsense political answer.

"Did you sell anything? Did you share ideas with some current customers about improving their operations? Did you move closer to changing someone's life other than your new waitress friend?"

Shane shook his head from side to side and said, "We delivered some stuff."

Randy pointed out, "Strategically, we could find others at half Ernie's salary to deliver stuff, but there is some efficiency in combining delivery with the sales call process."

"I got a call from the Bacon Brothers manager. He was upset over some nonsense about a browning infraction in their feed. We got them through the $1.50 difference. Trying to fight simplistic problems with complexity will usually hurt your real intention," said Randy.

Borrowing a line from his lesson with Magpie, Shane told Randy, "Ernie is a good guy, but he isn't very happy because he is not winning, and his confidence is certainly in a valley." He felt cleansed after his first innocuous comments.

Randy explained that Ernie knew precisely how he and Duffy saw him. "It is unfair to anyone if you are unclear about how they perform." He went on to say they told him he is a C minus performer and the specifics of why they feel that way. Ernie needs the most work prospecting new customers and finding ways to help current customers be more profitable.

He thanked Shane for riding with him and for the valuable but unsurprising information. "And oh, thanks for loading up Dingo; nice to see you jump in without someone asking you."

"You are welcome." Shane was sure this was as close to an endorsement one would ever get from this guy.

Randy moved on to the interviewing process happening later that day.

"Have you ever interviewed someone other than your new waitress friend?" Randy always seemed to need to deliver a jealousy-driven poke in the ribs.

"No sir. Been interviewed but have never done the actual formal process."

Randy went on to say that it is one of his most important roles and treats it that way because it is the most immediate and impactful way to improve or hamper your business. Randy also believed you must take it seriously because of your reverse impact on potential employees and their families. He pointed out that it must also be a good fit for them. Leaving a successful career to go to something that is not a good fit puts some of life's most adored things at risk. To be sure that was not the case, he only did 'multiple touches interviewing' and required potential employees to engage whenever possible with the role for at least a day. In this case, the candidate would spend a day selling with Randy instead of Ernie in the field. That would be uncomfortable for everyone. His theory was that he wanted to give them every chance to tell us that this is something they have dreamed about or could not see themselves doing. The multiple-touch team interview aspect is to get as many experienced sets of eyes as possible on the prospects. It also provides the most fertile knowledge platform for the prospective employee to ask questions to aid in their decision process.

Randy inquired, "So do you do much dating?"

The question flushed Shane, as he awkwardly responded, "I suppose you could say I am at the middle of the bell curve on total numbers."

"Do you know where the term dating comes from?"

Shane's silence and uncomfortable posture showed he didn't know the answer.

Randy helped him by saying, "It is the process of gathering DATA. Our job is to create comfortable environments where the prospect will provide DATA about how they think, would act, or have acted in the past when presented with specific circumstances."

Randy asked another question to elevate the premise, "Do you deer hunt?"

Shane explained that he had killed some smaller Whitman County bucks with the guidance of his dad, but he was no trophy hunter like Randy.

"You know how I have killed so many big deer like those you see in the offices and show space?" asked Randy.

Before Shane could respond, Randy emphatically and firmly replied, "DATA."

Shane looked perplexed.

"Deer need certain things to flourish like you, and I do," volunteered Randy.

In a finite order, he provided more insight into those things: "Number one is the **cover** that nature provides and the chance to use their instinctive advantages of **scent and sound.** Deer uses the habitat the earth gives them in terms of brush, trees, and topography to protect themselves. They also can avoid danger with their superior sense of smell and hearing. Number two is **food.** Deer survives on forbs, the leafy portion of woody plants, and human-induced food sources like corn, alfalfa, sugar beets, wheat, etc. Number three is *water*, a needed resource for everything on earth."

Shane locked eyes with Randy and nodded intently.

Randy continued, "Where I win the battle most often is when I have been out for months, sitting in an observation stand before the season starts, with a pair of binoculars gathering DATA on prospective deer. I scout food sources that are also accessible to cover and water. I will go out to different locations after work three nights a week from mid-summer until the season starts, watching their patterns."

"Patterns?" asked Shane.

Randy elaborated, "Like in our lives, I tend to go to the same restaurant, or you sit on the same side of the room in college classes. Deer tends to travel similar paths depending on cover, predator pressure, and food and water. Male deer, bucks, will change patterns during the breeding season, known as the rut, but most of the time, they will stay in a three to ten-square-mile pattern or routine. Without the DATA of that routine, my chances for success decrease."

"So the data you get from the questioning gives you a similar advantage to know which employee you will be hiring?" inquired Shane.

"It certainly helps, but yes, something like that. Your assignment today will be to observe the process I walk the candidates through. When I ask you if you have any questions, I want you to be prepared with a question that YOU will ask the candidates. Remember, I will call on you."

"What do you look for specifically in the interviewing process, and is it different for different roles?" Shane asked.

Randy elaborated, "While the concepts are similar, I will approach each with a different set of scenarios to attempt to extract data for a warehouse worker versus a salesperson."

Randy then pointed out that he looked for five areas in that he wanted to gain data on a salesperson. The five he outlined were: 1. *Ego drive level*. This he described as a controlled passion for success, fire in the belly, or a friendly win-at-all-cost demeanor. He emphasized that this is the cornerstone of what he is looking for. 2. *Responsibility*. He illustrated it as; your word is your bond and how you use versatility to generate constantly ascending trust by your customer. 3. *Goal setting*—the essence of time management, strategic thinking, and organization. Randy emphasized, "All people on earth have the same amount of time in their lives. How the salesperson values and disburses their time allotment will directly correlate to their success". 4. *Leadership.* Randy pointed out that the key is for the salesperson to recognize what it is and how comfortable they are demonstrating it. Their willingness to put themselves beyond where they usually go to take charge of a situation or opportunity. 5. *Basic business thinking*. Areas that Randy gave as examples to explore include margins, animal production business economics, credit handling, commodity pricing market trends, and what effect inventory has on a successful business. He wanted to make the interview process more conversation than an interrogation, and he estimated that if things were going well, the candidate could be in discussions for over two hours with just him.

Randy had one unique request for Shane. "I will meet the prospect, by myself, at the bottom of the stairs to my office. You can be upstairs in my office."

Shane was even more curious but obedient, "You bet."

All that setup reaffirmed that the salesperson is to be one of the more specialized hires. Randy required at least three interviews to acquire differently filtered candidate data. As to technically designated interviewers, there was only one. Randy provided some details of the mysterious 'Herd Bull.'

FEED YOUR LIFE

His name was Jimmy Heard. He served in World War II and was part of a small regiment, ordered to hang around the European stage for more than two years after the surrender to help ship war support equipment home. When considering iconic figures, you might think of King Kong, John Wayne, or a mythical 'Captain Agriculture,' but it would be Jimmy Heard in the Moses Lake region. His legend germinated and flourished with each chapter the natives told of his life. The nickname 'Herd Bull' had high brand awareness, and he loved wearing it like a birthmark. After he returned from the war, several local patrons believed he might have won the conflict single-handedly. He was hired as the first farm gate salesperson at Caldwell's. His legacy of calling on farmers had much to do with their success that continues today. Jimmy, at the request of his customers, ran for political office, became a state representative, and later a Washington State Senator. This took him to Olympia, Washington, and away from Caldwell's. He is most well-known for physically knocking out a fellow senator on the Senate floor with one punch for insulting a female colleague during a heated discussion over welfare reform. The 1962 fracas was captured by television cameras and was played for weeks, multiple times a day on the only three TV channels with evening news that covered the State of Washington. He was expelled for one month and paid the injured sparring partner, 'the right honorable Senator's' hospital bills. When asked about the incident, Jimmy calmly responded, "Some lessons in civility are more theatric than others." A hero was born. Shane heard his dad talk about the episode, but the enormity of the story was lost on a kid not yet in grade school. Jimmy now was the county fire inspector "for something to do" after he retired from State government service. Randy and Duffy still had a great relationship with him, and some people believed he might still be on the payroll in some way at Caldwell's. Randy explained that if Jimmy Heard disapproved of the sales hire at Caldwell's, that person did not have a chance to succeed. So, it was easier to have him in on the selection process than to have to establish, or worse yet, rebuild his endorsement later. Shane would sit in and watch him interview one of the three candidates.

Randy had concluded Shane's briefing, his interview philosophy, and the chronicle of Jimmy Heard. Metaphorically, the earth seemingly started to shake, high pitch angelic music blared, and retina-piercing background lighting outlined the darkened figure of, you guessed it, 'Herd Bull.' He was standing in the doorway to Randy's office. It was interesting to see Randy's demeanor change from an aggressive world leader to an intimidated first private in the company of this celebrity.

"Bull" Randy screamed like he had met a classmate at homecoming.

He was about six foot two, and his shoulders seemed nearly as wide. His shadow barely fit through the door. Every hair on his body was whiter than bristles on a new toothbrush, roughly a similar length, and all straight. Shane assumed the hair was too nervous to grow in any direction but straight. His skin shined like the seat of a well broken in saddle, and his tan overemphasized his white hair. He wore jeans, a Caldwell Feeds vest, and a button-down pressed white oxford shirt.

Randy jumped in again, almost nervously, "Great to have you here!"

Timing is everything when you are a legend. Jimmy waited for his response to ferment and, in a rich baritone voice, replied, "Better to be **seen** than **viewed**." Randy about choked on his excited laughter.

"How you been, Bull?"

"Well, the sweat beads I develop run a slalom course on the hairs on my head. My prostate has the elasticity of a pair of thirty-year-old underwear. However, I expect a call as I have four years of eligibility, and I heard the Cougs are looking for a Free Safety."

Shane thought to himself that from the looks of him, special teams or practice squad player may not be out of the question. He was in great shape.

Randy introduced Shane and said he was an Alumni Feed intern from Washington State.

Mr. Heard stuck out his hand; Shane swore Bull could 'palm' a propane tank without grabbing the handle. "Son, nice to meet you. I'm Jim Heard. Do you know Professor Borsellino over there in Pullman?"

"Sure do, sir; I took his economics class my sophomore year."

"Did you pass?"

"Yes, I did."

"Of course you did; he is a damn softy. He did help me a lot with a couple of my election campaigns. Where you from, young fellow?" said Jimmy.

"Northern end of Whitman County, sir," said Shane

"Oh yes, where heaven blessed the lentils." Mr. Heard could romanticize a cancer diagnosis.

"Mr. Heard Randy told me that you have led a life of public service and recently retired. What have you been doing since?" asked Shane as he wanted to pay homage and see if he could learn more.

"Well, let's see. I try to catch at least one limit of perch a week from the lake, and I read too much about politics. Those Seattle papers make me swear every morning." He finished with, "There has to be a twelve-step ramp-down program for former politicians, but I haven't found it yet."

"What was it like serving in the Government, sir?"

He paused to reflect on the question and, after a long pause, replied, "How long you got?" He added details by saying, "Well, there are two parts to it. The first part is when you are working on issues that help people because there is no better feeling than when you get something done. The other side is when you are working on identifying these issues. The ineptitude and deceptive opposition encounters make you want to quit and render dead animals every day for the rest of your life. An example of the lack of practical thinking in government would be driving down the road in your car, and the engine starts smoking and making noise. The normal government reaction is to get out and pass legislation about **how you should wax the smoking car.** You have armies of people getting involved in stuff they have no business in. Armies are great for pulling stuck locomotives out of the mud. But give me a few passionate people with a common vision, and I will give you productive legislation."

"Sounds frustrating," said Shane.

In his trademark dominant tone, Bull elaborated, "Too many people with less real-world knowledge and an overdose of personal motivation makes for a carnival of misguided decisions. It is no different in the company you are working for or any of those that wanted to donate to my campaign."

Shane looked on, nodding like he knew the exact circumstance. He really had little understanding or experience with any of it, but he thought the lesson might move faster with his affirming action.

While 'The Bull' monopolized smoothness, coolness, and swagger, Randy had a powerful recipe for impatience. "Time to process this pen of calves, gentlemen." This was his saying; that we needed to prepare for the interviews.

Copies of resumes were passed around, including a current high school agricultural teacher, a former dairyman looking to change careers, and a second job crop chemical sales lady expected to be in her mid-20s.

The playbook was reviewed for Bull's benefit. Randy would

focus on the candidate's personal drive, as he stated to Shane earlier. He thought he would spend at least ninety minutes with each prospect. The Bull would focus on technical and sales skill knowledge and take 45 to 60 minutes. Duffy was to focus on business knowledge and character. Shane would sit in on the rotations to meet each candidate and learn from each interviewer's approach. Much thought had been given to the one question he would ask, and he had a plan.

Randy met the first candidate at the bottom of the steps. After a pause, the thundering rapid rhythm of running up the steps was heard in the background. One set of audible footsteps stopped, and the other continued at the same pace for another five to seven seconds. Shortly after that 'minor cardio,' Randy entered the office where Shane and Bull were waiting for him and the Ag teacher. Troy Jacobs was the first to interview. He was trim, tan, five foot ten, and the father of three boys. Troy was on his summer break from teaching high school vocational agriculture in a city 45 miles away. He wore a coat, tie, and jeans, likely standard school teaching attire. He looked appropriately comfortable and was in his mid-thirties. When Troy recognized the celebrity of a former State senator sticking out his hand to greet him, he calmly shook Jimmy's hand and said in a solid tenor voice, "Mr. Heard, many thanks for your service to the people of Washington State, sir." He continued, "I especially want to thank you for your proud representation of agriculture and the Future Farmers of America."

Bull nodded as an act of appreciation for the comments and then asked Troy about his FFA Chapter and how long he had been in the teaching profession. His answer reaffirmed FFA's impact on young people joining the organization. It also illustrated how FFA is the 'headwaters' of future Ag teachers. Many of the Ag teachers today are the kids who once played grab ass and secretly smoked a cigar at judging contests, just as Shane had done less than three years ago.

The conversation reminded Shane of 'McCutcheon' and the positive impact he made on Shane and his classmates.

Shane was introduced and explained that he would stay for the interview. Randy wanted to throw out the question on everyone's mind before the process began and with Bull in the room. "So Troy, why would you want to look at this job when you have such a successful Ag teaching career?" It was easy to see that he had thought about this a lot, and his answer reflected it.

"Thanks for asking because it would have been a red flag to me if you hadn't." Troy swallowed to adjust his voice and collect his thoughts. "I will try to be concise. I love what I do, and most days, even ten years later, are fantastic. More than occasionally, I reflect on the reality that the best teacher in the entire State and the worst teacher get nearly the same salary and benefit schedule." Bull nodded approval with the same cadence as an empty rocking chair still in motion. Troy appreciated the acknowledgment. "The role here at Caldwell's appears to pay rewards based on my performance, which attracts me. The second thing is a deeper personal reflection. I have three boys. The oldest is ten, then eight and four. While I love coaching and supporting them individually, I simultaneously see the challenging and uncomfortable task of being a parent and teacher. I love FFA, but if there is some profession out there that can use my skills and I can better my family all the way around, I need to learn more about it."

Randy said, "Great, let's find out what we have in common." This was Bull's cue to excuse himself.

Randy checked for comfort levels on bathroom, water, and coffee. All systems were go. Randy positioned himself on the outside edge of the table next to Troy so there was no barrier between them. Sitting across from him at a table or behind his desk would create that barrier. Shane observed from the other side of the table. His position in the room didn't matter.

Randy picked up Troy's resume, which he had read several times before the interview, and now he held it up symbolically and started his questioning with a comment and a question. "A nice resume of all that you have accomplished. What are you most proud of and why?" Conversation flowed freely, and Shane was more observant of the questions than Troy's answers since he was learning more about interviewing than making the decision. The questions typically started with the phrase, "Tell me about a time when..." One that stuck out to him was, "Tell me about a time when you had to demonstrate leadership when you didn't expect to..." Troy talked about having to perform CPR on a fellow teacher. With most responses, Randy would follow with a comment or question to develop further discussion or clarification. In the CPR scenario, he wanted more details to understand better how the others reacted to his commands and how it turned out. The good news was that the teacher recovered and stabilized until help arrived. Troy's actions: instructing others to call for help; and directing first responders, probably saved the teacher's life.

What Shane noticed most was the conversational nature of the process. There was no interrogation, instead lots of follow-up dialogue and questions to dig deeper into Troy's answers allowing for more understanding of who he is. From Shane's early observations, Randy could be an impatient guy who likes to get things done quickly. Shane thought that if Randy were a surgeon, he would skip a scalpel for a backhoe to get it done quicker. But today, questions were smooth, deliberate, and thoughtful, with genuine curiosity and plenty of active listening to allow the candidate to think and speak. Shane also thought that if he had seen this side of Randy earlier, he might have liked him better.

Randy changed the tactic slightly to reveal the prospect's

passion for winning and drive. "So Troy, you were coaching livestock judging teams in FFA?"

"Yes sir," responded Troy.

"Soil judging?"

Again, "Yes sir."

"Parliamentary procedure?"

"Yes sir. When you have a program with one teacher, you do it all".

Randy took the topic where he wanted it to go, "Did your teams win?"

Troy's chest started to swell like a three-day-old corpse, and the corners of his mouth elevated more than expected as he was ready to respond. "Two-time State Champion in livestock judging; District champ in meat judging six times; parliamentary procedure state finalist four times; and several district public speaking champions, plus too many others to mention." He wrapped it with "We did good."

"How did it make you feel as their coach when your team won?"

"They say heroin is addictive. I would have no way of knowing that, but I will tell you that seeing the kids' faces and their excitement when they achieved something they had worked so hard for would rival any drug for me."

"How did you achieve this success?" Randy followed.

"It starts with selecting the kids willing to put in the work and creating a vision that it is good for them to win, but not mandatory."

"How do you create that vision?"

Troy touched his fingers and named things off like a checklist. "We hung felt banners from the ceiling showing previous generations' successes and wins in our ag class. We also did this in the high school hallways to ingrain in the participants what others had accomplished. We made sure to attach the team members' names to humanize the achievement. I also asked them to sign a commitment-of-time document to ensure they understood what was expected. We then practiced, sometimes twice a week, several weeks before the events, and attended several smaller contests before the state meets."

"How did you feel when you lost?" Randy went deeper.

"That is tough because the kids don't want to disappoint. You are shaping them for the future. I always tried to understand how we lost so that I could better prepare kids for the next group of contests. I learned long ago that **how you feel when you lose will often determine how long it is before you win again.** So, I would keep it as upbeat as possible".

Randy brought the conversation closer to home. "Have you ever sold anything?"

"Every day, multiple times a day." Troy paused with a reassured look on his face.

"How so?" Randy said, realizing this guy may be more than the lifetime Ag teacher.

"Well, let's see. I have to sell my plan and budget to the Superintendent and, sometimes, the school board. I have to sell the parents that I am the right guy to handle the most important capital they have ever created, their kids. I have to constantly sell students that participating in class will help them for the rest of their lives. I have to sell my own boys that doing the right thing and who they hang out with is the most important decision they will ever make." Troy looked at Randy and Shane and said, "Everybody sells."

"What makes you successful in selling everything you just talked about?" quizzed Randy.

"Well, I have learned that nobody in the history of the world is going to buy something because I want them to buy it because it will benefit me. It is always about them. If I haven't thought about what is important to them, I don't have a chance to sell them anything.

The second thing is that the perceived and most obvious reason they should be buying is not always the real reason they buy."

"Tell me more about that," Randy was now leaning forward, shifting his weight.

"Take the kid that will raise an animal to show at the county fair. Why do you think they want to do it?"

Randy was willing to play "To win and receive money for selling their animal to be used for school. Also, to have bragging rights with friends and to develop some responsibility."

"Those are all good guesses, and if you were a parent, you would be right," said an animated Troy.

He then turned to Shane and said, "How about you, Shane? "

Shane paused briefly and said, "To get out of school and meet girls."

Randy burst out laughing and thought to himself that this is all this college kid thinks about and how far wrong he was.

To Randy's surprise, Troy shouted, "Bingo, that is exactly right. While all those other things are a by-product of the experience, I sell Randy's list to the parents and Shane's list to the kids because that is exactly what is important to them."

After a few more questions about past behavior, which could lead to a vision of future performance, Randy paused, looked at Shane, and said, "Your turn, Youth Intern. Got any questions for Troy?"

Shane felt his vocal cords tighten from the symbolic notion of pulling up his big boy pants above his shoulder blades to ask a question of someone almost a third older than him. But he liked Troy and his approach. One thing he thought was fair was to see how this guy would handle some of the day-to-day nonsense and occasional light bullying that Randy loved to pass out.

The way he thought about digging for that DATA was, "Tell me about a time you had to deal with a type A personality, hard-charging tyrant, and occasional jackass that liked to call you out without much reason." However, this seemed like it might be a bit obvious, so he took a less direct route.

Shane swung for a triple. "Tell me about the best practical joke you ever played on anyone?" Right out of the Interpersonal Dragnet playbook!

The question caught Troy off guard, and in deep contemplation and memory search. The silly giggling and obtuse smile let Shane know that Troy might have something behind his amused but formerly vacuous expression. The ten-plus seconds of deliberating silence were seasoned with the occasional devilish giggle.

Troy developed traction, "This one time." In Rural America, those words have been the precursor to some of the world's greatest stories, often delivered with a juvenile grin. Shane hoped this would be one of those times.

Troy launched, "When I was younger and working summers on my dad's farm, he was asked to help a friend and neighbor move to a different farmhouse. I came along to help. We assisted a neighbor and his wife move furniture, appliances, and household sundries. Inside the house window garden were three older but colorful taxidermy rooster pheasant mounts. They stood prominently on a six-inch square wooden base, with striking tail feathers proudly pointing with a slight skyward angle."

Randy was smiling, leaning forward, showing no sign that Shane had asked a ridiculous question. That was what Shane feared most.

Troy took a swig of water and continued, "What are you gonna do with these beauties?" my dad asked the lady of the house. Without hesitation, she looked over her shoulder to ensure that her husband was not within earshot and, in a hurried whispering voice, said, "Give them to you. I have been trying to get them out of this house for ten years".

Another pause with a hearty smile.

"So Dad took them, loaded them into our pickup, and told me he had a plan." Troy transitioned to a bit more story setup. "Our mailman, Wilbur, and my dad had running feuds. My dad hated that his United States mailman drove a foreign-made vehicle and that he would get a military pension and a postal service pension. He didn't think it was right, even though they were on the same bowling team. So, in good fun, they played tricks on one another. One year my dad wrapped up a pig head from one of the hogs we butchered in butcher paper. Dad told Wilbur that it was a ham. Wilbur threw it in the freezer, saving it for Easter, and was shocked two months later when he brought it out to thaw and found it was the wrong end of the hog." Troy continued quickly so Randy and Shane didn't think that was the prank.

"Wilbur always carried a shotgun with him in his Toyota pickup even though it was strict Government regulation not to do so. He also was a notorious road hunter, though shooting within 100 yards of a roadway would get you a severe fine and potentially confiscating the firearm." Troy could see his story had them both engaged.

"That Fall on a Saturday, my dad called me into the home farm shop and told me that Wilbur would always be by to deliver the mail between 11:30 and 11:40 AM. One good thing my dad would say about Wilbur, he was 'undefeated on being habitual.' I was instructed to place the pheasant mounts in the hay field. The dry grass in the field was about three inches long due to that summer's hay removal. I was told to drive the pickup to the spot at about 11:20 and put these three pheasants in a random grouping about forty paces from the mailbox so they were within the direct line of sight of our mailbox. I was to drive back, and we would watch the festivities from behind some five-foot-tall round hay bales. Our position would give us a panoramic view." Randy and Shane were wiggling in their seats and smiling with anticipation like a kid in front of a rewarding gumball machine.

The smiling and giggling continued around the table.

"At 11:31 A.M., the Wilbur-driven red Toyota kicked up dust on the gravel road toward our mailbox. The brakes briefly squealed as Wilbur herded his vehicle in front of the mailbox about the size of a five-gallon bucket. Our mail was inserted in the box, and nearly as soon as the mailbox door closed, the engine shut off. There was little movement except for the slow creep of the gun barrel pointed out the window. As soon as the barrel became perpendicular to the ground, it blasted three shots in rhythm from his semi-automatic twelve gauge. The age of the dry-rotted taxidermy and the slightly windy day caused white clouds of talcum-like eruptions from each bird. Wilbur started the Toyota, pulled ahead, stopped, and abandoned the rig. He ran like he was landing at Omaha Beach, hurdling toward the dead birds. These meaty specimens would surely be some part of Wilbur's dinner that night. When he got to the carnage, he found the three bird bases upside down or on their sides. They were nestled in a carpet of sawdust and white straw-like stuffing accented with a substantial percentage of colorful rooster feathers."

Laughter was abundant in the room, and Randy asked the obvious, "What happened next?"

"As Wilbur bent over to inspect the base of his prize kill, my Dad yelled from behind the hay bale, 'Hey Wilbur, what time is dinner?' My dad laughed like he had pulled off the biggest heist in history. Wilbur stomped off to his truck to finish his route three shotgun shells lighter."

Shane composed himself from the prank discussion and asked

for a follow-up. The money question. "How do you handle it when someone orchestrates a practical joke on you?"

Troy reflected briefly, saying, "If it is a good joke with no malice, it can be a sign of love. However, I have little time or tolerance for mean-spirited events and language that puts others down."

Shane asked how he handles the negative type he was referring to, as much of Shane's experience with Randy was often a steady diet of negatives. He also wanted to give Randy a vision of when it is not working.

"When I was a kid, my classmates teased me by calling me 'Helen' because of my name being Troy, 'Helen of Troy.' I used to get so mad that I would even go as far as violence to make them stop. The approach had the opposite effect, and the heckling escalated. I decided to ask my grandpa about how to handle it. He gave me advice I still use today; …***Pay no attention to the barking dog and watch how much sooner it quits barking'.*** Even though it was killing me, I just started acting as if it was not bothering me and even went along with some of it. The result is that it stopped. The hecklers are just looking for attention, and just like the dog, when you pay no attention to them, they too will tend to lose interest and move onto some other nonsense."

Shane thought that could not have gone any better and hoped Randy consumed a full dose of that medicine. He doubted it would have much impact, but he had noticed that Troy's prescription of aversion to the nonsense was similar to how Brother Duffy treated Randy.

Randy shifted gears, "Troy, I got an exercise I would like the two of us to do together." Randy passed Troy an unmarked legal tablet and continued, "I would like you to take that paper and write out a list of things that motivates or drives people. Shane and I will assist if you get stuck, but I want you to make a list"

Troy took his No. 2 pencil and spoke out loud as he printed

them neatly on the page, "Let's see MONEY, but that isn't always a good thing."

"RECOGNITION"

"PERSONAL ACHIEVEMENT GOALS"

"PERSONAL HAPPINESS"

"CARRYING ON A LEGACY"

"COMPETITION"

"POWER/CONTROL"

"FAITH"

"FAMILY"

"HELPING OTHERS"

"RESPECT"

"HOW YOU ARE SEEN IN THE COMMUNITY"

"BUILDING SOMETHING AND BEING INCLUDED IN THAT BUILD"

"I am starting to slow down here a little," said Troy.

Randy said, "It is a great start; how about SECURITY?" Troy wrote it down.

"EGO," said Troy, who was back on track.

"LOVE"

"PASSION FOR A SUBJECT OR CAUSE, my wife is crazy about Longaberger Baskets." Troy was now slowing with more time between list additions.

"My kids are driven by FOOD." Randy fake laughed at that answer.

"SEEING OTHERS DO WELL"

"TROPHIES, PLAQUES, AWARDS."

"RISK/THRILL"

"STATUS"

"BUILDING A TEAM"

Randy was impressed with the list and outlined the next steps of the exercise. "Troy, I like your work. After you take a restroom break, I would like you to take that list and rewrite it using the same pad, but this time list from top to bottom which things are the most important to least important to you personally. Shane and I are going to step out while you do your work. We will return in fifteen to twenty minutes to discuss your answers."

After a bathroom and hydration break, secluded in the conference room with the door closed and outside of 'earshot,' Randy and Shane sat down across from one another after a bathroom and hydration break. Shane had learned that the first to speak in a conversation with Randy always needed to be Randy. "What do you think of the process there, Mr. Practical Joker?"

Shane thought momentarily about reminding Randy of the barking dog that Troy's grandpa had illustrated but thought better of that. "I like how you keep it conversational and flowing. What do you think of him?"

"Too early to tell. He has a lot of interesting characteristics, and I think he is trainable, but I am unsure if he is ready to leave *the Owl.*"

Shane knew exactly what he was talking about. In FFA, the advisor, Troy, is symbolized by *the Owl* as an example of wisdom and knowledge. In other words, can he move from teaching and FFA to a role like this one?

Shane asked, "Why did you have Troy write down his answers instead of just verbalizing in the last exercise?"

Randy supplied his logic, "Well, it gives an unfiltered glimpse into his personal organization, spelling, handwriting, and the basis to see what is personally important to the candidate. When we return, I think you will see why working on this as a group project is more beneficial."

Troy sat solo, scratching on his notepad, occasionally erasing and rearranging the order. He was into it. After about 15 minutes, Randy encouraged Shane to join him to review Troy's progress.

Troy said, "This is hard to get all of them in order, especially the middle ones."

Randy said, "Understand. Let's see what you have for your top five."

In descending order, Randy read them off the clearly printed tablet:

"FAMILY AND THEIR SECURITY," to which he also had added the word (IMPERATIVE) in parenthesis.

"Number two on your list is the word FAITH."

"PERSONAL ACHIEVEMENT GOALS was number three."

"HELPING OTHERS SUCCEED was number four."

"MONEY is number five."

Randy continued, "An interesting group of selections. So, what made you put 'FAMILY SECURITY' first, number one?"

"My biggest responsibility is to do everything I can to ensure that the thing I had the most personal involvement in creating is not disadvantaged by something I may want to do or pursue selfishly. There are many long hours involved in what I do, but I try to involve my wife and kids in as much of what I see as enhancing their lives as well."

Randy probed, "Why isn't money higher on your list if providing for the family is such a key component of what drives you."

Troy pondered momentarily and returned with, "I have a buddy who is a major trust fund recipient, lifelong bachelor, no kids, and he frequently says, 'the only thing money can't buy is poverty.'" After a short pause, he continued by saying, "And he just might be, the most miserable son of a gun I know. More than likely a result of having no one to share his success."

Randy pointed out, "Controlled greed is a good quality in a salesperson."

Troy vehemently agreed.

Randy wanted more clarity for discussion's sake, "So why 'PERSONAL ACHIEVEMENT GOALS' at number three?"

Troy pointed out that you don't often achieve without 'HELPING OTHER PEOPLE,' which was number 4. He pointed out that they are connected. He also sheepishly admitted that he was super competitive, and it was vital for him to succeed if he was going to invest in his career. He also noted that investment in himself could be defined as reading or classes that could help him.

Randy continued, "What would be your favorite reading that helped with that."

Troy didn't hesitate *"How to Win Friends and Influence People"* by Dale Carnegie. One of my dad's friends gave it to me with twenty bucks in it for high school graduation and told me it was the most valuable reading other than 'Gideon's.' "

Randy confirmed, "A great read. Which part did you get the most out of?"

"Easy. The importance of enthusiasm. **To BE enthusiastic, you have to ACT enthusiastic.**"

That answer made Randy smile as he continued, "So if we look at what you have at the bottom, I see you have 'TROPHIES, PLAQUES, and AWARDS.' This is an unusual answer, especially when you made the banners hang in your Ag room and school hallways to motivate students to join your judging teams. Tell me more about the logic".

"I didn't mean to discount the impact of awards and incentives. They are good for some people but don't drive me. My kids have never told me they want me to win another plaque so mom could prepare it for a special meal."

Shane recognized that Troy had picked up the importance to someone at Caldwell with the deer head mounts on the wall when he said, "Now, every time I go out deer hunting, my kids always want me to come home with one for the freezer. I must say, I have never come home with anything as nice as what you have on the wall here." Randy acted calm, but Shane knew his ego was swelling with pride like a rising loaf of bread.

The drill around 'the list' went on for another 15 to 20 minutes, and Randy shifted gears to the next part of the interview when he said, "For the next 15 minutes, you can ask me any question, personal or business, that you want. In the future, I may not want to answer your questions, so make them good ones."

Randy later told Shane that the fundamental objective of the questioning period was to reveal the candidate's curiosity. He thought this was especially true for someone in sales, as it would be a practical reflection of how curious they may be with customers in solving their issues. The fifteen minutes were to build a bit of urgency to ensure the questions were a priority and not turn into a visit.

Troy squared up in his chair, got his notebook, and started with a metaphorical high-hard-fastball. "What would you say is your organization's biggest problem today, and what will it be in the next ten years?"

Randy raised a right eyebrow, almost like he was preparing to look through a scope on his deer rifle. "A good question. There are always many issues in an organization this size. I would say it is being able to continually *scale* the organization to meet changing farmer needs vs. competition and to be able to win more of the herds and acre supply needs for the next decade. Things I invested in last year will be obsolete in ten years. One thing that won't be extinct in my lifetime is the personal relationship between Caldwell's and the farmer. Jimmy Heard, whom you met earlier, taught me that when I was a high school dock employee at Caldwell's, working for my dad"

"So how does this role affect that problem?"

"Our ability to build relationships and meet the 'scale schedule' are behind where we should be. I want to accelerate that rate of growth. I believe sales is the most profitable way to do that versus buying someone else's business, especially if the other guy doesn't want to sell or is more profitable than we are. If we are more profitable, their comfort with selling will benefit Caldwell's someday."

"Are you profitable today?" Troy followed up.

Randy leaned back in his chair for the first time as though this was the question he had waited for all day. "Yes, we are profitable. Our debt is limited to working capital, and we have a small banknote on the last phase of construction for the feed plant. That debt goes off the books next year. Our percentage net is two times the industry norm. So yes, we are blessed on the profitability front."

"Explain what my first month will look like if I take this job."

"Your first day will be planned like a wedding. My brother Duffy believes that new employees determine whether they made the correct decision on their new position in the first four hours. It would be better to tell you that in the first ninety days, I want you to spend at least 80% of your time on customers' farms asking questions and understanding their needs and goals."

"So, what does success look like to Randy?"

"A great question with no easy answer. Let me give you some context by reciting a list that might help you understand my thoughts: 1. I want people to call you, not me or Duffy, when they have issues. 2. I want you to close gaps in the feeder's nutritional program needs with stuff they aren't currently buying from Caldwell's 3. Help us identify service gaps that we have as an organization. It is essential to get farmers what they want, in the quantities they want, with accurate billing. 4. If we offer a new product, I want you to ensure every feeder and potential feeder in the marketplace knows what it is and how it will benefit them in the first sixty days of introduction. 5. Probably the most important, I

FEED YOUR LIFE

want you to love what you do. If you don't love it, you won't be here long"

Troy's time was running out on his fifteen-minute question pass, so he decided to test the limits of what Randy might answer, "What is the biggest goal you have yet to achieve either personally or professionally, and how could a guy like me help you achieve it ?"

Long pause.

"Steal my brother's wife and move to Cancun." A long, serious stare followed. "By the way, you can tell him that when you meet him later today."

Shane thought Troy might have hurt himself with the question. Randy later told Shane he loved the question because Troy sought a way to close.

Troy played along, "Not sure how much I can help with the brother's wife, but I can supply a couple of bottles of diarrhea medication and an exchange rate calculator for that Mexico stay."

Randy reset, "With a deadly amount of seriousness, I can tell you that I want to be leading the most dominant Ag supply organization in the Pacific Northwest. How you could help me in that journey will all be determined by whether you would be willing to join us or be a lifer in the teaching profession."

Troy had developed a bit of sweat that collected above his upper lip. Shane had just noticed it and thought the last comment might have accelerated it.

Troy wisely remained quiet. Randy decided to probe. "I know it is early in the process, but are you interested in this career? You noticed I didn't say the job."

"I will tell you, when I came here, I didn't know what to expect, but our discussion enhanced my interest. What are the next steps?"

Randy explained that he would conduct two other interviews later today and then ask Troy to ride with him for the day, calling on customers to get a feel for the role, and following that, they would have another interview to see how Troy felt about the fit.

Randy closed the interview with one last question for Troy, "I have a scenario for you." Troy nodded and grinned, "Let's say I was at the diner this morning, reviewing your resume, and a guy comes up and says whatcha reading? I respond and say I am preparing to interview Troy, the Ag teacher. She or he would then respond with, what an amazing coincidence as Troy, the Ag teacher, is my best friend. What would they say about you?"

Troy smiled at the unlikeliness of the scenario, looked out the window momentarily, and said, "I think they would say that I am loyal, there for them when needed, fun to be with, comfortable with who I am, in love with my wife, family, and savior."

Randy then upped the stakes, "Same scenario. What would your boss say." Troy's tone changed to be more serious.

"He is good with the students, challenges both administration and students appropriately, is not a defender of the status quo and is an asset to the school's agriculture education program." He smiled like he made a perfect gymnast dismount and added quickly like he forgot, "And oh, by the way, he can sell!"

Smiles gave non-verbal recognition for the quick wit. The rest of the discussion bogged down with vacation, compensation approach and theory without specifics, pension, and other human resource elements that would be covered later, all of which showed there was interest.

Soon after the handshakes, Troy went to see Bull. Then Duffy's secretary stuck her head in and said, "Is there a Shane here?"

"Yes ma'am?"

"When you get done, a Karla would like you to call her. She said you would know who it was. She wants to know if you have time for lunch."

Shane's ears rang, temperature accelerated, and his pulse

tachometer headed toward the 'red line' as he replied, "Thank you, ma'am."

"The number is on my desk in front of Duffy's office."

Randy's mouth was slightly open, with a devilish smirk as if he was mildly stunned and highly envious. He opened his desk, pulled out a ten-dollar bill, slapped it on the desk before Shane, and said, "You *are* my hero. Take her to lunch on me and re-enter the interview rotation with Bull and Duffy afterward."

"Thank You, sir, I will. I want you to know I appreciate it, and by the way," ...a well-timed pause followed, " I also want you to know that I would never cheat on Ruby," holding up the number she had slapped in front of him earlier that morning.

Randy could only muster a laugh and a stern order to return at 1:15 to meet with Bull and the Dairyman.

Shane's Learnings

On Relationships: Men insult each other and don't really mean it, and women complement one another and don't really mean it either.

On not dealing with underperforming employees: "It is not fair to anyone if you are not crystal clear to them about how they are performing." Too often, people avoid conflict by not telling someone they are not performing. This delay, in truth, is never beneficial to either party. If you are a doctor and someone has a disease, not telling them because you might offend them could be considered malpractice. The same is true for your employee that is not being effective.

. . .

On handling problems: Trying to fight simplistic problems with complexity will usually hurt your real intention. Keeping things simple can be hard work and requires discipline to remember your goals. Simplicity is always a desired approach.

On what your fundamental objective is in interviewing: Interviewing is the process of gathering DATA. Our job is to create comfortable environments where the prospect will provide DATA about how they think and how they would act or have acted in the past when presented with specific circumstances. Past experiences and actions often help predict future performance.

On creating productive interview environments: Like deer in the wild, people develop routines and norms. The interviewer's job is to create opportunities for beneficial and detrimental behaviors to make an appearance. This DATA *aids* the decision-making process.

On how great stories in Rural America flourish: "This one time." Often delivered with a juvenile grin, those words have been the precursor to some of the world's greatest stories. Analogous to the "hold my beer" precursor to ill-advised life-threatening stunts. "This one time" in the hands of a great storyteller is worth listening to.

On the challenge of governments: "Too many people with less real-world knowledge and an overdose of personal motivation makes for a carnival of misguided decisions." Successful organizations capitalize on a shared vision. Smaller, more nimble organizations, opposite of governments, often have a more straightforward path to this vision with limited distraction or diffusion.

On the interview process effectiveness: Most successful interviewers try to keep the process conversational. No interrogation, lots of follow-up dialogue, and questions to create scenarios that can highlight past performance and help the interviewer predict future performance.

On why people really buy something: "Well, I have learned that nobody in the history of the world is going to buy something because I want them to buy it because it will benefit me. It is always about them." This often is the most misunderstood fact that new salespeople miss. Genuinely understanding why someone is buying something will help you in your approach to being successful.

On the area of practical jokes: Practical jokes: "If it is a good one with no malice, it is a sign of love. However, mean-spirited events and language that puts others down are the ones the world has little time or tolerance for."

On handling that pesky teaser or bully: How to take the obnoxious practical joker: *Pay no attention to the barking dog and watch how much sooner it quits barking.*

. . .

On Interview tactics that engage the prospect: Asking the interviewee to participate in an exercise that shows actual writing, spelling, and personal organization skills can provide deeper insights than the standard question-and-answer format.

On giving interviewed prospects a questioning time period: Provide a defined short time slot for the interviewee to ask questions to see where you are with them and how curious they are. You can also gauge the depth of their thought process by the quality of the questions they ask. It also provides a way for them to feel closer to the interviewer because the ability to drop your guard is a way to build relationships with others.

On the philosophy of winning vs. losing: *How you feel when you lose often determines how long it is before you win again.*

On the most important thing you can teach your kids is: Who you hang out with is the most critical decision you will ever make.

On buyer's remorse regarding the prospect's decision to join you: New employees determine whether they made the correct decision on their new position in the first four hours. Make sure you plan productive activities and a schedule of what they can expect right after you show them where the bathroom and breakroom are.

11

"THERE'S A FEELING I GET WHEN I LOOK TO THE WEST" – LED ZEPPELIN

Lunch with Karla was a simple trip to the **Chicken in a Tub Drive-In,** which was close to Caldwell's main office and specialized in homemade root beer and chicken strips. She was a willing participant in continuing with Interpersonal Dragnet from the short briefing at the Pothole Diner. The two shared an array of great laughs and commonalities in the hour they had together. The Dragnet was productive, and Shane confirmed that Karla was an undergraduate biology student in her junior year at the University of Idaho with hopes of attending vet school. She attended high school in Tacoma but lived with her parents in Ephrata this summer. Her mom and dad moved there for a drier climate and the chance for her dad to drive a swather, cutting and windrowing hay in the irrigated alfalfa fields around Moses Lake. He was getting plenty of work with ten-hour days and the occasional night shift. She said it beat the snot out of driving a cab for twenty years in the rain-soaked streets of the Seattle-Tacoma metro. She loved the music of the Ozark Mountain Daredevils, wearing snug Wranglers, and being in the country, which brought her to Moscow, Idaho, to go to school. Shane liked the contour of her jeans as well as her wit. And from the different experiences she highlighted, he was attracted to her willingness to experience life. She asked him about his internship, family, plans to use his major, and how long he would be in town. He told her one more day and then off to Spokane to meet with his boss.

The introductory lunch seemed to be going well, but soon Shane would have to join Bull for another interview. Following the consumption of a bucket of chicken strips and premier vintage root beer, the silence morphed from acrobatic into clumsy, as neither of them knew how to evolve their discussions into the next steps.

On her side of the table, Karla looked down and rummaged through her black and white handbag constructed from Holstein's cowhide. She secured what she was looking for. A round cylinder that was about half the size of a hockey puck: it was a can of Copenhagen chewing tobacco!

"Need a dip?" she nodded at Shane as she banged the can on the table, prepared a portion for herself about half the length of a butterfly larva, and massaged it in her mouth. She wiped off the excess sprinkles with a wipe from her wrist to her index finger. She rolled her eyes back, looked toward the ceiling, and doubled her average voice volume to proclaim, "Wallaby Fire King. Man, that is the dessert of the South." Karla slowly lowered her head to watch Shane's reaction.

It was hard to be stoic after the unprecedented events of the last few moments. Shane knew he would have to rise to the occasion by taking his normally fertile mind to a condition of decomposition. He thought about the unpleasantness of cleaning out a hog barn in August. He became sober as a statue. These thoughts helped generate a focus not to look repulsed or surprised by what had just happened.

As his mind processed a truckload of conflicting thoughts, he summarized that while nothing inappropriate would happen between Karla and him, her choice of tobacco delivery might inadvertently be the best birth control ever made.

It could be considered a dangerous event for a young college-age man to rationalize things. However, sometimes breaking some rules and letting the boys expound is necessary. How could this petite symbol of femininity be putting something in her mouth that only a handful of baseball players and rodeo cowboys could find redeeming?

"Nah, I am good," said Shane referring to the repulsive offer. His face was emotionless, trying not to show her how uncomfortable he was watching her squish that finely ground nastiness across her beautiful pearly dentistry.

"I have to work tonight until about 9:30 at the Pothole. You want to get together after that for coffee or something?" she asked.

"Man, that sounds great, but I have to meet with my boss in Spokane early the next morning. I gotta leave around six and clean up some work before I meet with him."

She winked, laughed devilishly, and said, "I'd have you back before 6 am."

Shane thought it would be better to take a rain check until they returned to college. She reluctantly agreed. They shared information and set a date to meet at the Corner Club in Moscow when they returned to Pullman/Moscow in September. "Gonna hold you to it," she said as she moved to kiss his cheek. Man was that uncomfortable.

Ten minutes later, he sat across from former Senator Bull, trying to sanitize his short-term memory.

"Randy said you had a lunch engagement. How did it go?" asked Bull to pass the time.

Shane appeared reflective and distant, saying, "I did what I was supposed to and gathered data."

Bull had interviewed Troy and was impressed with him. He thought he would be a good fit if he could purge the Ag teacher from his system.

"Our next individual, I know somewhat from calling on his parents and cousins as dairymen. Not sure if he is a fit, but I would like to see what you think." Shane liked Bull's way of engaging him.

"What are you looking for in the candidates, Mr. Heard?"

"Competence, confidence, and their ability to understand the customer's needs. Do they know what they are talking about? A customer with much livestock experience will know quickly if these candidates understand their needs."

The two reviewed Elmer Blunt's resume showing twenty years of dairy labor and herd management but no college degree.

Elmer was clean-shaven and, on this day, added the accessory of excessive Old Spice. He checked in at six feet and about two hundred thirty pounds. He entered the room in jeans, experienced Red Wing work boots, and a blue western-cut work shirt with pearl buttons. He sported a slightly soiled 'Select Sires' dairy trucker cap featuring mesh and a plastic adjustment missing a couple of pegs. Shane and Bull introduced themselves, and it was explained that Shane was there to observe.

"Mr. Heard, it is great to see you again. I remember when you used to call on my dad. I know he would want me to give you his best."

"Gracious and appreciated. And how is the rest of your family?"

"Gramma passed last year, but she had many health struggles."

"Sorry to hear that. We don't get to choose it all, do we?"

After a moderate pause to acknowledge Gramma without appearing short, Bull explained that he would ask some questions to get to know each other better, but there were no incorrect answers.

"Elmer, you have much experience with beef cattle?"

"No, not really," answered Elmer.

"How about horses?"

"Never have eaten one, never have ridden one, and never have liked them a lot."

"Any experience with pigs?"

"Raised a couple of them for show projects with my kids."

"So let's take those pigs. How did you decide what to feed them?"

"We went down to the co-op and got some pig feed."

"How did you decide on what you wanted to feed them?"

"Basically, I asked which brand was the cheapest. We didn't want to spend much money on them. We did have to switch them to another brand close to the end to get them to put on enough weight to make the show. I think we got it from you guys."

"Did that feed cost more?"

"Quite a bit more."

"So, at the last dairy you worked at, what criteria did you use when switching feed programs?"

"A lot of times, it was heavily driven by cost or the forage we had on hand to supplement."

"So, if you were going to walk onto my dairy farm to help me and my cows increase overall milk production and improve the health of my dry cows and heifers, what would you recommend that I do?"

"I would start with knowing as much as I could about your current production and what you were currently feeding."

"Ok, good start. What next?"

"Try to find out what you want to accomplish."

"I like your approach. So, if I told you I want ten more pounds of milk per cow in the next year and calves getting into the milking herd two months earlier, what next?"

"It would take some pretty hot feed to make that happen," said a reasonably unconvinced Elmer, who was developing a pretty healthy sweat from the exercise.

"So, If I told you it could be done, but it was going to increase the cost of production by 8-10%, could you sell that to somebody."

"Wow, Mr. Heard, that feels like a tough proposition."

Jimmy had gotten to the root of the issue in that Elmer saw all feed being the same and giving similar performance no matter the price; for many salespeople, not recognizing that primary difference is a fundamental flaw and is very difficult to overcome. The Herd Bull backed off his questioning, knowing Elmer would not make the cut. He then asked a few questions about Elmer's family. What he really wanted to do was help him find a role doing something better suited to his capabilities. He was helping him by not pursuing this further. Not a fit. Pretty sure Randy came to the same conclusion.

After Elmer departed, Bull turned, looked at Shane, and asked what he thought.

Shane said in summary, "The guy you already have, Ernie, is better than this guy."

Bull got a bit philosophical. "Yep, let's not dwell on this one. Sometimes when interviewing, you quickly know it is not a match, so you change the subject a little, like changing bait when fishing. Elmer would not fit this role, but Caldwell's needs truck drivers and warehouse people. It is beneficial to see what they want to do."

Because of the shortened interview, Shane had a few free minutes before he moved to Duffy, and Bull felt like sharing additional wisdom relating to Elmer's issues with pricing.

Bull saw this as a chance to share some collected experience, "People in any industry must have a certain amount of belief in the product or system they are selling. Without that, they rely heavily on either personal relationships or price. In Elmer's case, it will almost always be price."

"So, is there an approach to help evolve these folks that focus on the product's price?"

"Education is the key to selling any premium product. That education is for the customer as well as for us. Experience, through usage, facilitates the education and creates belief." Bull put extra emphasis on the pauses.

"Not sure I am following?"

"Have you seen the Burt Reynolds movie *The Longest Yard?*"

"I have not."

"Excellent. Tell me about the movie," said Bull firmly as if he hadn't heard that Shane hadn't seen it.

Shane was puzzled and looked for clarity in the former Senator's request.

"It is hard to do, isn't it?" Bull professed.

"I guess I would say impossible," Shane countered.

"That is the same condition that afflicts Ernie. He has never seen the movie. Ernie could not discuss the value of products because he had never seen them work. His dad had a similar thought process when I called on him years ago."

"How do you break the thought process?"

Shane could tell Bull was a bit irritated with the question. "Experiences. Feeding or using the value-added products and seeing success can be transformative. If Elmer had fed those show pigs better feeds from us during their growing period, which indeed cost more, he would have seen that he saved money by feeding less *and* made the weight deadline. Once they have seen it work, you build that confidence and competence I told you I was looking for before this interview started."

"So how do you know how to price the products you are selling so they are a value?" asked a curious Shane.

"Well, that question could take months of classroom work to get your head around it. Let me give you some quick tips to remember: **People consciously charge what they think their product is worth.** Also, if you shear a sheep, it will continue to be productive, grow, and give you a return. *If you skin the sheep, you only get to do it once.* THE SAME IS TRUE FOR YOUR CUSTOMER."

"So if you price feed to keep you and the customer in business, is that the ideal scenario?"

Bull calmly and fluidly summarized, "I have never seen a good business transaction where both parties didn't prosper."

Shane thanked him for the explanation.

Bull backed away from the table, reached down, pulled up his straight-leg denim pants to expose his sock, and pulled out a can of Copenhagen, "Need a dip?"

Shane wondered how many more times he would be asked today, "No thanks, I already met my quota today."

Shane spent the next couple of hours pulling together the feedback he had received from the Alumni dealers he had interviewed as part of his summer project. Then he moved to Duffy's area to learn the details of the final interview of the three for the farm gate selling candidates.

Duffy was reviewing the resume of Connie Sinclair. This crop chemical sales rep had adequate agricultural experience, but it appeared more in crop inputs through dealers and distributors than in actual farm animal nutrition sales.

"The talk of the office is that you met some girl for lunch and eloped to Soap Lake to start your honeymoon. Any truth in that?" asked Duffy.

"We joined a commune," Shane said, playing along.

"Good to have a strong support system for your relationship," Duffy followed in intricate sarcastic formation.

Switching gears to the interview that would begin in a few minutes, Duffy asked if Shane had an early favorite. They compared notes on both Troy and Elmer. They had parallel and synchronized ideas for both candidates.

"So if Randy was looking for desire, and Mr. Heard was looking for competence and confidence, what is it that you are looking for in your interview?" asked Shane.

"Mostly hyper-demonic behavior and hygiene," laughed Duffy as he poked a little fun at the process.

"I look for characteristics of their work habits and what kind of people they would work best with and the ones they wouldn't. How they manage their day, and how they understand business fundamentals. I probe for character strengths and flaws."

"I am excited to watch the process."

"Well, you won't see an Interview black belt in action because I mostly enjoy a conversation. And, if you have a question, jump in there. It is great to have a tail gunner in an interview so I can listen and gather thoughts while you ask a question."

Connie Sinclair was seated in Duffy's office, commenting on the mobile with the E's levitating in the shared area of the office. Duffy similarly explained the significance as he had to Shane.

She asked Duffy, "Which E are you most versed in?"

"A good question, probably execution and economics would be my field of medicine."

Connie had shoulder-length red hair, a very fair complexion, and an athletic build. She was taking a break from work and mentioned that this was her only chance to do the interview. She seemed comfortable wearing work boots and paired them with a yellow collared tennis shirt embroidered with the chemical name 'Xylofil.' Her belt buckle sported the local FFA chapter logo. After small talk and an explanation of the roles of everyone at the table, Duffy began the interview.

He asked about her work history and what she learned in each role. She needed more time to prepare for and disliked her first role in a biological research firm. She heard about the 'Xylofil' job from a neighbor. She commented that you often appreciate your second job more because of the mistakes you made on the first one. A very mature and insightful answer thought Shane.

Duffy shifted gears a bit. "Connie, tell me about a time at work or church with your family when you had to show leadership. I will let you think about it for a minute and be sure to share details that led up to the leadership moment."

"Kind of an easy one. I am a widowed mother of a 4-year-old boy, so I try to show leadership daily. He spends days and some nights with my mother or mother-in-law, who both live here in town. This allows me to have a career and support us."

"Sorry for your loss," Duffy said, shaking his head, lamenting that he had asked the question. Then he commented, "Communities, they rally around their own."

From his own experience, Shane was intimately familiar with the power of the community back on the Palouse but did not want to derail the discussion.

"If you had your choice of working with a group on a project or by yourself, which would you prefer and why."

"I like both as I can get more done with groups when it is a large complex project; however, when I have to think through stuff, I prefer to think through strategy and tactics on my own."

"Any examples?" asked Duffy.

She talked about an extensive rollout of a new herbicide and how she would get the most out of the process. She worked through the plan, then brought in others to execute with some timelines and expectations.

Duffy asked her to line out her day, show any to-do lists she might have, how she set up her day, and how she followed up with customers. It was an inquiry into activities. Then he switched to more business questions.

"In the business, you are in today, do you follow margins?"

"Not really, because that is not my role. I am given a price list but not information about how pricing is set," she outlined.

"Do you have a feel for the difference in markup and margin?"

"No, never really gave it any thought."

Duffy briefly outlined the differences and how the two calculations can profoundly affect the business's bottom line. It did not spark any further conversation.

"I just sell the stuff I am told to sell and don't give it a bunch of additional thought."

"So, how do you know what to sell?"

"Whatever they tell me to sell is pretty much it." It appeared that she was not comfortable talking about the business side.

Duffy asked for several scenarios where she had to collect money, deal with demanding customers or employees, and how she reported to her boss.

The alarm bells went off with anything related to conflict. She said that she hated to collect money, and she dealt with difficulties in a very passive-aggressive way.

The rest of the interview was strong on selling chemicals but light on versatility to handle conflict issues. Duffy did not make her feel uneasy with his new perception, and the interview rolled to a polite conclusion with her asking about benefits, vacations, flexibility with childcare, salary, and policy. She did not exhibit much high-level curiosity. However, she might want to change careers. The process wrapped up, and she moved on to the next interview.

"What did you think of her?" Shane asked Duffy when it was just the two of them.

"Let's wait until the Roman Counsel."

"Roman Counsel?" asked a curious Shane.

Duffy clarified, "After the interviews are all done, we will be asked to give a thumbs up or thumbs down vote on each candidate, and then we will talk about why we voted the way we did. Saves a ton of time instead of circling a bunch of small talk".

All Shane could think about was how differently they do things at Caldwell's.

Duffy also mentioned, a bit sarcastically, getting to see the 'patented and self-coveted Randy Caldwell Led Zeppelin method.' "It is related to Stairway to Heaven, and you will recognize it when we get in there."

The interview wrap-up was set for 6 PM in Randy's office after the retail store closed. Shane asked the Herd Bull questions about campaigns and governance while the others collected for the wrap-up.

Mr. Heard was taking a liking to Shane's curiosity and even started asking him questions about his internship. Shane mentioned he was to write a report and present the results he had received from dealers and asked if he had any pointers for him on either.

Staring hypnotically at one of Randy's massive deer mounts, he said, "The written word, tailored with brevity, is evidence of thought." He then turned and smiled as if some of his proposed legislation passed the House and the Senate with unanimous yes votes.

"What do you mean?"

"You will figure it out," he laughed in a tone a little like he had hidden the missing clue to a life-or-death treasure hunt. He followed that with, "Ask your boss the question. It will be interesting to hear the answer."

Shane grabbed a notepad and wrote down what he remembered

to ask Mr. Gilmour in their next meeting. The act of writing this profundity down accelerated Herd Bull's laughter.

Randy, Duffy, and Monty entered and shut the door. Randy asked about the laughter, and Bull said, "Just breakin' the colt." The importance of the other matters at hand and the ambiguity of the response satisfied the newcomers enough to move on to the wrap-up.

Duffy entered, nodded, and smiled as he arranged his interview notes on the five-foot glass table resting on a rustic wagon wheel. What interested Duffy most was making sure he could hear the radio. He asked Randy to tune in to KGA radio for the day-end stock market report. Randy skipped across the AM dial on the Zenith portable behind his desk, achieved his target, and adjusted the volume to just above background noise.

Randy joined the group at the table and was kind enough to explain the procedure for what was about to happen in the wrap-up. As a reward to all the participants, he passed out a Heidelberg beer from his refrigerator behind his desk to everyone in the circle. "We used to spend too much time discussing candidates and beating our perceptions to death. After reading about the governance of 80 A.D. Rome, I instituted a similar process. After a fight was completed, they would allow the audience to vote whether the loser would live or die with a simple thumbs up or thumbs down."

Shane looked puzzled at what seemed like a cruel approach.

Randy added, "If there is unanimous agreement that someone isn't going to make it or fit here, why spend much time talking about it?"

"So what if it is split?" said Shane in a tone as if he had just found a dead goldfish in a tank.

Randy clarified, "We share findings and then debate to decide the next steps with the candidate."

Randy started the process, "Elmer Blunt, the dairyman." In unison, the votes were in.

Four thumbs down from the Caldwell group and Monty with Shane sticking a fist out straight, signifying neutral. He could not bring himself to think he was killing someone.

Randy added logic to Shane's process: "So you are moving across the country to start a business. Is Elmer Blunt one of the folks you would take with you as your *first* employee?"

Shane's thumb now felt the gravity and pointed straight down to mimic the others.

"Anybody want to say anything?" Randy sternly asked.

Shane knew better. Bull thought that he might make a truck driver or warehouse person.

Duffy asked Randy, "How many steps?"

"Twenty-Six," he said with one eye squinted closed to indicate that was not good.

Bull immediately said, "I take back the warehouse or truck driver."

Shane was puzzled by the *steps* comment but thought better and kept his mouth shut. Duffy could sense Shane's curiosity and helped him out. Duffy asked, "Do you know what we are discussing with steps?"

"Sure don't."

Duffy clarified, "Randy has a patented system that he has used for…"

"Twenty-two years," interjected Randy.

Duffy encouraged, "Why don't you share your cardio theorem there, Jägermeister." Thus, giving the floor to Randy. Duffy knew that he wanted to expound on it anyway.

"My experience is that I can tell a lot about what kind of employee I will hire by two things. One is if they are friendly. Number two is how far they get up the steps to our offices when I reach the top. There are forty-eight steps from bottom to top. As you have seen, I quickly ascend and turn around to see where you are when I reach the top. I use it to reflect on getting things done, aggression, and agility. The record is forty-five, which was 'Muskox,' and he was the best fertilizer salesperson we ever had. Anything below thirty-five, and I get nervous."

Shane was starting to think about his performance on the steps.

Randy knew Shane was curious and said, "You were thirty-five. However, Choppers (pointing at Monty) was in front of you. So, I award you five more steps, putting you in pretty good standing at forty."

Duffy pulled his fifteen-inch-long hair back into a ponytail and sarcastically added, "Thus, the reason I call it **Randy's Stairway to Heaven.**"

"Laugh if you want there, Buzz cut, but every time we hired anyone below twenty-eight steps, they were a disaster," Randy defensively proclaimed. Shane knew better than to ask where Ernie, the farm gate salesperson, came in.

This whole exercise of 'step math' was a data point, but everyone, except Randy, was silently questioning the validity or whether a human resource tribunal would agree.

Bull couldn't help himself, "You know I have heard you explain your stairway system with great conviction, and I guess I never recognized it…" A long pause purposely followed.

"Recognize what?" asked an excited and smiling Randy thinking that the highly intellectual Herd Bull would knight him for his brilliance.

Bull let the timing incubate a bit longer and delivered the gem no one expected, "I guess what I didn't recognize is the fine line between genius and moron."

Duffy, who was taking a drink, spit beer on his papers and the glass wagon wheel from laughter. Monty smiled as he always did.

Bull did what legends do. Shane returned to cleaning the hog barn to keep from rolling around on the floor. Randy fumed and took another pull on his bottle of Heidelberg.

Randy was ready to move.

"Troy Jacobs, the ag teacher."

Four thumbs up emerged, and Bull was neutral. They talked about what they liked about Troy with his competitive nature, friendly spirit, and work ethic. Bull wanted to see how Troy would be on a farm situation. "My concern is he might try to do more educating than selling." A valuable point was noted and something to look for as they go to the next steps. More comments about the positive conversations they had with Troy lasted over ten minutes and got Shane excited as he liked him.

"How many steps?" asked a curious Monty as he beamed like his son had just thrown a no-hitter.

"Oh, so I guess it is important now?" they all laughed, even Randy.

"Forty."

Whistles and grunts followed with approval as Bull helped himself to another 'Heidelberg beer' or hand grenade, as he called them because of their round and stout bottles.

"Connie Sinclair, the chemical salesperson."

All hands in showed two up, two down, and Shane was neutral. This, of course, made Randy pick on Shane first. "From the great republic of Switzerland, what say you there, Tiger Beat?" looking directly at Shane to make him more uncomfortable than expected after the earlier laugh had happened at Randy's expense.

Shane was growing less fond of Randy but maintained his composure to say, "I think she can sell, but she didn't seem comfortable with animals, and I felt it would be hard for her to deal with the unknown."

Duffy, who was thumbs down, piped into Shane's defense and

said, "I agree with him that she has talent, but she would never be able to deal with you there, big brother. I must look at the candidates through that lens that you can't."

Randy grumbled, puffed up a bit, and recognized that Duffy was probably more right than wrong. "Bull, you were thumbs down as well. What is your logic?" Randy was working to flip an ally.

"She is a tough lady, and raisin' kids on your own is it's own monumental righteous assignment. However, she works a lot more with retailers in the chemical world than she does with the farmer. When I asked her to list things she liked about her job, the farmer face-to-face mailbox call portion was absent. When I added the on-the-farm cold call as an option along with three other things and asked her to rank all of them, the farm gate portion was dead last. If I had added a dental cleaning as a choice, I guess farm calls would have ended in the same location. A big percent of life is just *'showin' up,'* and I don't think she can rehab herself into getting excited about standing toe to toe with a dairyman that has gone feral over his changing milk production."

Monty chuckled like he was watching an episode of Leave it to Beaver and finally got Ward's lesson for that week. "Can I change my thumb?" everyone laughed but Randy.

Duffy then asked the magical question of Randy, "How many steps?"

"Twenty-nine," said Randy a bit reluctantly.

Duffy followed, "So, following your own rules, isn't she a bit questionable?"

To irritate him even further, Duffy mockingly piled on, "SO, if you were moving to the other side of the country…"

"Thanks, Don Rickles, I got it. I was working off the info from a farm supply dealer in Ritzville that said she did a good job working with them. That is why I gave her the benefit of the doubt. Bull, your logic swayed me. I am a thumbs down."

Randy plowed ahead. "So the next steps are to see if Troy, the Ag teacher, gets charged up working with me for a day in the field. If he is a fit, we put together an offer to try and pry him loose from his teaching career. I will want you guys involved with our strategy to get him to our camp if this heads that direction."

Monty asked, "What about Ernie?"

Randy answered, "He knows exactly where he stands and is in a probationary mode. If he turns it on, we keep him; if not, he needs a fresh start." All understood.

For a few long moments, the silence of the five of them was punctuated by the musical sorcery of Ronnie Milsap's ***Any Day Now*** oozing out of the radio. That masterpiece was cut short, giving way to the market report from KGA.

"Turn it up, Randy," asked Duffy excitedly.

The monotone voice of Burl Quarterstick, backed up by the rhythmic chatter of the fake ticker tape, indicated that the day's economic news was coming to the Inland Empire.

"Today, stocks closed slightly higher on positive economic news and job growth forecasts in the housing and manufacturing sectors. The winners of the day included Robin T. Widman Industries closing up two-and-one-half percent on news of the potential merger with Brazell & Company, which caused Brazell to be off one percent. Hunkler Home products closed up three points on the news that their mac and cheese was voted best in America."

The rest of the report became hypnotic for Shane, and he started drifting and thinking about thanking Caldwell's, Bull, Troy, and Monty. He also wanted their contact information to match what he had from Ernie so he could send them thank-you notes. He was also thinking about his two-hour drive to Spokane that night. He had taken a beer but used it as a landmark instead of consuming it because of the long drive. His trance was interrupted as his attention returned to the warbling Quarterstick on the radio.

"And to finish our financial news. U.S. Tobacco Company finished in record territory today on news that demand is accelerating for its Skoal and Copenhagen smokeless chewing tobacco."

A wry smile crept onto Shane's face as he turned, looked out the window at the barren sagebrush of Moses Lake, and in a low-level whisper, recited, "Wallaby Fire King, the dessert of the South."

Shane's Learnings

On how to maintain your composure when it is ill-advised to show displeasure: It is great to have a lighthearted approach to many things in life. But sometimes, you need to maintain *being in character*. This can especially be true when dealing with very sober situations or events. Another circumstance can be with bosses or important clients that are less admired for life's jovial nature. Shane took his mind to clean the hog barn to sober his circumstance and meet the current tone of the meeting with others. When I say, he went to the hog barn, cleaning the hog barn was one of his least enjoyable tasks. He could get there by experiencing the smell, the texture, and the occasional splatter of the manure again.... Find your own 'inner hog barn' to go to in those moments.

On saving time in the interviewing process: Just like a bull rider will say you can't ride two bulls the same way because of the tendencies of the animals, you can't always interview the same way. Example—I had a middle-aged man interviewing for a sales job, and he drifted into a nap while in the interview process. What a stimulating interviewer! Sitting in a warm room, he relaxed between questions and was out, dead asleep for over 90 seconds. This seemed like a month to me as an interviewer, but it was evidently a result of a medical condition that caused this reaction. I waited until he woke and asked him the next question like nothing had happened to prevent embarrassment. Again, they are not all the same.

<u>On If you are really on the fence about an employee</u>: Ask yourself this simple question…. So you are moving across the country to start a business. Is *this person* the first one you would take as your first employee?

<u>On the subject of knowing quickly that the candidate doesn't fit</u>: Sometimes, in interviewing, you change the subject quickly when you know it is not a fit. It is a little like changing bait when you are fishing. Elmer (the dairyman) was not going to fit the role of the salesperson, so there was no reason to drag that out by asking the same questions that you would for the full interview. The reason to explore other interests is that you don't want to disrespect the candidate, especially if they are your organization's potential or current customer. It is beneficial to see what they want to do and get passionate about so you can see where there might be a fit somewhere else in your organization. Almost everyone has a hidden talent or passion that makes the world better.

<u>On how to deal with price vs. value discovery</u>: Bull saw this as a chance to share some collected experience, *"Most people in any industry must have a certain amount of belief in the product or system they are selling.* Without that, they rely heavily on either personal relationships or price. In Elmer's case, it will almost always be price." The process of the successful seller relies heavily on the *transference of feelings and experiences* as a significant part of their process to gain new business. The more you have seen your products work and genuinely believe they can solve the prospect's problem, the more success you will have. Selling premium products is about education. SEE YOUR PRODUCTS IN ACTION OFTEN. Again, it is hard to explain a movie you have not seen.

On how to think about pricing your products: The shortcut in philosophy in setting pricing (especially in multiple-use products) :

1. **People consciously charge what they think their product is worth.** *If the price it too cheap, the customer imagines inferiority. The higher price DOES NOT dictate superiority. Knowing what the seller thinks about it by how they price it better reflects quality when you have little experience with the product. The sooner you can prove the product's value (mentioned above), the easier it is to defend your price point.*

2. *If you shear a sheep, it will continue to be productive, grow, and give you a return. If you skin the sheep, you only get to do it once.* THE SAME IS TRUE FOR YOUR CUSTOMER. *Price the product to keep both of you in business. The key phrase that should guide your short-term pricing strategies: the only good business transaction is one in which both parties prosper. Price for that to happen.*

On team vs. individual interview processes: Team and group interviewing has become more popular. It is great to have a tail gunner in an interview so that they can listen and gather thoughts while you formulate and ask a question.

On How to speed up the wrap-up/decision-making process on interviewing: After all the interviews are done, we will be asked to give a thumbs up or a thumbs down vote on each candidate. Then we will talk about why we voted the way we did. It saves a ton of time versus circling a bunch of small talk about each candidate. Your first instinct is often your best and allows a brief interpretation of the candidates.

On the unique attributes that some look for in the hiring process: We heard Randy say, "I can tell a lot about what kind of employee I will be hiring by two things." He elaborated; one is if they are friendly. Number two is how far they get up the steps to our offices when I reach the top. There are forty-eight steps from bottom to top. As you have seen, I quickly ascend and turn around to see where you are when I reach the top. I use it to reflect on getting things done, aggression, and agility. This is a system that one of my dealers would use on *every* potential employee or candidate. While it was his system and unconventional, he had excellent employees who were willing to work and friendly. You may find a plan that aids your interview process, as we discussed in the last two chapters.

On the idea of using chewing tobacco as the cornerstone of attracting a mate: This action may need some refinement if you think it is your significant advantage in attracting a love interest.

12

THE LOST TRIBE AND THE HARMONY OF THE CRICKETS

As the sunset flaunted her luminary swagger at darkness, Shane decided to make a clean break from the compelling beauty of Moses Lake and coerced Emmitt back toward Spokane. With windows down and gas station sunglasses assisting his drive, Bob Seger serenaded the journey on Interstate 90. Shane imagined this was the freedom that citizens of other countries could only dream of. Bob's vocals on **'Night Moves'** sifted like suspended flour from the speakers while Shane's screaming accompaniment pierced the evening air. The music competed with the pipeline of road noise pouring through the triangular window side vents. These vents directed a seventy-mile-an-hour wind and the occasional stray bug bouncing inside the truck cab. At times like this, the wind blowing through his flowing mane added another check in the plus column of why he had elected to keep it. Changing into ragged gym shorts and a Fram Oil filter t-shirt made the 85-degree evening heat bearable, and his style points accumulate.

As an un-helmeted male motorcycle rider propelled by at over ninety miles an hour wearing only a pair of gym shorts, he weaved in and out of lanes and dodged other travelers. Shane muttered in a voice that represented his disdain for the dangerous action.

"Frickin organ donor."

As it relates to the bugs, dusk in the summers of eastern Washington means the peak hatch of every type of mercenary insect willing to give up its life to add accent and color to the canvas known as your windshield and hood. Emmitt looked a little like a 4th grader's watercolor. Every low spot on the highway that traversed a damp stretch of ground would result in a bombardment of hundreds of new insects self-selecting for their final trip to Spokane. Once settled at a hotel, he located the coin-operated car wash to return that 67 Chevy pickup to Saturday night splendor.

With his squawking remote device, Shane checked the answering machine and listened to a couple of messages to his dad about combine parts that Boxcar had evidently ordered. There was also an invitation from the organizing committee's pre-harvest potluck get-together scheduled for Friday of next week. Shane had repeatedly shown his dad and brothers how to run the answering machine, but the lessons appeared ineffective. He knew he would have to call to remind his dad about the combine parts. But he was also sure no family member would attend the potluck due to the hurdle of creating a dish that would pass a 'group dining' safety or taste test.

There was a message from Mr. Gilmour, the Dreamweaver. THIRD MESSAGE: *"Shane, this is Ron Gilmour. I hope you had a good week at Caldwell's; I am sure you have much to tell me. Please plan to meet me at the Spokane feed plant on Monday around 9 a.m. A marketing person from the home office is coming by around 10:00. I think it would be great for you to sit in on our meeting. I hear nothing but good things about what you are doing. Can't wait to hear about the aphrodisiac fish and chips."* The end of the call was punctuated with his mischievous chuckle that trailed away to an abrupt BEEP. CALL ENDED.

Shane knew Choppers had been sharing the extracurricular activities of Moses Lake.

Being a hip, fashionable young bachelor in Spokane with a freshly washed truck has unlimited possibilities. Dick's Drive-In had offered a sole Spokane dining location on Division Street since before the Nez Perce Indians whipped the cavalry in the 1800s. They probably celebrated their win with a bag of Dicks 29 Cent hamburgers. The hand-cut shoestring fries, cod fish and chips, and fourteen different flavors of milkshakes were a magnetic draw. The dining experience at Dick's was unusual because lawyers, hookers, homeless people, and Samaritans stood shoulder to shoulder under an overhang fifty feet wide by thirty feet deep that protected them. At the same time, they ordered from one of eight walk-up windows. Radiant heaters hanging from the ten-foot ceiling in the winter and fan blades the size of wagon wheels in the summer made the ordering process bearable and moved some of the air around to limit and disperse unusual odors. After you get your food, your car or one of the fryer-grease-preserved picnic tables vacated by former diners punctuates your dining experience. This outdoor dining drew a few nasty seagulls from the coast, craving a consistent food source. A double order of fish and chips, a whammy burger, and a vanilla shake was as wild as this bachelor would get. Back at the hotel, under a streetlight, Shane threw an overdue coat of wax on Emmitt.

Going to the Alumni Feed office in Spokane meant wearing the awkward company tie and white shirt. He reasoned there were worse sentences, and getting paid to wear it made the requirement more tolerable. The part he was dreading was Gilmour's hoosegow of an office.

Monday morning, as he pulled into the plant, he considered protecting Emmitt by parking the truck under the only tree in the parking area. He noticed pigeons sitting in the tree and thought their surgical targeting defecation was not ideal for the new coat of recently applied wax.

The first person he encountered was Mary Tempo, Mr. Gilmour's secretary.

"The prodigal 'Coug' has returned. How is your summer going, Shane?" she seemed genuinely interested as her hazel eyes stared through him, and she grabbed his paw like a ranch hand that had been processing calves every day of her life.

"It has been great, Mrs. Tempo." After he said it, he thought his response inadvertently had undertones of Eddy Haskell addressing June Cleaver.

"Please call me Mary."

"Oh, okay, it has been great, Ms. Mary thanks for asking."

"Better, but still a bit uncomfortable," she reiterated with a smile.

Shane had never been around a woman as confident and outgoing as she was. He didn't know how to act around her.

Mary sensed this and asked Shane to tell him about going to Caldwell's, Cap's, and several other dealers he had been surveying. This familiar discussion was gradually sanding off the rough edges of awkwardness by switching the conversation to things he had experienced, and only he would know. She knew that being an expert or having firsthand experience in something allows communication to flow smoother because of the gathered increased confidence by the communicator. She was one intelligent lady.

The Dreamweaver, who had been in a meeting about the plant's manufacturing issues, swaggered into the room, beaming as he had just won the grade school spelling bee. "How is the finest intern to ever walk the earth?" Of course, this was followed by his signature water pump handshake, mildly sinister but playful laugh, and high beam smile.

As he frequently did, Gilmour looked at Mary and began a

third-party conversation to pull someone's chain. "Mary, did you know our young friend Shane here is a fish connoisseur?" He elevated his voice slightly at the end of the sentence for emphasis.

"No, Ron, I had not heard that," she replied, turning toward a blushing Shane to see if she could gain more depth. She also had been around Gilmour enough to know he wanted her to do just that. "Do you have a favorite?" she asked.

Shane had learned from watching Uncle Bo back on the farm that when someone is *'yanking your chain,'* and you know it, sometimes it is better to deflect the whole chain back at them and give them exactly what they want. This seemed like an ideal time, as Gilmour knew he would be slightly embarrassed by it, and this tweak was his way of getting some mischievous mental cardio in.

"I have a strong and defined palate for Aphrodisiac Cod," Shane shared in a snobbish nose-in-the-air response.

Mary and Ron laughed generously as Shane told the story about the Pothole Diner. He did that to get Gilmour to where he wanted to go on Shane's terms, not on Gilmour's, and to make sure he got his side of the story public. He had no idea what Monty had told them.

This mildly childish discussion continued longer than it deserved, and thankfully it ended. Shane's meeting was moving upstairs to Gilmour's dark paneled cave. As they turned to leave, Mary grabbed Shane's arm and leaned in close so Gilmour would not hear and said, "You handled that brilliantly. Well done."

He looked at her more confidently and said, "Thanks, Mary."

"That's better."

The feed plant hummed as they were manufacturing rabbit pellets and cattle blocks on their manufacturing lines at the same time. It was going to be a hot day in Spokane. The noise of the manufacturing and the honking forklift was beyond chatter. Shane nearly ran to the top stair like he was glued to the back of

Gilmour's obnoxious plaid sports coat. When they got to the top of the landing on the second floor, Shane had a personal realization that Randy Caldwell's stairway to heaven had impacted him.

The meeting was not in Gilmour's office but in a conference room five times the size of his office/holding cell, with an entire wall of roof-to-floor windows resembling a terrarium more than a conference room. The table was the size of two pickup beds and was made of laminated pallet wood constructed by one of the forklift drivers in the mill. The Mortar Board logo with tassel dominated the 'fifty-yard line' of the rectangular table. Compared to Dreamweaver's office, this was a four-star resort.

Shane arranged the thirty-plus surveys that he had completed, mainly by phone, in a pile, assuming Mr. Gilmour wanted to get into the elements of the results.

"My, you have been working hard, young man. Did anything surprise you about the process of doing the survey?"

Shane confessed that the dealers were more open to answering the questions over the phone than he thought they would be. His biggest concern was what to do with all the data once it was completed.

"We can talk about that later, as I might have an idea to get you thinking about how you will approach your presentation."

"Do you know Senator Jimmy Heard?"

"Herd Bull?" Dreamweaver was grinning like he was three drinks in at a happy hour. "Yes, sir. One of my all-time favorites. Did you meet him?"

"I was on the interview team at Caldwell's with him, Duffy, Monty, and Randy."

"That is a solid crew. Did you go through the Roman theatrics on the prospects?"

"Yes, sir, I also got to spend some time talking about the Senate, and he gave me some advice for my report."

Gilmour's smile grew, like inflating an inner tube, a slow but increasing grin now showing nearly all of his teeth. "What advice did he give?"

"Well, he told me….." Shane reached for his notes for the exact words and recited…"The written word, tailored with brevity, is evidence of thought." Shane explained, "Senator Heard laughed and told me to ask my boss what that meant."

Gilmour was smiling and belly laughing as he looked out the eight-foot-tall bank of windows overlooking the parking lot, where they loaded trucks.

"Why is this funny to you?" Said an innocent and curious Shane, who wanted to understand the relevance, if there was any.

"Well, the Bull and I learned that from the same guy. The guy who got us both into the Alumni feed business was Stub Porter. Everyone called him Stub."

"Why Stub?"

"He was over six foot seven inches tall and played forward for Drake University basketball in the late '50s. He was no slight guy."

Gilmour expanded, "Stub was a great communicator. He was the regional manager for Alumni and hired me. He also found Mr. Heard and got him placed at Caldwell's."

"So that is the connection," said a smiling Shane.

Gilmour immortalized Stub for nearly ten minutes with stories about their work together on meetings and campaigns, plus extra-curricular activities, including driving an Oldsmobile off a loading dock and running a golf cart into a lake. He kept emphasizing the important thumbprint that Stub had left on his career. Shane wanted to move him along, so he set one on the tee for Gilmour.

"Sounds like he made a huge impression on you?" Shane knew it was an obvious question.

"He was such a great leader. Most people would follow him

through the gates of hell with a squirt gun full of gasoline," Gilmour replied.

Gilmour continued, "Stub used to say you need to boil the ocean down to a salt shaker to get anybody to appreciate it. He also said if you could get the Bible onto a note card, many more people would become clergy."

To reinforce this point, Gilmour said that when you brought Stub an idea, he wanted it to be as close to one page as possible, at most two. This, of course, reinforced the brevity portion of the statement. The written word segment was Stub's way of saying your idea, your initiative, *whatever* it is, needs to be playschool simple. A 7th grader should be able to explain it to the head of General Electric. There were five simple parts to how Stub wanted the written words to flow. Gilmour wrote them on easel paper and briefly explained each of the five points. Shane took notes like a junior

1. <u>What is the Situation/Background?</u> In other words, what is happening? Use as many facts as possible and not much personal feeling, bias, or premonition. Stub told me that facts are like fruit; they are the only part of the tree or plant you want to consume. Often the facts are apparent, and you may consider them optional. Stub refers to critical points driving the central themes for the reader's support. Remember, you are educating the reader. Sometimes the one to be educated is you, don't leave out the obvious.

2. <u>What is it you want to accomplish?</u> This may be an overriding goal that can be adapted, but it needs to be as specific, measurable, attainable, realistic, and time related as possible. The description of the

goal must be connected to the facts. **We will create delicious, naturally grown, stackable watermelons by the decade's end.** This section is the stratosphere level regarding the elevation of your thoughts.

3. What needs to happen for this to be accomplished? "What is the summary of a very detailed plan? Think of it as a newspaper, as the headlines of an article. You have compressed your big idea into a select group of headlines necessary for the reader to assimilate what you are thinking about quickly." This is at the 10,000-foot level.

4. What is the timeline of activities, and who will do what? These specific initiatives must be completed, by whom, and when. Think of these as being at trapeze height versus on-the-ground tactics.

5. Budget (if needed): This is not spreadsheet work. Spreadsheets may be used to support the summary numbers you calculate. The numbers shown often estimate anticipated spending and the return you expect.

The discussion took about twenty minutes, and Mr. Gilmour had many examples sprinkled throughout. He also asked Mary to bring the notes highlighting these five points. Everyone he trains in this area gets a copy. Shane needed to figure out how all this related to his survey presentation. So he asked just that.

Gilmour smiled and collected himself, acknowledging he had looped the orbit some. "You will be surprised how good presentations go through the same process. Writing out your _situation/background_ in bullet point form should include all the facts that you know. In your case, it summarizes important feed dealer input data. It would also include an analysis of what you know about your audience. Your *objectives* are what you want the audience to leave with or take away on completing your presentation. Ask yourself, w*hat needs to happen?* What tools, tactics, props, verbiage, etc., will you need to convey your message? *The timeline prepares you with a timing roadmap for* what you need to pull together and by when. *A budget* recognizes the costs of the elements you will need for the presentation. Simple stuff if you stick to a similar pattern."

Shane could hear 'Fronk the Wheat Gansta' holler at Shane's inner animal. "Act like you got this!"

The whirling confusion of this process was interrupted by the Alumni marketing teammate who was there to present marketing programs to Dreamweaver. Shane immediately began cleaning up his survey clutter as introductions were formalized.

The teammate entered the conference room with a smile that looked to be in direct competition with Gilmour. The gentleman was about thirty-five years old, sporting total Alumni attire: white shirt, mortarboard tie, and a finely tailored herringbone gray double-breasted suit. His dark brown hair looked like a freshly harrowed field back home and had been lightly and tastefully garnished with clear glistening mineral oil. His voice was deep and loud. It would not shatter glass, but it might scare it. As Uncle Bo would say about someone that talked this aggressively and loudly, 'Either he can't hear himself, or he learned to whisper in a sawmill.'

"I see someone is straightening us out with survey data," said the new loudest man in the room as he observed the surveys on the table. He extended his hand to Shane and said, "Greg Bonejack."

Shane could see Gilmour was not smitten with his approach. Shane greeted Greg with appropriate enthusiasm and introduced himself as the summer intern.

Gilmour quickly re-directed attention back to the marketing teammate. "Greg, thanks for coming. I think you will like the information that Shane and the interns are pulling together for us."

"I am sure I will, Ron. How many dealers have you interacted with over the summer, Shawn?" Greg asked.

Shane let the miscue on his name slide, but it wasn't increasing his affection for this guy. "About thirty I have interviewed in person and on the phone."

"Well, Ron, I hope the intern program gives us a better internal ROI this year than in past years."

Mr. Gilmour, with instant deployment, lost his ever-present effervescence. He silently stared at Greg for what seemed like half a semester. Everyone was getting uncomfortable. Shane gathered his paperwork so he could leave and let these two come to an understanding or evolve into a full-blown hockey scrum.

"No, Shane, part of an intern's learning process is engaging in the whole experience. Shane, please sit." He continued, "And besides if we are going to get an internal ROI on the intern program, you need to get exposed to all aspects of what we do." Retorted Gilmour.

"Ok." Greg reluctantly accepts and is finally starting to sense the confrontation.

Greg is the marketing manager of the Specialty Animal Business for Alumni. He is well educated and creative, but as Gilmour later pointed out to Shane, he has needed more real-world experience. He also has a reputation for being a bit glib, demanding, and more than occasionally self-centered.

Calmly and deliberately, Gilmour sets the table for the discussion. "So let's get a feel for why you were nice enough to join us, Greg. I understand you flew from Omaha just to be here this morning. Thanks for coming all that way."

Greg began, "Well, Ron, let me get right to the point. This is the third year we have seen a decrease in the goat, cricket, and mink feed business in your sales division."

Gilmour gave an emotionless response of "Uh- huh," and deliberately stared at Greg like he was modern art hung in a biker bar.

Greg couldn't stand the silence and started to speak rather loudly. "It seems your sales force has no regard for growth in these important business segments."

Greg is now in justification mode and ramps up his displeasure with an even higher volume. "We have rolled out promotions to dealers to stock cricket crumpets and offered trade promotions like free box cutters to goat owners when they buy a bag. We even had a Christmas stocking offer containing Fred of Como barbeque sauces to mink farm operators. You and your team never ordered any of those for operators and dealers. Feels like they are not on board with the specialty business."

The silence was fermenting while an acknowledgment of such a meaningful conversation had to be gift-wrapped accordingly.

"Uh-huh," Gilmour deadpanned similarly to the former response he gave, knowing full well this repetition would continue to quicken Greg's cardiac cadence.

Greg shifted in his chair and made a critical error in judgment by laying out a veiled threat, "You know Ron if we can't get the results from your team, we need we will have to start looking for some folks that can."

"Uh-HUH!" This time a more rapid response from Gilmour with elevated emphasis at the end of his statement.

Gilmour looked over at Shane, who was in full anticipation of the entire field NASCAR crash that was about to happen in turn four. "You know, Shane, I think your first instinct might have been right; you should probably see Mary and see if she needs help." Following those comments, Gilmour slowly turned his head, blinked his eyes methodically, and stared at Greg.

Shane was viewing a Gary Cooper **High Noon** moment between a young hotshot gunslinger and a crafty weathered marksman, and he would not see the ending.

Shane strolled into Mary's office and did as Gilmour asked. She responded, "Is everything all right in there?"

Shane smiled and wryly responded, "I think Mr. Gilmour is going to teach a taxidermy lesson."

Mary looked at Shane without surprise and said, "Mr. Gilmour has said several times that Greg has always been very comfortable with himself."

Mary then shared the real reason Gilmour asked Shane to leave the room. "Mr. Gilmour has a solid rule, **recognize people in public, and admonish them in private.**"

Shane reflected with a nod and returned to correlating survey data, wondering if Gilmour was putting one of those box cutters to good use.

Meanwhile, the conference room was morphing into an arena; Dreamweaver and Greg sat at the pallet table between them. The table would help resist the temptation to trigger a severance package if punches were thrown on company time.

After several minutes of staring, Ron tells Greg, "You hear that?"

Greg looked from side to side as if it would improve his hearing ability.

"Not sure what you want me to hear?" he responded with slight indignance.

Gilmour closed his eyes, looked up, and said, "Listen." The two men were sitting there stoically, immersed in the morning sunlight, as the significant noise all around them was the banging and pounding of the feed manufacturing equipment in the adjacent plant. This plant noise was punctuated by the frequent honking of noisy forklifts scurrying around the warehouse with feed pallets.

"I hear the feed manufacturing process," acknowledged Greg with some reluctance.

"Glorious, isn't it?" With his eyes closed, Gilmour breathed deeply, still looking toward the ceiling as if he were reviewing a fine port wine. "Do you hear the rhythm to it?" asked Gilmour. "The deep bass of the pellet mill growling, along with the high pitch of the steam moving through the plant to make it all possible, is capped off by the treble and the unpredictability of the forklift honks, like a razor-sharp percussion section." The old gun continued, "THAT is one of the most beautiful sounds in the world. THAT, my fine young colleague, is the **harmony of the crickets.**" When on a roll, don't stop! He continued, "Because of your Specialty Animal business I assume you have a great deal of experience with crickets and probably know they are most productive when they are in rhythm. You know, I have fished a lot for crappie with crickets. When I drop the screened box that I keep them in, they stop making noise because they are unhappy."

"What does any of this have to do with the performance issues associated with the products I came to talk to you about?" asked an increasingly engaged Bonejack.

"Quite a lot, actually." Without raising his steady, consistent voice, Gilmour replied, "You were essentially asking 'what in the hell are you and your guys doing'? You flew four hours from Omaha on a Sunday with one or two plane changes. You were staring at those performance numbers the entire time, developing a more than mild irritation for me and the sales division. Then you brought me your facts in a rather confrontational attitude and a bit of a loud voice, I might add".

"Point taken."

"Greg. THAT noise out there? THAT is what my team and I have been doing—three full shifts a day, six days per week. I am a 'cricket herder'. The more our team sells, the more harmonious the symphony of the crickets is in the plant. When I don't hear that plant running, my boss and I get really upset. And if you have never heard this, write it down- ***the boss gets what the boss wants.***"

"I just wanted to know why the performance was not up to par," said Greg.

"And I will tell you. How many of the products you just asked about are manufactured in the plant we are sitting in?" asked Gilmour.

"All of them are manufactured in San Jose and brought here, you know that."

"Yes, I do. I have nothing against the products you are discussing, especially when they arrive on time and are easy for our dealers to get. The high level of product shortages in San Jose has been legendary. Dealers have quit stocking some of these products because when a hungry mink can't get feed, as you may have heard, the mink farmer gets pissy and looks for alternatives. Preventing those alternatives from happening at the mink farm wastes allot of productive selling time."

"Many of those mink farmers are bad managers, very bad." Greg wanted to use their poor organizational skills in forgetting to order as a reason the San Jose plant had its issues.

"Greg, there are several reasons for the loss of business. Unreliable supply is certainly one of the biggest. I will also tell you it is not a priority for our sales team about what my boss, the cricket herder, wants to be done."

"Well, how do we prioritize it?" asked Greg.

"That is as simple as fitting Wilt Chamberlain into a Volkswagen," retorted Gilmour.

He continued, "Let me elaborate. If we took all the crickets and all the mink in the eight western states that I cover and shipped all the feed to all the critters in those two species, would we be able to get the total consumption for the year on forty truckloads?"

"Probably about right," Greg said reluctantly.

"Ok, let me bring that into perspective. Today this plant will ship twenty-five truckloads of bags and ten truckloads of bulk feed. Nearly your total potential for all the West Coast in the groups we were talking about. I mentioned fishing earlier, and a very accomplished panfish guide told me a statement I carry in my head." A short pause was brought in for emphasis. "**You never leave fish when they are biting to find fish.**"

"But it doesn't seem like your guys are trying. They haven't ordered any premiums to help sell more of these items."

"Uh-huh. Back to where we were. On a recent visit, I asked one of our better feed dealers about the goat promotion with the box cutters as a gift."

"What was their response?" Greg wanted to know with more than mild curiosity.

"Well, he walked me into the tool section of his hardware aisle and asked me what he should do with the three different kinds of box cutters and carpet knives already on his shelf. If we were going to give them away to some of his customers, how many would he be able to sell?" Gilmour wanted to put the idea in its place. "I am not sure where the idea came from, but the execution was going to miss the mark."

"It was my idea," said Greg.

Now the Dreamweaver knew where the enthusiasm for these knives was rooted.

"Greg, I want to help you."

"Are you sure about that?" Greg inquired.

"Because candor saves lives, I think you have an auspicious career ahead of you, and I can help you."

"How is that?" Greg warmed slightly.

"You like Indian art?"

"Never paid much attention to it."

"But you have seen it? If not, go down to the plant manager's office; he has close to a full gallery of it down there."

"What does Indian art have to do with my career?"

"I try to read as much as I can about American Indians. Chief Joseph, Geronimo, and Sitting Bull can give some amazing leadership lessons. I am no fan of how the insurgent settlers treated the Indians."

"Me neither."

"As you look at the makeup of the various tribes, they all had certain norms and beliefs. Some reputations were earned, and some suffered from unfair and jilted propaganda. However, there is one tribe that has been lost from all the records."

"Which one is that?" Greg is mildly interested now.

"It was the Zealots."

"Never heard of that tribe."

"Exactly, there is no Zealot tribe left."

"What happened to them, famine or disease?"

"No, the other Indians shot them for being too obnoxious and self-focused."

Gilmour stopped to see if that was being absorbed at all. It was starting to, as Greg stared out the window.

The Dreamweaver would now try to help this talented teammate rehab his approach. He extended his right arm across the table like a lifeline to someone descending the vortex of a sewer drain.

Greg turned from his self-reflective window gaze, with a view that included a full bulk truck idling up onto the feed mill scale, to see the extended arm of who just ten short minutes ago was his resistance, Gilmour.

"What is this?" said a mildly indignant Greg.

Gilmour calmly neglected Greg's terse tone while still extending the arm and looking directly at him silently.

In a composed and steady pitch, he began his lesson with the same statuary stance, "Do you know where the idea of the handshake originated?"

"No idea."

"About five hundred BC, Greeks would grab each other's forearm as a physical indication that they had no weapons. This symbolic action helped develop trust between those less familiar with the other."

With arm outstretched, Gilmour announced, "I have no weapons."

Greg couldn't help fighting off a creeping grin accompanied by the stinging realization that this guy was interested in trying to help me.

Sometimes we state the obvious hoping to deflect reality. Greg took umbrage at it and said, "So I am obnoxious and self-absorbed?"

"No," said Gilmour after a purposeful pause. "You are passionate. The world can live with passion when channeled correctly." The neon smile was back on Gilmour to speed up the recovery.

"What do you mean channeled correctly?"

"A slightly complex answer awaits, but let me ramble here." Gilmour took a long pull on a tepid cup of coffee for effect. "You came here this morning with the premise of needing to fix *YOUR* problem, not *OURS*."

Greg knew he was correct; you could tell from his silence.

Gilmour expanded, "A passionate realist would have asked me how my team was doing and how they could help figure out how to turn the specialty losses around."

Greg asked the most challenging question, "What would a Zealot have done?"

Giving him a bit of a break, the Dreamweaver responded, "Well, Greg, there aren't any left, so I can't answer that." Dreamweaver continued, "Let's start with figuring out how we might fix the Specialty business right here at this plant?"

"How do we get it fixed?" said a humbled Greg.

"Hey, that's a good question; let's go down and see Dukie, the plant manager and see if he has any ideas for how we work on the shortage issues out of San Jose."

"While we are there, I hear he has a hell of an Indian art collection," Greg replied.

Gilmour smiled, "He is passionate."

Shane's Learning

<u>On helping the unconfident communicator:</u> When you encounter someone nervous or apprehensive about communicating with you, a tip is to get them to talk about something they are familiar with. Firsthand experience often primes the pump for more accelerated conversation. Familiar topics tend to make the conversation flow smoother because of the increased confidence of the communicator.

<u>On dealing with someone playing with you: When someone is 'yanking your chain,' and you know it, it is often</u> better to deflect the whole chain back at them by giving them exactly what they want. Getting angry or upset with the prank will often prolong the duration of the nonsense. In reality, your being uncomfortable is their payoff. Justice is usually served by getting to the end of the prank before the teaser.

. . .

On helping someone who has trouble summarizing thoughts:
Boiling the ocean to a saltshaker to get anybody to appreciate it; or if you could get the Bible onto a note card, **many** more people would become clergy. This emphasizes the true genius of simplicity. A good friend who had a way of expanding the meaning of a simple paragraph into a full-day seminar used to tell me that if you asked him to do a two-day conference, he could prepare in ten minutes… However, he and his content would meander around like a calf in a pasture. If asked to do a ten-minute session, it would take him two days to focus and pull his thoughts together.

On how to help someone organize their written thoughts:
'Brevity is evidence of thought.' A simple five-step way of organizing your thoughts is as follows:

- ✓ **What is the Situation/Background?** In other words, what is happening? Use as many facts as possible and not much personal feeling, bias, or premonition. Sometimes the facts are evident, but you may not think they are essential. Make 2-3 pages of facts. Combine and condense your top ten facts into 5-8 key points driving central themes for the reader's support. Remember, you are educating the reader. Sometimes you are educating yourself.

- ✓ **What is it you want to accomplish?** This may be an overriding goal that can be adapted, but it needs to be as specific, measurable, attainable, realistic, and time related as possible. It should also be related to the facts when describing, *"We will create delicious, naturally grown, stackable watermelons by the end of the decade"* This section is defined as the stratospheric level.

✓ **What needs to happen for this to be accomplished?** In other words, what are the steps necessary to get the *whatever?* Completed. There can be many pages of support for a very detailed plan but condensing them into a select group will be necessary for the reader. This is at the 10,000-foot level.

✓ **What is the timeline of activities, and who will do what?** Straightforward buckets of initiatives must be completed by whom and when. Think of these as being at trapeze heights versus on-the-ground tactics.

✓ **Budget (if needed):** This is not spreadsheet work. Spreadsheets may be used to support the summary numbers you come up with. The numbers shown are often an estimate of expected spending returns.

On using the process to create presentations: You can improve presentations when you go through the same process. Writing out your *situation/background* in bullet point form should include all the facts. In this case, it is the summary of essential data. It would also include an analysis of what you know about your audience. Your *objectives* are what you want the audience to leave with or take away from your presentation. List what tools, tactics, props, and verbiage you need to convey this message. *Timeline* prepares you with a timing roadmap for what you need and when you need them. *The budget* recognizes the costs associated with delivering the presentation as you would like. Simple stuff if you stick to a similar pattern.

. . .

On giving different kinds of feedback: *'Recognize people in public and admonish them in private.'* While feedback is essential to a person's development, it should be positive when possible and correctional when appropriate. Community broadcast of correctional issues is leadership injustice. The person on the receiving end will resent it, even though they may do little about it publicly. It is doubtful that this unproductive criticism will have the impact you desire as a leader. The tangible result is that you will likely lose the rest of your team. They frequently rally around their peers unless they are entirely incapable or disruptive. Your team knows who those people are but want you to handle their improvement in private. Positive feedback or group goals achieved should be unrestricted, public revelry. A mistake organization make is that they don't celebrate their successes as hard as they work. An effective public celebration is an underappreciated source of momentum.

On staying focused on what is working: *"You never leave fish when they are biting to find fish."* Said another way, if the strategy works, stay with it versus losing focus and moving on potentially lesser return projects.

On the importance of giving meaningful feedback: "Under the premise that candor saves lives, I think you have an auspicious career ahead of you, and I can help you," was what Gilmour said to Greg. Why is such a thought process meaningful? If you have a doctor who diagnoses an unsuspected, potentially life-altering disease, you wouldn't want the doctor to diminish any detail, even if it would raise your anxiety. Gilmour viewed Greg as being in danger long-term and wanted to ensure he knew why.

. . .

On "The boss gets what the boss wants." A prolific strategy for staying with an organization and being promoted is to make your boss look good. A foundational premise is to follow what the boss wants. As a boss, you must provide clear and concise direction on what you want accomplished. Gilmour's boss wanted a full and productive feed plant.

On the real meaning behind the handshake: About 500 BC, Greeks would grab each other's forearms as a physical indication that they had no weapons. This symbolic action would help develop trust between those less familiar with each other..... *The handshake was born.* Use it with similar intent.

On the fine line between passion and zealotry: *A passionate realist* would have asked me how my team was doing and how they could help determine how to turn around the specialty losses. Being a **zealot** for your cause at the expense of other larger projects your company has will be recognized as a selfish tactic.

13

PUT THE POTATO IN THE FRONT

The cab of a combine can be compared to an isolation booth on a game show. It is temperature controlled, the rampaging diesel engine's roar is fourteen inches away, drowns out most of the sound, and provides the solitude of a mother's womb.

The uniformity of the ten-to-twelve-hour daily experience of harvesting the carpet of wheat attached to the hillside can lead to boredom. The specially engineered hillside combine allows the driver to keep the eight-ton feat-of-engineering splendor operating on terrain steeper than a goat's face. In contrast, the driver is as level as sitting in a church pew.

Shane needed threshing time away from his internship on the weekend to sort out many clustering items. He only had a couple of weeks left in his summer odyssey. He had two more dealer trips ahead and had to sort his project presentation into 'a saltshaker'.

The time back home on the combine and the chance to catch up with his family over the weekend was a welcome distraction. Even though he was only there for a day and a half, it was worthwhile to curb the potential envy his family members might have over his summer activities.

His sister had been driving a grain truck to the elevator for nearly eight years. Her hundreds of trips per harvest year had helped her develop an intimate familiarity with every crease of excess gravel; the diameter of every pothole; the depth of every ditch; and the pitch of every corner. When meeting another truck on the gravel road built to accommodate one and-one-half car widths, these things were critical to know. The traditional rule of the gravel road was that the empty truck returning from the grain elevator would pull to the curb and stop so the loaded truck could pass in the opposite direction while keeping momentum. This is because the chance of an accident is high when both trucks continue unyielding. The loaded truck has a higher level of difficulty restarting its journey from the edge of the road should it have to stop. This is compounded if the loaded truck goes up a hill on a gravel road. The most perilous hazard is when the dual rear wheels of the loaded truck become mired in a ditch past the skirt of the road. The truck can tip over because it runs out of road. These safety scenarios needed to be reviewed with anyone driving a truck due to the recent arrival of a group farming the place following Mr. Rossow's retirement.

T-Rex Farms was a farm organization near the Idaho border, expanding its operation into Whitman County. They secured the Rossow farm lease through ancestral bloodlines. Boxcar had hoped Mr. Rossow would offer him the opportunity to farm it. Genealogy floated to the top on Mr. Rossow's wife's side. This meant a nephew had a clear runway to lease the land. He was a part of the T-Rex group.

The T-Rex group farmed and drove their equipment, in football terms, like they were in a blitz package. Everything was fast and slightly reckless. This included the bright orange tandem axle diesel Ford grain trucks they herded down the gravel road like the out-of-control horse-drawn buckboard wagons you see in the old black and white western movies.

Shane's sister had experienced the formerly mentioned courtesy violation from these trucks twice in the last two days. The unloaded orange three-axle missiles nearly caused an accident because their unwillingness to share the road in congruence with the unwritten rules of gravel road etiquette. Safety is paramount when driving a grain truck with nine tons of wheat in the back. Prayers at the evening dinner table for a safe harvest had taken on real meaning.

Shane left at 2 p.m. to get to Spokane to catch an evening plane to the San Francisco Bay Area. His instruction from Dreamweaver was to connect early Monday morning with Noel Bowman, the twenty-year veteran Alumni Feed Salesperson. Noel was a legend in Alumni Feed for his savvy street real-world wisdom and because he had spent some time in the Alumni marching band when he was based in the Midwest.

Noel had a wavy mane of dark hair smattered with gray streaks. Both colors highlighted his buckskin tan complexion. He reminded Shane a bit of Michael Landon, who played Little Joe Cartwright on Ponderosa, but he was more barrel-chested like Loren Green, who famously played Ben Cartwright or "Pa" on the same long-running series. When he smiled, he produced dimples where you could stick a roll of quarters.

Noel picked up Shane at the Holiday Inn Embarcadero at Fisherman's Wharf. Shane was up early, walking the docks. Your first time seeing the ocean, even if it is an inlet, is a moving event. The smell of boiling crab and sea lion excretion from those hanging around to get fish handouts convinced Shane that living in the Embarcadero would not be a high priority. It almost made him miss the hog odor from back home. Noel was getting a kick from listening to Shane talk about this inaugural experience. It helped him reflect, reconstructing memories of his naivety when he started.

The new car smell in Noel's root-beer-colored 1980 Cutlass with the landau top and plush low pile cloth seats provided a great ride toward the wine country, north of the bay area's congestion and diverse neighborhoods. Shane hardly noticed the great ride. He was too busy absorbing topography and agriculture that he could never have imagined existed. He and Noel got acquainted as they traveled, and Shane learned about his three boys, his stint in the Navy submarine corps, and his success with Alumni Feed.

Noel talked about his passion for his job, working with dealers, and calling on customers. It was a much more desirable job than being in the Alumni head shed. He had been there. He had orchestrated several dealer and marketing programs while in Alumni corporate. When the opportunity to go to the field in California arrived, he jumped on it. He said he didn't care if the relocation would hurt his career. He punctuated it by saying, "The closer you are to the customer, the closer you are to heaven."

While driving, Noel reached into the back seat with his right arm. Without his eyes leaving the road, he opened his briefcase with octopus dexterity, pulled out the folder he wanted, and dropped it beside Shane. It was a green-colored folder with the words **Bowman district** in the tab. He boasted that a prolific salesperson could maneuver this briefcase without swerving or losing visual contact with the roadway. He also warned Shane that he was a trained professional and should not try this tactic alone.

"OK, enough sightseeing; I need to provide you with some background so that Gilmour knows I did my job. So my young man, someday you might have a job like mine or one that requires you to provide a simple but thorough explanation of what you do?"

"Curious what the purpose of that would be," Shane questioned as he sifted through the various papers in the green file.

"Do you like my car?" Noel asked.

"Rides great," Shane commented.

"So before I bought this car, I knew little about it. I had only noticed a few on the highway. I went to the dealership and talked to a salesperson. He told me a lot about the car's virtues and took me for a test ride. Before I left, he gave me a very detailed brochure. It had all the features, the performance data, and the engine and drivetrain data. It contained many specifics and the color options available for the exterior and interior. It also had various glamour shots with beautiful people driving and enjoying the car. In other words, they were trying to convince me that I was making the right decision buying this car."

Shane nodded to signal his understanding.

"That is the same thing that is in the green folder. In my job, customers must buy into you every day. Many people in my role forget that they also have others to sell every chance they get. The others I am talking about are your boss, your company, and its support staff."

"Why do you have to sell Gilmour?" Shane asked.

"A great question; I love Mr. Gilmour. He is my seventh boss in my twenty years at Alumni. You don't know who your boss will be tomorrow, so you are prepared with your brochure, like the Oldsmobile dealership, to explain to them what you do and that you know what you are doing. And most importantly, that **they don't need to worry about you.**"

"Worry about you; I may not be following?"

"So what is a boss trying to accomplish?" Noel asked as they passed a winery that looked like a German castle.

"I am not sure, harmony?" Shane knew he was freewheeling on this one.

"That may be one of the benefits, but I would break that into a few categories that would vary by individual. However, for nearly all bosses the core of their desires would be similar."

Shane nodded, hoping this would signal his desire to learn more.

"Bosses all want to be successful; never met one that didn't. Some judge success as making more money. Some want to be promoted for notoriety. Some want to develop people and help them be successful. They all have bosses too. They aim to make their boss look good; the rest of the benefits will normally follow."

"So why the green file?" Shane had glanced at it enough to get a general idea of the contents.

"Offense."

"Offense?" Shane repeated in question form.

"Yeah, I want to shape the impression of me and what I am doing in my sales territory. Let me give you an example of where I learned that."

Noel told Shane that he had done a great job creating annual plans for an essential dealer program when he was in headquarters. He had thorough, sound understandable strategies to support the project and created a detailed work plan and budget. He made a compact illustrative document with elaborate backup reference materials. He gave it to his boss and asked him if he had any questions. The outcome was more of a two-hour interrogation than a discussion about this well-devised annual plan. A crafty veteran, Helms, who worked in corporate support, sat in on the meeting. He could tell the inquisition wrung out Noel. After the meeting, they went to an alcove by the cafeteria, had coffee, and discussed what had happened. Helms explained that Noel had done excellent work, the best he had seen all year. Then he offered, "However, Noel, you did not control the content or the delivery of your great ideas. You let your boss, who only knew about a tenth of the project as you, get control instead of you guiding him through your work the way you wanted". The lesson was to go on offense. You walk through all the items how you want them to be interpreted. Helms continued, "In the absence of your offense, the boss sometimes must be a *boss* and fill the leadership vacuum by taking control. You know, 'smartest guy in the room stuff.' That was the reason for all the questions and the difficult meeting. Remember, in a meeting like this, you educate your boss to look good in front of others. The lack of offense allowed the interrogation by the boss to get the education needed to move the project forward. The veteran's tip was that there is an endless need to make your boss look good. It's life's ladder of vanity."

Noah recalibrated, "So the folder is my way of going on offense. Data includes my top ten customers with their historical performance, the top ten product sales, and total product sales charted by year. A comprehensive map shows the location of all my customers. The map also shows major competitor outlets with write-ups on each manufacturer and retailer in the territory. I also list my top five objectives for the year and note my work history."

"This is very impressive; even I understand what I am looking at," commented Shane.

"That is part of the process. I get many people riding with me that are feed industry newborns. I want them to leave with one major thought on their mind."

"What thought is that?" Shane asked.

"I want them to think, 'Man, that guy knows what he is doing.' That is what going on offense means." Noah continued, "Your boss wants you to do a few things. One main thing to understand is that a boss doesn't want you to bring them problems or surprises. They want to understand problems, but they want you to bring them the solution to those problems. Problem solvers eat at the big kid's table. Surprises are for birthday parties. And by the way, nobody REALLY likes surprise parties."

"Is there an art of problem-solving?" asked Shane.

"A question that can take years to answer. Let's start with **what** you are bringing to your boss. Is it worth their time? For example, if you call Gilmour to ask him what he thinks you should do for lunch, you will probably have the word 'terminated' beside your name very soon."

"That seems obvious," Shane reinforced.

"This might help when you think about bosses. I had a great boss tell me something once, and I have never forgotten it. He said he could NOT stand working with only two types of employees. **One is the employee you cannot tell anything, and the other is the employee you must tell everything.**"

Noel continued, "A perfect reminder to progress in any role is always to do more than you are asked to do. A statue has never been built to honor those who have done what is expected of them. Bring your boss big ideas that can scare him just a little and provide a plan of how you can help pull off this big idea. You will be viewed as a valuable employee."

Shane acknowledged the wisdom as only an intern can, "Makes sense, but you mentioned you might have a bad boss along the way. How do you handle that?"

Noel momentarily took his eyes off the road to look at Shane, "They told me you were a sharp little fart."

Shane added, "And that my haircut makes me look like someone's sister."

Noel chuckled and said, "I mentioned I had seven bosses in twenty years. That is a boss about every two and a half years on average. Most last eighteen months."

"Seems quick," Shane added.

"It is the way corporate organizations work. I had a 'cousin of

Satan' for a boss in HQ and thought about quitting. A long-time great employee gave me some sage advice when she saw my frustration by telling me that the organization would smell this guy like a feral coyote in a den, accelerating his demise. She reminded me that POWs last for years behind bars. By comparison, you can spend eighteen months executing what you should do with a difficult boss. She also told me that if you like the company, don't let someone else's incompetence drive you away from it. She was so right. He was gone in six months."

Shane changed the subject. "You mentioned that being closer to the customer is like being closer to heaven. Why do you say that?"

Noel pointed out that some people don't like meeting the farmer at their operation. He pointed out that at least **50% of the sales process is 'showin up.'** He pointed out that if he doesn't go to the farm, the chance to get the farmer's business is a little like the chances of taking down a rhino with a BB gun. Very small. He commented that there has never been a trip to a farm when he didn't learn something. He also mentioned that if he brings the business to one of his dealers, the chance of the dealer shifting more business to him increases exponentially. He said that he tried to make sure he made it part of his routine.

"What is it like working in corporate headquarters?" inquired Shane.

Noel told Shane there were many factors to this, but the leadership often sets the tenor of the working environment. It can vary from a trip to summer camp to a gulag. This wide variance is set by the attitude towards the employees being able to develop their leadership skills; and often by how much the employees intimately understand the business they are in and what fundamentals make it work.

Shane asked for more clarity about employees knowing what business they are in, as that just seemed so fundamental to him.

Noel became quite expressive, "You can tell someone that we are in the feed business, but unless they have been with customers or dealers and see how the entire purchasing cycle plays a role in our commerce, their ability to be effective can drop exponentially."

"Is there a lot of that?" asked Shane.

"Depending on the organization's size, there are variances. I have compared notes with friends in several industries, and there is diversity in cultural approaches. In some entities, roles get created in corporate organizations. Sometimes it is trendy for leaders to feel that the more people they have reporting to them, the more important their role and the better chance to be promoted. In other places, they work on skeletal support structures and grind employees until they quit without corporate concern."

"You are kidding?"

"Wish I was. The common denominator in all this headquarter talk and working in corporate is that daily, you must be able to swim the eight-hundred-meter medley in a festering septic tank of politics. By the way, there are no life jackets. In many organizations if you don't like political GAMESMANSHIP, stay out of corporate and remain close to the customer. Most customers don't have time for politics in their purchasing decisions. Maybe that is why I think it is heaven."

Shane and Noel arrived at their first destination, Comrade Feed and Garden. The outside appearance differed from most feed dealers Shane had seen this summer. It had no tall elevator leg, manufacturing mill, or grain tanks. There was a large warehouse with attached greenhouses and pallets of merchandised pet food. Mulch and other garden supplies were under the eave near the store entrance. On top of the reader board, designed to distract the commuter traffic frequenting Gier Way, stood a life-size quarter horse and border collie. This was to remind and educate travelers using this road a couple of times a day what the focus of this operation was. There was a haybarn filled with bales of alfalfa and straw where cars and pickups backed up to get single bales to take home. Shane saw a Mercedes with two bales of three-wire alfalfa shrink-wrapped in plastic and sticking out of the trunk, and he realized that he wasn't in Whitman County any longer.

Noel parked out of the way of customer parking spaces to limit the congestion already occurring at this location. Noel asked before leaving the car space, "You ready for sensory overload?"

Shane's puzzlement showed on his face.

Shane noticed the difference in merchandising as they entered through the front.

The most unusual visual he had ever seen in any store was rotating over his head. The store incorporated a continuous rotating track purchased from a bankrupt dry-cleaning store. The tracks hung at various levels to make the customer's eye level vacillate up and down as the trail meandered around the store. Like a dry cleaner store, the continuous chain had hooks; instead of carrying clothes, this conga line moved dog treats, horse tack items, empty jugs of supplements, and shampoos. It had small sample bags representing the dog food and horse feeds that Comrades sold. It carried bird feeders, hay hooks, small propane tanks, small dog carriers, and much of what was on sale. If the store had it, it was seen circling up above. The looping dry-cleaning display has been updated with nylon glides to limit its clanking noise to avoid annoying customers. It indeed captured most of their attention upon entry.

Down the central aisle were at least twenty different large-bag dog foods. All were stacked ten high with a sign behind them to identify their makeup and pricing differences. It appeared an obsessive-compulsive architect organized them. Shane saw a man dressed in a uniform with a Comrade Feed and Alumni Feed patch on each sleeve. He walked into the aisle with display replacement bags on his cart. After a customer purchased and removed one, he grabbed one off his cart and stacked it on one of the piles to return it to ten-bag height. Having stacked the bag, he held a well-shined, two-foot by three-foot piece of plywood equipped with a three-foot handle made of a two-by-four. He hit the replacement bag he just placed on the stack with that paddle contraption with the finesse of someone beating the dirt out of a rug hanging on a clothesline. After three to four spankings, the bag was perfectly shaped, and the pile looked like it had been sited with a sextant. It was square and perfectly shaped, with little chance of tipping over in the busy store. The horse aisle was similar in structure and design, perfectly displayed with information, pricing, and cost per feeding for your animal behind each stack.

Shane was drawn to an unusual section by a chopped-down and transplanted seven-foot-tall maple tree. Its wide-reaching branches were filled with every imaginable bird feeder. An impressive variety of wild bird food, sunflower, and various bagged seeds were merchandised nearby, with the distinct benefit of the cart boy's flogging.

Jeans and work clothes were stacked on the wall by brand, type, color, and size along the entire upper-level section, in full view from the lower level. The pants display nearly touched the top of the building. A young lady was babysitting these jeans and folding all the clothing with the exact organized symmetry created by the bag spanker.

Every Comrade employee uniform displayed the embroidered Alumni feed logo.

Hundreds of scented candles adorned the animal and farm-themed gift shop, enriching the scent of the entire store.

Background music wafting through the rafters of Comrade was a classic country theme, with Don Gibson crooning "Sea of Heartbreak" and Johnny Cash's portfolio. The Nashville masterpieces were interrupted by a reverberating sound of a six-inch bell mounted by the door. The sign by the exit door says, "If we exceeded your expectations today, please ring the bell." Regardless of anything else, when the bell rings, the staff screams in unison, "Thank you, comrades!"

This store buzzed like a hive. Customers, primarily women, meandered in almost every aisle. Some wore English horse-riding apparel, some in tennis or golf attire, and some in jeans and denim shirts. Ten-thirty in the morning must be shopping time in California. Noel commented that this was light traffic. On typical Saturdays and Sundays, customers are at the counter register ten-deep until they close.

Noel took Shane to the office of the one and only Lyda Shapiro. She was on the phone expressively flirting and teasing whoever was on the other end about getting her saddle order by Friday or she would travel to spend the weekend with them. She motioned Noel to come in and sit while she continued her call. Her office was a photo gallery of events at Comrade hosted by her and the staff. Centered on the intimate pink walls was a hand-painted oil of a black and white border collie sitting at attention.

Lyda wore Western clothes that Shane thought might be out of the Porter Wagoner collection. Her hair was nearly maroon, shoulder length, heavily teased and framed the pancake makeup and pink blush generously applied, perhaps to disguise a few years she wished she had back.

Her phone call ended; she jotted a note to herself and added it to a few things on her desk that were **in process**. She took a deep breath and looked the two of them up and down.

"Gentlemen, the Chippendale dancer tryouts were this morning; you all must come back next Monday."

Noel said, "I brought this guy from corporate to model the new Alumni underwear lineup."

Looking back at Shane, she paused appropriately and said, "He is capable. I like your hair there, cutie; spin around for me there, darlin." Shane was terrified but reluctantly played along. As he slowly turned around, his cheeks turned the color of Lyda's hair. She offered some wisdom for that modeling career. "When you wear that tight swimming suit, remember to put the potato provided to accentuate your curves in the *front* of your pants." She capped off this choreographed exercise in embarrassment with a wink. Shane wondered if the eyelashes she sported would classify as a cardio workout because of the length and girth.

Noel enjoyed quota-size giggles being on the sidelines of Lyda's predictable teasing of Shane. He felt only mildly guilty for not warning him. He knew from years of experience that she was harmless, which was all part of her act.

Noel introduced Shane, offering some background and his objectives for the summer. He praised Lyda for being the most innovative feed dealer he had ever worked with. He pointed out that she inherited the feed store when her dad passed away in his 50s. Her mom didn't know what to do with it, and Lyda spent much time there with her dad growing up. She had to make it work for her and her mom's survival.

Lyda transitioned out of burlesque mode to talk seriously about the business. "My dad loved serving the area's commercial egg producers and turkey growers. Even before Dad's death, they got pushed out by suburban housing and small farm dwellers escaping the nonsense of the bay area. I looked at this migration and saw that these folks coming to suburbia wanted companion animals to fulfill this lifestyle. I am twenty-five years old and have been gifted this old wooden feed mill to serve bulk commercial growers and the few agricultural stragglers that frequent the store. We had more traffic from transit travelers stopping to ask directions than customers coming in to buy lifestyle feed supplies."

"Well, it appears to be quite a successful transition," Shane offered and continued, "How did you go about it?"

She laid out the playbook, which started with retaining as much commercial business as possible to help generate cash through the transition. She knew this part of the industry from riding shotgun with her dad. From when she was five years old, she tagged along in his beat-up pickup or the bulk truck to serve his customers. Wherever they went, he would always introduce her as his **comrade.** To honor their relationship, "Comrade" became the namesake and brand of the new entity. She highlighted the tactics of the store's evolution by noting that the main thing she did was go directly to the hobby farms to meet these folks and learn what they were looking for in caring for their animals. She took riding lessons; she bought a goat she named Goliath and a hutch of rabbits. If she was going to have tacit knowledge about these animals, she had to become like Ellie May Clampett, with all her passion and affinity for critters. She already knew a ton about chickens but nothing about retailing or other companion animals.

"Lyda, please tell Shane how you evolved the retail space," asked Noel.

"I first went to as many feed stores I could locate that were catering to these suburban companion animal owners. I wanted to see how they were doing it and asked many questions. Looking back, most of the questions were borderline ignorant. Next, I brought in as many women as possible who had animals or who gardened and were in the retail business. Megan owned a flower shop and had Quarter horses. Renee was in the hardware business and had purebred Columbia sheep. Another lady owned a nearby drive-in burger joint, was the local 4-H leader, and had forty head of brood cows."

"Just curious, why all women?" asked Shane for clarity.

"Great question there, jailbait," she said with a wink, returning to her Mae West persona.

Shane's cheeks were feeling uncomfortably warm again.

"From what I could tell from my store visits, most of the purchases were done by women. If the animal operation was male-oriented, the women were still most likely to come in and pick up supplies for the rural operation." She continued, "These ladies that I made my transformational advisors would come over after we closed, and we would drink a bunch of wine and talk about what the new retail space should look like and what it should stand for."

As she continued and reflected more about these guidance sessions, she pointed out the watershed moment that came one night after the wine had flowed like Niagara Falls. One of her strong-willed friends challenged her to explain what kind of business she had. Lyda recalled that her answers were about retail, supply, nutrition, etc. Her friend kept saying nope. Every guess missed the mark. The advisor finally said, "Who is your competition?" Lyda listed the usual suspects, such as other feed stores, manufacturing mills, and the big discount farm store.

"My moment of enlightenment was when she explained that my competition was customer's activities and hobbies such as reading a book; going to a movie; bass fishing; entertaining grandkids; major, minor, and little league baseball." Lyda arose from her chair, leaned her head back, spread her arms wide, emulating someone on the stage, and rhythmically declared in C minor, "I am in the entertainment business." She dropped her head and flapped her fan-palm-sized eyelashes channeling Liza Minelli.

"Entertainment business?" asked Shane with innocence in his tone because the concept seemed so out of place.

Lyda provided context. "My friend explained that the lifestyle animal owners, rural dwellers, sundowners, or whatever you want to call them, were deciding how to spend their disposable time and income on something entertaining. Hobbies are entertainment, TV, sports, knitting, scrabble, and skiing are all obvious entertainment. What helped me understand was that I was also in the entertainment business. People like animals, people like gardening, people like landscaping or feeding birds. They are not doing it for financial reasons. Ninety five percent of all those activities are negative cashflow. People participate in these endeavors because it makes them happy and relieves stress; for some, it is a little about competition, just like the entertainment industry. She laid it out for me, straight, like an Alcoholics Anonymous sponsor. She said to **make your store entertaining or die**".

"So how did you do that?" asked Shane.

"Merchandising in a fun way. Education and seminars that help them do a better, more enjoyable job of gardening or animal care. Live events like trail rides, pet parades, animal swap meets, animal Halloween costume nights, and pictures with Santa and their pet. You name it, and we have tried it here in the last eighteen years." She pointed to the photos taken at those events that covered the walls in her office.

"You mentioned merchandising. I have been in almost forty stores this summer and have never seen anything like this one. It is amazing."

Lyda posed, turned her leg in, looked at the floor like she was embarrassed by the comment, and responded, "Ah, marry me, precious pubescent intern boy." The flapping lashes followed close behind to add sarcasm to such an unpredictable moment.

Shane responded with light sarcasm but determinedly to deflect the insanity of her request, "My family negotiated an arranged marriage for a new combine, and I can't break the contract."

Lyda pouted for effect.

Shane said, "If the John Deere Reaper deal falls through, I know where to go."

FEED YOUR LIFE

"Noel, you better hire this guy before someone else gets him."

"10-4, Lyda. Any other questions there, pubescent intern?" Noel took his turn at the sarcasm.

"Yeah, I am curious about something."

"Shoot," she said.

"You appear to be very successful. What drives you after seeing this kind of success?" asked Shane.

She paused momentarily, which was not out of character for her theatric nature. "Seeing my customers happy and being at the top. I am as competitive as a famished wolf in a self-serve butcher shop."

Noel raised his eyebrows and nodded in affirmation.

Lyda then went on to list several achievements. "For the last seventeen years, we have been in the top ten in lifestyle feed sales for Alumni Feed. We are currently number three on the west coast for Ballam Rabbit Feed." Shane looked at Noel and winked. She continued, "We are in the top five in the United States for Veeder's high soak shavings and number six in the country for Mr. Bigg Bowen's gardening magic fertilizers."

"What an amazing success story."

Shane got Lyda's tour of the facilities and was introduced to every employee as Lyda's future husband. They all knew the gag and fed the beast by playing along. The bell in the store signifying a great experience rang so many times it was like 'noon in the village.' Soon Noel and Shane were headed out to the car. The Sons of the Pioneer's music bounced around the rafters.

One final thing caught Shane's eye through the overabundant, flamboyant visual stimulus. A two-foot by three-foot framed poster in a sepia tone hung high above the exit door, highlighted with a high-velocity spotlight. The image featured a large man in a pair of bibbed overalls in a candid photo shot, looking slightly away from the camera. He's kneeling in a building full of turkeys, holding a large white tom in one arm and working on a poultry waterer with the other. Standing behind him in the picture, viewing his actions with a posture of benevolent admiration, is a five-year-old girl wearing overalls and a felt cowboy hat with stitching around the brim. You could tell this image was truly meaningful, or it wouldn't be there. The words on the frame said, "Thank you for everything, Daddy."

As they were leaving, Shane turned and looked at Lyda, pointed at the picture, and, remembering Noel's comments about going on offense, said, "He would be so proud of you."

A tear squeezed out and ran down her cheek, starting an avalanche of pancake makeup.

"If that marital combine your father procured ever breaks down, you return here to Lyda, my adolescent intern male." She blew him a kiss like she was on stage.

As she always was when she was in the store...in the entertainment business.

Shane's Learnings

On the rules of grain hauling by truck: The traditional practice of the gravel road is that the empty truck returning from the grain elevator pulls to the curb and stops so the loaded truck can pass in the opposite direction while keeping momentum. Gravel road safety needs to be adhered to.

On the value of knowing the customer on their turf: "The closer you are to the customer, the closer you are to heaven." You will find the most learning, perspective, and often monetary gain by how well you know the customer. You can rarely ever learn that behind a desk or in meetings. Some people don't like going to meet the farmer at their operation. Fifty percent of the sales process is *showing up.*

On educating others in your company on what you do: Prepare a simple but thorough explanation. Show updated and simple results of your actions and the things that make you or your role successful. Educating those you will encounter who don't understand your business is essential. You want the recipient of this information to realize "this person really knows what they are doing."

On the psychology of bosses: Bosses all want to be successful; I have never met one that didn't. Some judge success as making more money. Some want to be promoted for notoriety. Some want to develop people and help them be successful. They all have bosses too. The number one goal is to make their boss look good; the rest of the benefits to them will generally follow. Help them in their quest, and you will be rewarded as well.

On the value of voluntary supplementary effort: An excellent reminder to progress in any role is always to do more than you are asked to do. Remember when Shane cleaned the chicken brooder? There has never been a statue that was built honoring those that have done just what is expected of them. Bring your boss big ideas that can scare him just a little and provide a plan of how you can help pull off this big idea, and you will be viewed as a valuable employee.

. . .

On employees bosses abhor: "There are only two types of employees bosses cannot stand working with. One is the employee; you ***cannot tell anything***, and two, the employee, ***you have to tell them everything.***" Avoid being either one of them.

On working environments: There are many factors to the working environment. The leadership often sets it. It can vary from a trip to summer camp to a gulag.

On corporate organization staffing: Roles get created in corporate organizations, sometimes because it is trendy for leaders to feel that the more people they have reporting to them, the more critical their role and the better chance to be promoted. Many great organizations will exhaust their resources with fewer but better people and constantly strive to streamline work to avoid bureaucracy. This constant evaluation is hard but necessary work.

On dealing with the problematic boss situation: Corporate organizations often have a great deal of employee churn or rotation. There will be bosses you will have for short periods; some are not quality leaders, or you don't particularly like working for them. You can learn something from almost everyone. However, if you like the company, don't let someone else's incompetence drive you away. The tenure of the incompetent is often less than eighteen months.

. . .

On listening to the customers: Many great small business retailers make advisors of target customers that can help entities think through what they look like and stand for.

On how to learn the needs of a customer you don't understand: Lyda illustrated the playbook of her store evolution by saying the main thing she did was go out directly to the hobby farms to meet these folks to understand better what they were looking for in caring for their animals. She purchased animals, took riding lessons, and gained experience and knowledge by owning them. She became part of that community.

On the deep analysis of what business you are in, Truly analyze and think about your business and how the ramifications of that analysis can lead to strategic approaches that can help your business win. Lyda found out she was in the *entertainment business* because most of her customers were spending *disposable* time and income on their animals.

On male swimsuit modeling: And oh yeah, if you have to do any swimsuit modeling, be sure to 'put the potato in the front.'

14

THE SEVEN WORDS YOU CAN'T SAY IN A FEED STORE

It was a whole week in California. Such a beautiful, diverse, and confusing genre for someone reared in the cocoon of the inland Pacific Northwest. Shane saw more agriculture than he could have ever imagined existed. The place has a broad and colorful canvas, from tomatoes and almonds to squabs and artichokes.

During the trip, one blessing appeared from the 'Patron Saint of Interns,' which seemed to be a prophetic event. Who knew that the subway tile-lined shower at the Modesto Holiday Inn could be the incubator that gave Shane the idea of how to formulate and deliver his internship presentation? It is amazing the clarity that can come from a rhythmic aqua drizzle. He stayed in that shower for nearly an hour, afraid this creative sequence would vanish. His fingerprints had wrinkled and looked like the prunes his dad would gnaw on to stay 'regular.' What reinforced the validity of his idea was his recall of Egyptian history and their belief that they received power from the Pyramids. Yep, there was a shape involved. He was finally excited versus intimidated by the project. He scratched out a version of how he might approach the presentation. It is incredible the productive impact that time in the bathroom can have due to prunes or showers.

Shane was gaining a graduate degree of real-world experience from Noel. He went with him to a sizeable competitive feed dealer near Visalia. Noel had been trying to convince the dealer to become an Alumni dealer for three years. He lamented that he had unsuccessfully used various tactics over the years. He and the Kampdog family that owned the prospective dealer had become respected friends during the courting process. But they had never pulled the trigger to handle Alumni brands. Part of their decision was loyalty to their current Muckraker brand of feed. However, a more significant portion was because the other Alumni dealer, two markets away, was very aggressive, if not predatory, in their pricing strategies. Mitch Kampdog feared they could not make adequate margins on Alumni products because of this competitive dealer.

Noel had presented margin guarantee programs, new distribution offers, and four-month credit terms on their purchases for the first year. Today was different. He asked Mr. Kampdog if he could meet him in their conference room for thirty minutes. It was agreed. They arrived fifteen minutes early so Noel could greet the ladies at the front counter. He had gotten to know them well over his years of trying to turn the account.

The facilities were over forty years old, and improvements stopped shortly after being built.

Mitch Kampdog entered the conference room that was the size of the back of a flatbed truck. The room had a distressed barn wood finish with three green porcelain wharf lights hanging evenly over the conference table. Noel asked for that specific room as it was decorated with several awards, photos, and maps of the battles in Europe where Mitch's dad was involved during the German conflict. Shane guessed Mr. Kampdog to be slightly over sixty. His dad had started the business after WW2, and Mitch worked alongside him until his dad's passing during the Kennedy administration.

A burgundy-brunette dye job on Mitch's hair was the first thing you noticed. The dawning of a gray ring on the hairline around the top of his forehead provided ample evidence. He has dressed in dark chino pants and a white untucked, cropped work shirt. His work boots were well-oiled and showed minor wear. As he sat, he gave Noel a strong ribbing about having to bring reinforcements.

"That is exactly what I came to talk to you about, Mitch, reinforcements," said Noel. He introduced Shane and explained his intern project and how he was a tag-along for this meeting.

"Mitch, you and I have talked at length about your dad's military service," Noel continued.

Mitch commented, "He served a great country, and because he met Mom during his service, I guess you could say it was important to me being here as well." Mitch was certainly sentimental regarding his father.

"The objective of most any military is victory, correct?" asked Noel.

"It should be your only objective."

"You have told me that having the resources to wage efficient and powerful battles is also essential to achieving those objectives."

"Agree." Mitch was apprehensive in his answer because he didn't know where Noel was going with this discussion.

"Your objective is to win your feed business over the four feed competitors in your marketplace. One has a milling operation, one has bulk and liquid feed handling capability, and the two others are stores like yours that have been around for many years," Noel summarized.

"A couple of those guys give me a license to hate, but as you know, I am much too big a man for that," Mitch said sarcastically.

Noel pulled a backpack onto the table and said, "If you don't mind, I would like to paint an illustration of how you can win this battle."

Mitch agreed, and Noel brought out a bag of green plastic army men. Most were standing one leg in front of the other, holding a gun, and were about as tall as a sandwich lying on its side.

Noel took an army man, put it before Mitch, and said, "This is Margaret, your sales lady. She is very talented, but she is only one soldier."

Mitch commented sarcastically, something to the effect that she would be delighted with the likeness.

Noel added three other army men in front of Mitch, representing his relationship with Muckraker Feed. He pointed out that one of the army men was tied to their service, one to their pricing, and one to consumer knowledge of their brands.

He added nine army men on the other side of the table, representing the salespeople that worked for his competitors. Several other army men were added, describing the attributes of these competitors, such as local service, milling, liquid feed, and bulk product sales. There were four times more army men on that side of the table.

Mitch acknowledged the disparity.

Noel opened a bag of gold-colored army men. They are the exact plastic figures, spray-painted gold. Noel identified the gold army men as the assets that Mitch could deploy to defeat the battalion of competitors across from him. Noel listed off the attributes or benefits that Alumni Feed could provide him if he made the switch "Highly researched products," Noel added, a gold figure. "Liquid feed," Noel added another. "The Prerequisite Research Farm selling trips," Noel added another. "Feeding Trials," another. Soon the gold army was dwarfing the competition with the list of benefits and attributes related to Alumni.

Mitch was starting to nod his head and was uncharacteristically quiet. He was thinking.

Noel then pulled out a model plane, again painted gold, with an Alumni Feed logo on the tail and said, "With Alumni, it is not just a ground game." He listed National advertising and brand recognition. He added a model tank spray painted gold with the Alumni logo. He said, "The innovations we have in researched products that provide customers with more value can help you with the most powerful ground game in your market." He pulled out another gold army man with a miniature party hat glued to the top of his helmet. "This signifies the award trips we offer dealers and spouses to acknowledge their market performance and growth."

Mitch said, "How much do I have to ship to win one of those trips for my wife?" Noel explained the program's rules and noted that quota achievers would go to Hawaii for five days this year. When Noel asked how taking his wife to Hawaii sounded, he responded, "Better than Turlock."

Turlock, California, was where Muckraker Feeds had its annual dealer meeting.

Noel stopped, looked silently over the battlefield of army men, and said, "What military decisions do you think your dad would have made looking at the battlefield that lies before you?"

After a long, deliberate pause, Mitch replied, "You have given me more to think about than all your other visits combined."

Noel asked for the chance to earn the right to change over the business to Alumni Feed Mitch answered, "Come back in two weeks with some pricing and profitability data for this market. I must be sure I can sell your products profitably."

Noel agreed and packed up his gold arsenal. Mitch stepped out to help a counter person with a customer. Noel placed one gold army man on the pen and pencil set, which was like the hood ornament of the desk in the conference room. He hoped that Mitch would see it often.

They all shook hands and departed.

As Noel drove away, he looked at Shane and asked, "Whatcha thinking there, Hoss?"

"It was amazing to watch. I think you got his attention. How many times have you used this approach?"

"First time for everything. I must tell you I was nervous. Without the proper familiarity with the prospect and the market, that exercise could have been like harvesting a beehive in your birthday suit."

"What gave you the idea?" asked Shane.

" The respect he has for his dad's war service, as well as the need to try some other type of visual to get his attention versus the typical bland rhetoric."

"What will you do next?"

"First, I will send Mitch a follow-up letter as a reminder of what we have to offer. I will include the award trip rules and the last three program folders for recent award winners. And I'll send it to his home address."

"Why to his home?"

"Easiest answer of the day. So his wife can see it. That was the point in the discussion when I knew we were making a breakthrough. He was picturing how he could show his spouse that he was successful. It was all triggered by his question about the incentive trip. I might also send a picture of me in a hula skirt with a Mai-tai in my hand and a caption that says, **come join me in Hawaii.**"

As part of the learning experience for Shane, Noel decided that after a week of taking Shane to mostly celebrated feed dealers, a trip to an underperforming dealer would be suitable for comparison. It was also good for his research project. They arranged to visit with one such feed dealer outside of Fresno.

Sizemore Feed carried several competitive lifestyle and companion animal feed brands, including the Alumni brand. Lilly and Greg Sizemore had been in the feed business for many years after inheriting it from his parents. The building and surroundings had deteriorated since the transfer within the family. The paint was faded, and the parking lot and landscape had a collection of blooming and late-stage weeds accentuating it. The shelves needed to be cleaned and reorganized, and the inventory had more holes than Swiss cheese. And like good cheese, a lot of the merchandise was aged.

The Sizemores were not happy to be there. They seemed to let it be known with several derogatory comments about the business and the customers and ample vitriol about Alumni Feed.

The disparaging comments about Alumni Feed focused on supply issues, occasionally broken bags, prices too high, and the fact that Noel and others tried to get them to do things to grow their business. That bothered them. One of the things they commented on during the visit is that Noel wanted them to go with him to call on prospects at the farm gate. They had no interest in anything past their parking lot. Alumni Feed corporate would not extend them an endless line of credit, which seemed unfair to them. Noel would expect them to sell and service customers that Noel brought to them. They were still upset and even sour when they were getting full margins on those products.

Shane asked clarifying questions that seemed to irritate them. He was trying to be polite but was inquisitive. The strategic mixture of having Sizemores in this growing market was as embraced by Noel as a mobile home park acceptance in Beverly Hills.

Noel let their adverse discussion go on for about forty minutes and then diplomatically delivered the exit tactic with disguised sarcasm. "You know Greg and Lilly, I have heard a sage man say that *feedback is a gift.*' In the spirit of that concrete proclamation, I can reliably say we have opened many presents today. Thanks for sharing your valuable thoughts, but I need to get Shane to several more stops today."

The Sizemores were now quiet, and a bit puffed up because they interpreted that as if they must have done something meaningful.

Walking to the car, Noel exhaled his frustration loud enough for Shane to hear, "What a couple of role models."

"How do you deal with them going forward?" asked Shane.

"Aimlessly," Noel said disgustingly. "I won't spend any time with them the rest of the year. Nothing different would happen there, even if my family and I moved into their warehouse and I was there every day. This doesn't sound kind, but they are on hospice and don't know it. I have tried to get them to understand that, but they prefer their downward glide path and misery. I don't need to participate."

Shane said, "So what do you do about them in your role?"

Noel explained that his role was to find the right people to be the best dealer in every market. Sizemore's market was a good one but not his top market to focus on. Once he had the right people to replace them, he would evaluate the situation and decide to either have someone attempt to buy out Sizemores; or start a new entity and move the Alumni Feed dealership to the new business. He had no second thoughts or remorse that his solutions were not the best for the market and the Sizemores. He stated that everyone involved in this scenario was in misery, but he would do something about it. And said the change might give the Sizemores an opportunity for a happier life.

Noel thought that Shane's last stop in California might be his most eye-opening and prefaced it by saying that he had never been to a dealership where he hadn't learned something he could use elsewhere. He encouraged Shane to continue his pattern of questioning and curiosity.

After about an hour's drive, Noel pointed out several customers he had or was attempting to acquire when they approached a feed store called **The Commissary**. Under their store name, the sign said, **Your suburban and rural supply store**. The stand-alone building sported a twelve-foot-tall front over the porch entry with an Alumni Feed logo on each end. The Commissary logo graced the rest and looked like it might be visible from space. The store alone was nearly forty thousand square feet. Shane thought it might comfortably hold his whole grade and high school back home.

The business sat on over five acres, with many outbuildings and plenty of parking. Bulk fertilizer, hay, straw, gates, and livestock panels were in various buildings. They all matched with gleaming white metal siding trimmed in black and gold. Alumni Feed colors. The parking lot was free of debris and pristine. Backed against the side property fence were three matching one-ton delivery trucks, all painted white and gleaming with more chrome than a paint horse. Noel pointed out that there were twice that many trucks out making deliveries. Shane noticed there was a good crowd of cars at the front entrance. A young man with a five-gallon wash bucket wielding a car window washer and squeegee, aggressively removing bugs from the windshield of customers inside shopping.

Noel remarked that the store owner, Ken Krakoviak, was a service genius, adding, "He got the idea on the window cleaning when he realized there was 20-minute drive time for his customer to get to the store. He loves a clean windshield, so he reasoned what better way to get twenty minutes of subliminal goodwill on the customer's way home than to give them a whole new way of looking at the world."

FEED YOUR LIFE

"Do the customers notice it?" asked Shane.

"Ask Ken; he will shoot you straight."

Noel parked the Oldsmobile near the delivery trucks to avoid Friday traffic while they were in the store.

As they walked toward the main store, Noel detoured to an open-sided shed with a one-ton delivery truck in it and said, "Follow me; I want to introduce you to Carnivore."

"Carnivore?"

"A trip worth taking, believe me."

As they approached the shop area, the radio blasted Aerosmith. They could hear the high pitch and occasional groan of a machine trying to wrestle the airwaves away from Steven Tyler. Shane followed behind, recalling the trauma of the crazy Dutch dairyman's wet T-shirt contest earlier this summer.

Noel hollered, "CARNIVORE!"

A gruff voice answered, "Friend or foe?"

"Ed McMahon… Bringing a five-million-dollar check from Publisher's Clearinghouse," responded Noel.

"Bullhork, he was here last week," echoed the same gruff voice. He turned down the music and came into the light holding an industrial car buffer under his arm.

Carnivore had enough hair covering most of his body parts to make a black bear cub envious. The follicles on his fingernails might even need a trim occasionally. He was a generous 160-pounder, standing about six foot tall, dressed in straight leg-painter pants and an Alumni t-shirt with the arms cut off to show his proud and errant follicles. His mullet, beard, and shaggy leather hat were all covered with a spattering of car wax or rubbing compound from the shining process he was performing. He had a chunk of deer horn hanging around his neck by a leather shoelace. He lit up a bare-ass, no-filter Lucky Strike and pointed the pack to offer up a smoke toward Shane and Noel. Both declined.

"You all related to the Surgeon General or somethin?"

Handshakes and introductions were necessary as Carnivore was a bit edgy around strangers. Shane commented on the music he was playing, and they found common ground in that they both had seen Aerosmith on tour.

"Ken, have you put some wax on the trucks?" Noel inquired.

"At least two times per year. You know the drill. I did the forklifts last week."

This caught Shane's attention. "So you wax the forklifts?" asked Shane.

Noel and Carnivore looked at each other and smiled. "Give him the story Carnivore," said Noel.

"Have you met Ken yet?" said Carnivore.

"I have not," Shane replied.

"Well, he is a bit of a 'Mr. Clean' without the physique or the earring. Don't get me wrong, he has done me great, but there are some things that he may be the only guy in the world that looks at situations the way he does."

Carnivore went on to say that Ken wanted delivery trucks washed and waxed. Carnivore had intense resistance to the value of this. To add objective evidence to his opposition, he told Ken that he was recently at the local oval racetrack. The guy that won the seventy-five-lap main event and had the fastest time in the trial had no time or funds to paint his Chevelle stock car. The point Carnivore tried to make was that painting a race car doesn't make it go faster. So why wash and wax the trucks? Ken was intrigued not for the point Carnivore was making and called the track to see who this guy was and find out more about the unpainted racer. He thought he might learn something or, for a bit of his advertising budget, strike a deal for a painted race car sponsored by the Commissary. He arranged a meeting at a coffee shop with the car's owner/driver. Ken quickly found the driver to be one of the more repulsive individuals he had ever met. He was unbathed, with no dental plan and a *screw-the-world* attitude. Ken asked him why his car was unpainted. The reply was that 'sponsors' are a pain in the ass, and he preferred a rust-colored vehicle with the number "17" spray painted on the side rather than dealing with those parasites. Ken bought his coffee, returned to see Carnivore, and explained his new philosophy based on the enlightening fourteen-minute discussion with this Neanderthal.

Carnivore stopped the story to either collect his thoughts or for effect. Shane couldn't tell which but did not view Carnivore as an accomplished thespian.

"Did he get the sponsorship?" asked Shane.

"Heck no. But he gained a new philosophy that drives the reason I am washing and waxing forklifts."

"What is that?" asked Shane.

A new and foreign deep voice resonated from behind all of them. "We love sponsors, and we will do anything to make them proud of who we are and what we do," stated an approaching Ken.

"Shane, meet Ken Krakoviak, the owner of the Commissary," said Noel as he turned and shook hands with the man whose voice had been interjected into the story.

"Glad you guys are here." He recanted and continued, "Carnivore does great work; don't you think there, fellas?"

"Thanks, boss." It almost looked like he was blushing and hoping he didn't get canned for telling that story.

After introductions and the purpose of the call by Noel, Shane couldn't help but ask, "Can you please tell me more about your comments about loving sponsorships?"

Ken was intrigued that someone that looked like he was closer to being on the high school prom committee than the job market would ask for more definition of his thinking.

"Well, Carnivore was right. I met the ole boy with the race car and learned more than I ever thought I would. I got to thinking about his comment about the challenge that sponsors present. I thought it was such an odd comment that I started asking myself, "Do I or any of my people act that way towards others; do I have any sponsors? After about half a pint of Jack, I realized I had many sponsors. Sponsors like my bankers, my employees, the companies I buy from, and most of all my customers."

"Makes sense, but what does it have to do with what Carnivore is doing?" Shane followed.

"Well, I decided that if I had a race car with sponsors, I would want to represent them as well as possible. Clean car, excellent performance on the track, and a great attitude when I represented their brand. So, I want our bankers, employees, brand owners, and customers to feel like they are part of a great team. I want rolling stock to gleam, employees that sincerely smile, and customers that think our showroom and warehouse are so clean it would be a great place to have a wedding reception."

"Tall order. How do you think you are doing?" asked Shane, who was told to be inquisitive.

"Well, I mustn't remind Carnivore to wax the forklift. He knows, does an awesome job, and knows he is a big part of our success. Right there, Bigg'un?"

"Yes, sir," Carnivore responded.

"Shane, let me give you the tour, and Noel can catch up on some issues with our counter folks inside the store."

Ken asked a lot about Shane's background, internship project, and plans as they toured the well-merchandised and spotless facility.

Shane asked about washing the customer's windshield, and Ken said, "I have people stopping in here all the time just to see if we still do it. Since gas stations got lazy, we have grabbed the consumer's mindset of extra service of a bygone era. Frequently, they comment to us and their friends that it is a service they miss. We are known as the feed store that provides a new vision."

Ken's age was close to Noel's and Shane's combined. He was in great shape for being in his sixties and walked a bit sideways with his gait. He wore a pearl button-work shirt to accompany his pressed and starched Wranglers. His deep voice may have been a victim of his cigar habit, which may also explain his slim weight management build.

Noel joined them in Ken's office at the end of the tour. The office was small but elevated, with lucid visibility for Ken to view most of the operation's sales area. The decor was completely void of anything but a calendar on the wall, a notepad, an adding machine on the three-by-five-foot metal desk, and a picture of him with his family on the wall. The lighting was better than Dreamweaver's office; however, it smelled of molasses and cigars because it was located just above the cattle block inventory and infused with Ken's pungent tobacco routine. The ceiling fan's ticking sound was trying to keep time with the tunes from the country radio station playing in the background.

Noel presented a couple of new promotions from Alumni Feed that he hoped Ken would want to grab hold of to help grow their business. The first one offered a substantial rebate to customers that required two weight seals off the bags they purchased. It also required the participant to recommend a friend as a possible feeder to receive a $10.00 rebate check from Alumni Feed and the chance to win a national sweepstakes prize of a new Ford pickup. It was designed to stimulate feed sales and add new customers. It required the Commissary to run a minimum of four provided newspaper ads. They also had to build a display around the sweepstakes offering with a Ford pedal truck resembling the grand prize. The dealership could give the pedal car away as a local prize.

The other promotion was a rabbit feeding demonstration in the store to show customers the advantages of feeding Alumni Rabbit Crunchies. For performing the four-week trial, running a newspaper ad with the results, and providing proof of performance, Commissary would receive a dollar off per bag of Alumni Rabbit feed purchased for the next two months.

Ken sat up in his chair, made notes on his pad, and started hitting the keys on his adding machine, like Liberace at the piano on opening night. After about twenty-five keystroke entries, he excused himself, stuck his head out his office door, and hollered, "Florence, can you send up Spongecake?"

Noel leaned closer to Shane and whispered, "You are gonna cherish this."

Ken sat back down in his chair and shared the role of Spongecake at Commissary for Shane's benefit before he arrived.

"You like comedy, Shane?"

"Yes sir."

"Who is your favorite comedian?"

"Oh, there are so many good ones, but I like Steve Martin. Red Skelton was always a family favorite, and Richard Pryor is very talented at the opposite end of the 'potty-mouth' spectrum."

"You sure listed some good ones. I love comedy and try to watch as much as I can. I find comedy is the salve that cures life's imperfections. There is so much logic in good comedy that it is often more real than the world we live in."

Noel jumped in. "Tell him who your favorite funnyman is, Ken."

"It is easy for me. George Carlin," Ken replied.

"The seven words you can't say on TV. That is a classic," Shane enthusiastically responded.

"I mentioned comedy is sometimes more real. My favorite example is when George says ***Think of how stupid the average person is and realize half of them are stupider than that.***"

Shane laughed heartily, and Noel smiled because he had heard it more than once and agreed.

Ken continued, "The whole concept made me think that a successful organization needs to live by that fifty percent theory. So, I created a position I believe every organization needs—a 'Minister of Pragmatism.' The 'MOP' is as close to that average person as possible." He also pointed out that the Minister of Pragmatism can be one of the more competent people in your organization if they can forecast what will happen in a consumer's mind due to one of your organization's tactics. Ken concluded, "The process is much more art than science."

Ken's reasoning for the everyday role of the 'MOP' was that messaging, promotions, and customer communications need to be understandable and attractive to as many people as possible. The 'MOP' fulfills that role by reviewing it all for effectiveness.

Sporting steel-toed work boots with the leather wholly worn off the toes, auburn hair with a flat top, horn-rim glasses, camo pants, and a Jerry Jeff Walker logoed t-shirt, the six-foot four-inch Spongecake walked into Ken's office as though he didn't want anyone to see him. Besides his chest the size of a bale of cotton, his most striking feature was the full-bloom gray beard that contrasted with his auburn hair. It was a strange but natural occurrence. Ken joked that you must overthink if you have gray hair and an auburn beard. If you have Spongecake's combination, you talk too much. That seemed like a fallacy because this man seemed like he had been trained in a monastery.

Spongecake was introduced by his given name Warren Griffin, a nine-year employee of Commissary. He appeared to be about forty years old.

Noel had known him for years but finally thought it was time to ask where the nickname came from.

In a nasal-enhanced tone, Spongecake said that his grandmother gave him the handle because of the colossal amount of her cake Warren could eat. She also had the alternative premise that many people would forget the name Warren, but no one would ever forget the Spongecake moniker. Gramma made some sense. All Shane could think of was the Johnny Cash song, ***A Boy Named Sue.*** One thing was clear; this guy did not possess the enthusiasm of 'Camp Director' at Alumni Feed HQ.

Ken had Noel walk through the two promotions separately, step-by-step, to get an unfiltered reaction from Warren.

On the Weight Circle and Ford Pickup promotion, he had to say, "Dag gone, could you make it any more complicated? This will take a lot of our counter people's time to explain. We can discount current customers after completing two or three things. Way too complicated and a long run for a short slide. You would be better off having the local Ford dealer give everyone that test-drove a Ford pickup a ten-dollar off coupon for the Alumni brand feed. At least we might get some new customers out of it."

Noel loved the idea and wished what Spongecake suggested was the actual promotion. He would call some of his old buddies in the marketing department to see if we could test the execution of that idea right here. Ken said he had coffee with the owner of Saddam Padilla Ford and would check with him to see if this was a potential cross-promo.

On the Rabbit Trial promotion, Spongecake was a bit more receptive. "People always seem to take an interest in the animals. However, I am not sure they would be excited about the smell of a couple of 'reekin rabbits' in the middle of the store where they buy their feed. I would put them outside on the loading dock where they enter the store. To avoid predators, I can move them inside the warehouse with the forklift each night. The discount for us doing this is not gonna make us rich. Seems like much work again for a small return."

"Warren, thank you as always for your input," said Noel.

"You are the best, my man," complimented Ken.

The esteemed Spongecake exited the room as humbly as he entered.

Ken looked at Shane and decided to break off a generous slice of his frustration about the marketing department at Alumni Feed. He focused on Shane because Noel had heard it with regularity.

"He is right, you know. That is complex as a congressional farm bill. We have a scientific name for the marketing team at Alumni."

"What is it?" asked an innocent and smiling Shane.

"**Complexitorous Infinitum**," Ken proudly shared with a smile. "Our prized Minister of Pragmatism had improved a promotion by simplifying it to where a dealer could actually use it."

Ken beamed with gloat, but he really enjoyed providing a lesson to this young man.

"Son, I had a next-door neighbor who was a preacher. On the wall in his den, where he polished his sermons, was a framed embroidered inscription that I have never forgotten." Ken paused for added emphasis and slowly delivered his one-line seminar, "SIMPLICITY... NEVER GOT IN THE WAY OF GREATNESS."

Shane's smile was evidence that the tutorial may have been a triumph and encouraged Ken's continued teaching mode.

"Let me further illustrate the idea of simplicity by asking you a question. Have you ever used an outhouse?"

Shane shared that he had a substantial helping of that celebrated opportunity at scout camp, and the recall was vivid.

Ken held his fingers about two inches apart in front of his face to illustrate his point.

"This much water paired with gravity has saved millions of lives and provided the most underappreciated comfort the world has ever known."

Shane's brow wrinkled with curiosity. Ken expounded in an attempt to relax that forehead.

"A Scotsman patented the 'P-trap' the year before America was founded. Other than the wheel, that device, combined with a crooked pipe in two inches of water, is, in my opinion, the simplest and most effective device ever invented." He expounded, "That two inches of water," nodding towards his separated fingers "is why your toilet, shower, and sinks don't stink. Without it, every house with in-door plumbing would smell like a Dodge City, Kansas feedlot."

Noel had several years of working with Ken and knew his philosophy better than his wife's birthmarks. He decided to add to the simplicity principle in a way that could train Shane and also reinforce the value of Ken's organization (and most feed dealers) to their customers. He emphasized that the simpler you can apply products, whether it is feed, chainsaw operation, or garden seed planting, the more customer acceptance and feed store **return loyalty** you will get.

"Here is another example of simplicity having a major impact on the world." Ken moved his hand and arm upward slightly and dropped it a similar amount as he moved his whole arm horizontally. He replicated this several times and declared, "The simple shape of an airplane wing, combined with appropriate thrust, will help lift a multi-ton airplane into the atmosphere and keep it there across continents."

Ken illustrated a real-world feed store example. He threw a booklet that had to be at least forty pages long, with a frisbee flat spin. Shane snatched it out of the air and began to thumb through it.

"That there are the application instructions for **Terradactyl**, a new weed spray. Government regulations and fear of lawyers created this novel that only they will read. Our job is to decipher and map out the usage of this product for the producer. We give them a copy of the instructions. However, we hand them this pre-marked cup and tell them they use one for every five gallons of water. We tell them that it is too windy to spray if they pass gas and can't smell it. Not safe."

Shane laughed as if he had just heard George Carlin's opening joke. "What is Terradactyl supposed to do?" asked Shane, who had spread his share of herbicides.

Ken said sarcastically, "Remove all strategic noxious weeds, obliterate every, and all, non-productive broad leaf weeds, increase yields by two-fold, extend the life of all humans, and increase ACT scores for your children by a quartile."

"Lofty list of accomplishments," Shane panned.

"Our job is to keep it simple enough that they are not afraid to use it and to provide counsel to make the application optimize the product's benefits. It is true with your products as well. You all at Alumni make great products. We improve them by teaching feeders how to use them correctly and simply."

Noel needed to get to another appointment. He and Ken walked through a list of accounts he and his salesperson would target on next week's visit. He summarized their visit and asked Ken if there was anything else.

He turned in his oversized office chair, looked directly at Shane, and said, "Yea."

Shane fidgeted in his smaller secretary office chair with the newfound attention he was getting.

"You are a bright young man with what appears to be a bright future."

"Thank you, sir." Shane was a bit relieved that was Ken's first comment.

"Let me give you some advice that will help you immensely and make your career and your life more successful and enjoyable. As you can imagine, it is simple if it comes from me. I hope you find this impactful."

"I am sure it will be, sir."

"People will help you. LET …THEM." Silence followed and was only mildly broken by the commotion from the retail store below. Ken continued after an appropriate stillness. "One of the major issues I find with young people and sometimes with older people is they want to do everything themselves. This is admirable but causes self-inflicted difficulty for your growth and the organization. It is especially true for you in that you are young, and I hate to say the word *cute*, but people swoon over puppies because they are cute. Don't be afraid to use that in your learning process."

"Can you give me an example of the help you are talking about?"

"Do you know what an EMT is?"

"Yes, sir, they come to aid in emergencies."

"Do you think people injured or in medical despair let the EMT help them?"

"Feels like self-selection if they don't," agreed Shane.

"Well, think of the person trying to help you in business, your relationships, your career, or your life as wearing a white lab coat with a stethoscope around his neck. You are more likely to think about embracing their help."

"Thank you, sir. I have a use for that wisdom as I have to give a presentation on my summer internship in about ten days. I was told to visualize my audience as being naked. Now I will envision my whole audience wearing white coats."

Ken said, "Don't lose focus with all the white apparel and think they are asylum escapees that could disrupt your presentation."

Shane snickered, "I can see why you embrace comedy!"

Shane's Learnings

On ideas coming at unpredicted times: Who knew that the subway tile-lined shower at the Modesto Holiday Inn could be the incubator that gave Shane the idea of how to formulate and deliver his internship presentation? It is amazing the clarity that can come from a rhythmic aqua drizzle.

On using props to help change the delivery of the message in the sales process: Noel had worked for three years to gain commitment from Mitch Kampdog using multiple programs, discounts, and various versions of the written and spoken word. Today he focused on the use of props centered on the personal attributes of his passion for his father and his war record in his approach. He was utilizing the visual of small toy army men to make his point about achieving victory in a market they both knew a lot about. Noel lined up Mitch's attributes, referenced them as soldiers, and then created a similar approach to creating a competitive army to show him the size of the military he was up against. He then used army men designated as Alumni Feed soldiers representing the various attributes that could be used to go after Mitch's competitors. This visual and the nature of military combat opened Mitch's eyes to the possibilities. The other surprise was that one army soldier represented an awards trip Mitch could only get with Alumni. The idea of rewarding his wife with an awards trip they both could be proud of seemed to resonate unexpectedly with him. Props provide a new pipeline to the mind in the selling process. You will want to practice your approach before using this route.

. . .

On how to exit a conversation going nowhere: Noel and Shane had been with the Sizemores for an extended period, with conversation mired in one unsolvable problem after another. Noel decided it was time to exit, as no end was in sight. "You know Greg and Lilly; I have heard it said by a sage man that *feedback is a gift.* In the spirit of that concrete proclamation, I can reliably say we have opened many presents today. Thanks for sharing your valuable thoughts, but I need to get Shane to several more stops today."

On dealing with unproductive accounts as a salesperson: Noel has made endless attempts to help grow Sizemore's business. No matter the suggestion, there seems to be no attempt to want to grow the company at all. Shane asked how he would work with them in the future. "I won't spend any time with them the rest of the year. Nothing different would happen there if my family and I moved into their warehouse, and I was there daily. This doesn't sound kind, but they are on hospice and don't know it. I have tried to get them to understand that, but they prefer their downward glide path and misery. I don't need to participate. Sometimes it is just best to move on to another customer."

On washing the customer's car windshield at the feed store: "I have people stopping in here all the time just to see if we still do it. Since gas stations got lazy, we have grabbed the consumer's mindset of service of a bygone era. It is a service they miss, and they frequently share that with us and friends. We are known as the feed store that provides a new vision."

. . .

On how to treat the sponsors in your life and your business: After going to the auto racetrack and talking to a rogue driver that had a disdain for sponsors, Ken thought deeply and realized he had many sponsors. Sponsors like his bankers, employees, the companies he buys from, and my customers. Ken wanted these sponsors to be proud to be involved with his business. Ken wanted rolling stock to gleam, employees that sincerely smile, and customers that think our showroom and warehouse are so clean it would be a great place to have a wedding reception. As a result, all equipment, including forklifts, is waxed twice yearly.

On the impact of comedy: Ken's embrace of comedy led to this discussion. "I love comedy and try to watch as much as I can. I find comedy is the salve that cures life's imperfections. There is so much logic in good comedy that it is often more real than the world we live in."

On the idea and the value of the minister of pragmatism: George Carlin said in his comedy act to think of the average person and realize that 50% of the people are dumber than that person. The concept made Ken believe that a successful organization must live by that 50% theory. So, Ken created a position here, and every organization needs a *minister of pragmatism*. The MOP is as close to that average person as you can get. The reasoning that Ken gave for the everyday role of the MOP was messaging, promotions, and customer communications that need to be understandable and attractive to as many people as possible. The MOP fulfills that role by reviewing it all for effectiveness.

. . .

On the need for simplicity: Ken had a next-door neighbor who was a preacher. On the wall in his den, where he polished his sermons, was a framed embroidered inscription that I have always remembered. Ken paused for added emphasis and slowly delivered his one-line seminar, "SIMPLICITY… NEVER GOT IN THE WAY OF GREATNESS."

On the value of helping customers correctly use products: "Our job is to keep it simple enough that customers are not afraid to use the products and provide counsel to make the application optimize the product's benefits. It is true with your products as well. You all at Alumni make great products. We make them better by teaching feeders how to use them correctly and simply."

On life and career advice for young people: People will help you. LET …… THEM. One of the significant issues Ken finds with young people and sometimes with older folks is that they want to do everything themselves. This is admirable but causes many difficulties for your growth and the organization. Think of EMTs. People are mostly not afraid to let them help. View those trying to help you as EMTs.

15

A MILLION YEARS OF ANGEL TEARS

Re-entry from planet California for Shane was preordained. His commercial airline flight was without incident but was accented with Shane staring in profound appreciation of the wing's curvature. That simple chunk of machined aluminum smoothly maintained him and ninety-five of his flying compadres at 28,000 feet off the hardpan below. Simplicity truly is our friend.

The 'mission impossible' answering machine at Boxcar's house offered an installment from Mary Tempo sharing the things needed next week for the Regional Sales meeting. Shane will be joining the group on Tuesday. Dreamweaver's team would arrive with spouses on Sunday. On Monday, they would review the annual planning process, which was unnecessary for Shane to trudge through. Shane thought Dreamweaver didn't want him to see the less appealing part of the sales job. Mary shared the dress code and what he would need to bring for the meeting.

The second message was from the Dreamweaver himself. SECOND MESSAGE: *"Shane, this is Ronald Gilmour. I heard you were a real asset on the trip to California, and I can't wait to hear about what you learned. Mary Tempo has you all lined up for the upcoming sales meeting. I have you on the program for Wednesday afternoon to present your summer survey findings to the group. I hope forty-five minutes will be accommodating. We hadn't spent much time discussing your presentation at the mill other than when you were in Spokane. That was by design... I want to see what you come up with. I have faith that it is going to be fantastic. To assure you, I have been at this for many years. I have never had to take anyone to the hospital after giving a presentation at one of my meetings. You can conclude from this history that your presentation will be absolutely wound-free."* Mildly sinister laughter trailed off as the **BEEP. CALL ENDED.** punctuated the end of the message.

Shane's pulse quickened at the thought of forty-five minutes of firing squad activity, but he felt he was ready. He had been planning this all week while in California.

His old friend Elk had moved to Spokane and always had an artistic flair; Shane would tap into it. He would have Elk create five presentation charts on a chart paper pad for his presentation.

Mary Tempo gave Shane some final advice on his presentation the last time he was in Spokane. She helped him define the nuances of the audience. She also pointed out the need to practice and know the first three minutes of your opening like your own freckles. "When you master the opening, it will build your personal bank account of confidence for the rest of your presentation." She provided a template of what others had done in the past and what resources would be available. This is where the chart stand pad of paper originated. As he stuffed the chart paper under his arm to leave the Spokane office, her final comment was, "Have fun and remember two intertwined pieces of advice. **Plan it like a wedding, launch it like a battlesip.**"

That phrase was now stuck in his head like that *Afternoon Delight* song.

Shane drove the combine for his dad on Saturday and Sunday, giving him multiple hours to practice his content, delivery, and technique while purposely meandering in circles to feed a starving planet. On Monday, he decided to call in a favor and wiggled out of having to drive the combine.

Shane arranged to meet with his former sixth-grade basketball coach Dan Charles to get feedback on his presentation. Dan's job was the west coast representative for the Wolverine Chainsaw company. Uncle Bo and most of his close friends in the Palouse called him 'Jason' because of his career associated with the Texas Chainsaw Massacre movie franchise star.

Shane and Dan met for breakfast so he could get that last-minute advice from a guy who worked with dealers, many of them Alumni Feed dealers, and had put on hundreds of presentations. They met, of course, at the Grain Bin Grill. Shane brought the primary emphasis of his presentation on letter-sized paper so they could review it together. It would be a little awkward to do flip charts in the restaurant.

Dan was about forty-five years old and had a son that was Shane's age and was his basketball teammate. Hence the connection for Dan as a coach. Typically, one of the dads must coach these developmental teams in small-town environments. His coaching sixth graders were as close to a basketball career as Dan would have. Five foot eight and 180 pounds is not material for an NBA lottery pick. His denim pants accented his black and red lumberjack shirt. A patch above the shirt pocket prominently displayed a sinister feral wolverine gritting its teeth on a chainsaw! Quite a logo. Shane was sure the actual 'Jason' would covet this shirt.

After a couple of omelets, catching up on his son and Shane's family, Shane playfully asked if he was being recruited to coach the Seattle Sonics. Shane explained that he would make a presentation to the Alumni West Coast sales team and sought last-minute advice. Dan covered the West Coast for Wolverine.

"I am holding out for the Trailblazer's job on the basketball front. Is Noel Bowman in that sales group at Alumni Feed?" responded Dan.

"Yes sir, I rode with him last week."

"That is one good dude; I have been trying to get him over to Wolverine for years."

Shane shared the project's scope, what he was asked to present, and his forty-five-minute time frame. He then walked him through the content of his presentation and how he would show it. He waited for Dan's reaction.

"Did you think this up?" asked Dan.

"Yes, sir."

"Very impressive; maybe I should forget Noel and hire you."

"Always willing to listen, but today as you can imagine, I am pretty focused on this."

Dan offered input with a focus on one central area. "What does your audience want to hear or get out of your presentation?" Shane showed him his work on thinking through the Situation/Background, Objective, Plan, and tactics that the Dreamweaver had covered with him.

"You have done your homework. Your role in the presentation is to find creative ways to resonate with the message. I think you have done that. Let me give you some real-world advice on presentations that you might find helpful. Not saying you will deal with this, but if you are in meetings or presentations in the future, there is a strong chance you will."

Dan told Shane that the audience does not always have *friendlies* in presentations to customers, prospects, and peers. These spectators of your performance can become adversarial for strange reasons.

"I guess I am not surprised by prospects or customers, but you may need to add some meat in the stew on the peer examples," Shane said in search of expansion.

Dan explained that, unfortunately, tribal group dynamics often take place with peers. "Part of it is personal, and part is petty insurgency."

He gave some examples to support his experiences.

1. "**The Green Eye.**" Some peers think they should be giving the presentation, which is a form of envy. They are usually harmless; however, their actions often point to them trying to reinforce to the group that they would be doing it better.
2. "**Socrates.**" Some people want the others in the room to know how smart they are, and they ask the tricky question to elevate themselves. A way to decipher if you have a Socrates is to observe them

after they ask the question. They often scan the rest of the room to seek gratification from their peers to see if they recognize their uncompromised intellect.
3. "**The Bomb Thrower.**" They love to offer unanswerable scenarios or unachievable objectives. This is a complicated one because they often try to show the depth of their intellect by demonstrating that they recognize a problematic system but also insulate themselves from fixing it because of the complexity of this empirical circumstance.

This discussion made Shane nervous. "So you always experience this?"

"Heavens, no, but I want you to get the value of that omelet Alumni Feed will pay for from our discussion. I would be stunned if any of this happened to you with your group, but I do have some quick reminders to help you if you ever do."

"Would love to hear them," replied Shane, who felt a bit more at ease after the beginning of Dan's discussion. Yet he pictured a green-eyed warrior scholar with a Molotov cocktail charging the stage at the upcoming sales meeting.

Dan offered some simple things to remember when you encounter any presentation mutineer. The list included the following.

- **Stay calm.** Your composure is your pathway to synchronization with your audience. If you get rattled, the offender wins, and your audience friendlies are more likely to abandon you.
- **Acknowledge** the issue but always ask for **clarity**. A few examples: "A great question. There are many ways to

answer your query, so I would like a little more context as to what you are looking for, so I can do a better job of providing a helpful response." With the bomb thrower, "It is a tough scenario you have pointed out, and it sounds like you have thought about it a great deal. Are there some steps you think we should pursue soon to help us fix such a big issue?" In a structured way, with the big questions, you can throw the anchor back to them to catch.
- If your **audience** is friendly, enlist their support by involving them. An example, "Wilma brings up a good point. Do you all have any feedback or experiences that can help?" There is always more collective wisdom or experience in the audience. Let them help you.
- **Ask** about satisfaction after it has been addressed. "Did we get what you were looking for with your question?"
- Take it **outside**. If a scenario needs deeper engagement, ask that it get handled offline so we can ensure we get satisfaction for you and the rest of the audience.

Shane was taking notes like a shorthand champion. "Why the question about clarity?" he asked Dan.

"Well, actually, there are several purposes, but if you could give me a little more context around your question, I could provide you with a more satisfying response," Dan winked.

Both looked at each other and smiled.

"Ok, I will quit playing. Often the person that has asked the question hasn't thought about why they asked the question. This forces them to think about what they are asking by clarifying their thinking. Second, it buys you time to develop a potential response by returning some responsibility to the person who asked the question. Third, they will frequently explain the reasoning behind their question and often answer it for themselves. If not, their talking out loud often gives you more clues to formulate a proper response. The question you ask is your best ally when backed into a corner. Never be afraid to ask more than one question. Again, you want to make sure you fully understand the request."

Shane displayed a distant stare and then engaged, "Makes sense. Which of the three different folks you talked about is the most difficult for you to deal with?"

"Easy. Bomb Thrower."

"Why?"

"There is more exaggeration which is often unproductive. They talk about monumental encumbrances such as world hunger, government oversight, or some colossal or uncontrollable components in completing something productive. I guess I have the most problem with them because there appears to often be more malicious intent or at least pre-meditated detours in their observations. But it is also the easiest to diffuse by asking those clarifying questions. More questions normally result in more withdrawal on the issue."

They wrapped up most of the conversation, and Dan reaffirmed with encouragement that Shane was prepared and would do well in his presentation.

"You will know how you did by the restroom discussion."

"Restroom discussion?"

"An undercurrent runs through every organization called the *Jungle Telegraph*. It is the non-publicized communication network of organizational members. It is anchored by member perception and is a cauldron of emotion, pragmatism, and occasional rumor-fueled conspiracy. There often is some truth to the rumors, but for salespeople, the most productive meetings of the Jungle Telegraph can happen in the restroom following sessions in the meeting room."

FEED YOUR LIFE

"Why is that?"

"I think it is their safe place."

"I hate to be a naive intern, but why would men think a restroom is safe to share their true feelings?"

"I am not sure, but just think of it as a women's beauty salon with many more toilets and a more sinister aroma. Many ladies will tell their deepest, unencumbered thoughts to someone sculpting their mane. I think it is a form of follicle hypnosis."

Shane and Dan concluded their business with reassurance, encouragement, and thanks. Dan was off to Yakima to prepare for a chainsaw art convention. Shane would be sending Dan a note thanking him for his time. In the background, gliding subliminally around the house of coffee patrons was Glen Campbell's; **'By the time I get to Phoenix'** Shane had been talking with Dan with his back towards the door and did not see who had entered the grill. That music meant one thing.

Yep.

In his favorite booth, caressing a cup of coffee and demolishing a King Kong-sized order of biscuits and gravy was, as Shane suspected, John "Magpie" Wilkins. He looked up from his plate and smiled with a trickle of sausage-infused gravy dormant on his puffy chin. His smile was prompt and seemed liberating, as though John had something on his mind.

"Boxcar Junior. How is your summer goin' there, young un?"

"Great, Mr. Wilkins. How is the Interstate treating you?"

"Asphalt is my amphitheater," Magpie replied. "Have you given any more thought to joining Team Bigfoot Trucking?"

"I wanted to talk to you about that," said Shane, which made Magpie shift from a lounge chair position to a leaning-in business mode in the booth. Shane reached into his pocket and pulled out his wallet. He withdrew a business card and laid it on the table. The card had the contact information of Ernie, Caldwell's disgruntled salesperson that Shane rode with.

Shane tapped the card, slid it across the table before John, and said, "You indicated that passion is critical in a successful career. This guy is passionate about trucking; I will leave it with you to follow up."

"So, not you?"

"I never say no, probably not for a while. This guy is a much better candidate."

"I will follow up, and thanks for the lead. How is your dad's harvest going?"

"Pretty well, about eighty percent complete and no major issues or injuries."

Magpie and Shane shook hands. Magpie brought some gear-jammin wisdom to the summary. "Great news on the harvest. Until we meet again, may all your waitresses be former Miss Universe and all the weigh stations be closed."

Shane laughed like he was in a comedy club because he knew this was precisely what Magpie wanted.

Magpie ended with, "I still owe you a ride for the one you gave me to Ephrata. I need you to get in my cab and see if I can get you to catch the truckin' bug."

"Sounds like an ailment you can live with," Shane reassured.

Magpie, not to be outdone, completed the thought, "And a disease you can prosper from. Let us make that happen one weekend this next year." Handshakes again, and another thanks for the lead ended their reunion.

The Alumni Feed sales meeting was at the Coeur d'Alene Hotel on the shores of the lake of the same name. The hotel lobby was less than two football fields from where, in his youth, Shane had inexplicably won his pet duck by throwing a nickel on a plate.

Coeur d'Alene Lake is one of the most resplendent bodies of

water on earth. Shane's Sunday school teacher once said it was so beautiful that it was formed from *"a million collective years of angel tears."*

Over twenty-five miles long, girdled by serene valleys and virgin shorelines, the lake has had many purposes. It has baptized and fed families of Native Americans. It transported thousands of rough-cut timber logs harvested upstream and floated to a processing mill for framing and subfloor construction on someone's dream home.

The lake's tranquil waters have become the weekend home to enraged turbine-powered hydroplanes, sightseeing paddleboats, and pulsating floatplanes, creating the noisy aerial panorama above the crowd of power and sailboats below.

The Coeur d'Alene Hotel was now the collection point and headquarters of all the motorized annoyance.

Shane had never stayed in this hotel. He reasoned that Alumni Feed must think I am okay if they give me a room with a lakefront view. It indeed beat a cab view from a combine seat.

Late that afternoon was a scheduled cocktail event at a designated poolside covered area. Shorts and casual wear were the theme. The event provided the chance to interact with the sales team members, their wives, and Mr. Gilmour and his wife.

Since they knew one another, this was a new and uncomfortable experience for Shane. He now knew how a kid moving to a new grade school felt, with many folks sniffing the new kid to evaluate compatibility.

Shane caught up with the news from Monty (Choppers), Noel Bowman, and several other salespeople he had ridden with that summer. The sales team had three ladies who worked in parts of Oregon, California, and Arizona. All were highly communicative with Shane, and he found two of them had been interns themselves in the last four years. They gave some great perspectives on returning to college and telling others about the process they had experienced that summer.

In conversation, Shane learned that Caldwell's had hired the new ag teacher/salesperson. He felt even better about leaving Ernie's card with Magpie. He also heard a bit of rough news on Cap at H-D. His wife was having an affair with the basketball coach from the high school that Cap's high school was going to merge with. Life moves fast. Which mascot the merger may rally behind was probably not Cap's most significant issue.

While he knew many salespeople, their spouses were all new to him. Mary Tempo recognized this and escorted Shane around to meet the others. What a relief to have her guide the conversation with these ladies who vacillated between intrigue, to diligent matchmaking with their niece. You know, the one with a great personality.

It was a picturesque evening on the hotel rooftop while the sunset accented the lake's best side. As that sunset eloped with the earth, the powerboats and airplanes also took their exit. The water seemed soothed, maybe even relieved, to escape the tumult. As tranquility gained momentum, it was evident that mild to moderate intoxication of the sales team members and their spouses was also trending. Another observation was the number of smokers in the group. There seemed to be a direct correlation between alcohol consumed and those lighting up.

One of the wives, Ethel Bowers, who was in her sixties, had kept the bartender in tips most of the afternoon. Alcohol can sometimes bring the college co-ed out in a senior citizen. Ethel and her husband RJ were from the Boise, Idaho, area. Ethel took it as a personal challenge to see if she could get the intern to blush by being extremely flirtatious.

Savagely slurring her words provided additional evidence of inebriation. "Hey there, Spartacus, are we gonna dance later?"

"Uh, sure."

"Good, I like the slow, grinding numbers." She hit her right buttock with her open palm and proclaimed, "Purdy firm ain't she?"

Shane smiled to hide his terror, and in the most encouraging one-word statement he thought he could make, he said, "Igneous."

Ethel smiled, cackled, and sauntered off in search of someone else to annoy with her hard-earned tipsiness.

The team loaded up in a bus for transfer to the St. Orgion Steakhouse. They brought their cigarettes with them. St. Orgion served calf fries for appetizers and great beef, pork, and chicken cuts cooked over an applewood-fired open pit. It had to be hotter than Ethel's soused dance floor thoughts in that kitchen.

Shane was invited to sit with two older salespeople and their wives. They had yet to meet Shane, and he assumed they wanted to explore who this kid was. Shane was eager to reciprocate. He surmised that none of these four folks smoked and observed that Shane didn't either, so they were trying to create their smoke-free table. He was happy to be on 'team clean lung.'

Seymour was in year thirty-five with Alumni Feed, and Clyde was in year thirty-one. Like most other wives, their wives sported a gold charm bracelet. Each of the bangles jingling off their wrist signified a trip or award they had won as a couple from Alumni Feed. Seymour's wife had at least twenty-five charms rattling with each arm movement. This was much like war ribbons sported by soldiers…all worn with pride.

Seymour looked piercingly over the top of his half-glasses that he required to read. Choppers told Shane that Seymour made substantial sales with large feedlot and broiler operations over his career. His role today was mostly collaborating with Alumni Feed dealers in Oregon and western Washington. He was one of the de facto group leaders of the sales team. Many co-workers came to

Seymour seeking advice as he previously held a sales manager role in North Carolina., like Dreamweaver held today. Clyde looked up to Seymour like a JV ballplayer does to a Hall of Famer. There was little similarity between these two colleagues other than their rangy build. Both were in great shape, but Seymour was slightly taller at six feet, with a deep baritone voice, an extensive tan causing mild skin damage, and vanishing dark hair. Seymour didn't smoke cigarettes, but he did chew on a cigar and rolled the tobacco into balls the size of a marble. Clyde talked in a distinctive high-pitched voice that coordinated with his lighter complexion and receding blond hairline. He was about three inches shorter than Seymour and dressed like he was straight from the country club.

Seymour led most of the meaningful discussion, and Clyde followed his lead and seemed to say "Yip" frequently, which Shane interpreted as "Yes." Seymour asked Shane several questions about his background, schooling, family, girlfriends, work history, and the summer program. During this twenty-minute inquiry, Clyde did a lot of 'yippin', the wives shook their wrist rattlers and, in a separate conversation, tried to one-up each other's stories of grandkid superiority, as do most grandmothers. Shane answered Seymour's questions as best he could but was curious about Seymour's poker-face reaction to most of his answers. He didn't seem captivated by Shane's dialogue but occasionally smiled while focusing intently over his reading glasses. Shane reasoned that maybe the commotion from the restaurant made it difficult for Seymour to hear Shane's brilliant answers. Shane convinced himself this was why there was little reaction.

The stray smoke from the restaurant's open pit steak preparation, matched by the cigarette smoke volume, made Shane slightly edgier than usual. But he also saw this uncomfortable environment as the time to re-route related questions and career advice to these two veteran salespeople. His interest in their response would hopefully recalibrate his smoke-coated discomfort. So, over a Wilsonburger Ranch Montana cut medium-rare Porterhouse, Shane initiated similar background questions of these feed veterans. After picking up a historical background on these couples, Shane began to ask career questions.

"So, gentlemen, what advice do you give to a young salesperson looking to be successful?"

A long pause followed; Seymour chuckled and then began with a bit of sarcasm, "Well, you start with the easy stuff," as a wry smile migrated to his lips.

Seymour swallowed a bite of steak and said, "I don't want this to come across as flippant because it is a truism. It is the same thing I tell every salesperson that asks a similar question. For every feed salesperson, the rule is simple. **Whoever creates the most animal crap on earth wins.**"

Without breaking stride, Clyde reinforced, "Yip."

After consuming a fork full of baked potatoes, Seymour added additional observations. "If that is the objective, great salespeople should recognize different ways and opportunities to make that happen. All markets are different in how you win in those markets. But the single thing I have found in the 'win the poop race' is to multiply yourself through others. Key customers you sell, your feed dealers, salespeople employed by the dealer, and counter people at the feed dealership are your multiplication task force. Your job as a salesperson and how you make that happen separates a good salesperson from an average feed bin kicker."

"Yip," Clyde pontificated.

Shane acknowledged and added, "I have also been told a great salesperson knows how to be effective at the farm gate."

Looking over the top of his glasses, Seymour said, "Knowing how to do that so you can train others to do it is the most important multiplication there is." The conversation took on the same multiplication theme until it ran out of steam. Shane shifted gears.

"So I have a fundamental question to ask, and I ask it simultaneously out of respect and curiosity," Shane said pensively.

"Yip, fire away, young fella." The dessert course of rhubarb cobbler was brought to the table in a small Dutch oven to cool down.

"You both have a lot of longevity and great success with the company. What has kept you doing this with one company as long as you have?"

"A great question that I would love to hear the answer also," Megan, Seymour's wife, remarked. Clyde's wife nodded in affirmation.

Seymour paused, exhaled, and began his response with some context. "Megan and I have three kids, all in or have completed college. We repeatedly told them a few essential things we thought they needed to develop themselves. One of those things was *'**the most important decision you will ever make is who you hang out with**.*' Our youngest would associate with a couple of kids who didn't always think things through. One of those kids was named Colt. We would tell our son to use his brain, not Colt's, whenever they were together. Did you ever have any buddies like that?"

"Oh yes, sir. Your advice is savory."

Seymour raised his head to look at Shane through the eyewear. "Not sure what that means, but the point is that I had the same responsibility I was passing along to my kids for nearly thirty-five years. If the most important decision I have to make is who I get tribal with, I choose this group of people in this room and my dealers. It would be disingenuous not to live by the exact lessons we are trying to teach our family."

Megan added, "Alumni employees are as much family as business associates. I know as much about the spouses of the sales team as I do my cousins, nieces, and nephews."

Seymour agreed, "You know why Gilmour gets the spouses and sales team together?"

"No sir," said Shane.

"One word. Retention," Seymour punctuated.

"Yip. Other industries and companies have courted us all," explained Clyde. He said that he learned from a former colleague that a good test to put yourself through when you are wooed and pursued by another firm is to ask yourself, are the people good enough? The second acid test, which was even more critical, is to ask yourself, could you last in a fishing boat for two days with the person you would be working for? If the answer to that is no, then don't join them.

"So I hear the word 'culture' thrown around at college regarding organizations. Is this what you are explaining as an example of the culture "?

Seymour jumped on this question faster than any other Shane had asked. You could tell it was a passion accelerator for him.

"Culture is what the customer and the employees view it to be. The 'headwaters' of the characteristics of culture most often starts with leadership. The result of leadership, however, is most accurately interpreted by your customers, not by organizational leaders themselves. Culture in an organization, like a society, takes a long time to root, but if it is significant, it will withstand the storms of one bad leader. Most organizations are, at some point, going to have an **underwhelming leader**. Events and activities that reach the heart of the employee fertilize those roots that help make a great workplace. My job as a former leader and Gilmour's job today is that of a culture curator. That is why you see activities such as this that foster family engagement. People who only work for a paycheck will leave you for the next bigger one. People that work for and with families are more likely to grow a career with you."

"Is that why the two of you stayed?" asked Shane.

"Yip."

"He said it all," acknowledged Seymour.

As the rhubarb cobbler and homemade vanilla ice cream marched on, Seymour added additional input on the longevity issue. It may have been therapeutic to get it off his conscience. "Not everything about working this long with one organization is nirvana. It is inherent and necessary that youth be served. Young people bring fresh ideas, vigor, and new mental genetics to an organization. My job and Clyde's is to keep up and push ourselves personally to developmental improvement. I will say that the frustrating part is that Clyde and I have mountains of experience, filtered and fermented by failure and success, to share. When and if asked, that experience can truly help the organization. In most organizations, especially larger ones, experience doesn't always generate the same excitement that strategy and tactics from young people will. Said another way, sometimes when you have the most to offer an organization is when it has the most contempt for you."

"So what is the right answer?" asked Shane as the salivary glands tightened from the tart rhubarb he was consuming.

"Not sure there is a simple answer. However, a place to start when new corporate strategies or tactics come up that are internally attractive and appear to be the catalyst or some other business school fad, the best practice is to ask a few experienced men and women how these changes will affect the customer. This simple inquiry can keep the organization from real trouble and will often save millions."

Clyde concluded, "Yip, just ask us old crusties. We can help solve lots of issues."

Seymour and Megan pulled Shane aside as they left the restaurant, and Seymour said, "We have experienced many interns here. I just wanted to recognize how impressed I am that you are not afraid to ask great questions about issues that stem from your curiosity. Never lose that."

Megan said, "Good luck tomorrow in your presentation, and whatever you decide to do going forward, it was a pleasure to meet you."

"Those are very high compliments, and I will do my best to live up to them," said a grateful Shane.

Seymour had one more piece of advice for his new friend "You present tomorrow."

"Yes sir," said Shane.

"You will notice that a number of the sales team will be asked to leave the hotel bar at closing."

"Ok."

Seymour continued the lesson, "Probably not best for you to be one of them. Pilots have a rule of twenty-four hours from bottle to throttle for a reason. A rule I would give you is to beat at least half of your audience to bed. You need to be fresher than they are."

"Great advice; see you tomorrow?"

"Yip," winked Seymour

Shane's Learnings

On starting your presentation: Know the first three minutes of your opening like your own freckles. When you master the beginning, it will build your personal bank account of confidence for the rest of your presentation.

. . .

On how to approach presentations, marketing campaigns, or events: A rule of thumb to remember when engaging in any of these: "Plan it like a wedding, launch it like a battleship."

On How to deal with customers, prospects, and even your peers, there are not always "friendlies" in presentations.

1. Stay **calm**. Your composure is your pathway to synchronization with your audience.
2. **Acknowledge** the issue but always ask for **clarity**.
3. If your **audience** is friendly, enlist their support by involving them.
4. **Ask** about satisfaction after it has been addressed" Did we get what you were looking for in your question?"
5. Take it **outside**. If a scenario needs deeper engagement, ask that it get handled offline.

On the 'Jungle Telegraph': An undercurrent runs through every organization termed the 'Jungle Telegraph.' It is the non-publicized communication network of organizational members. It is laced with members perception and is a cauldron of emotion, pragmatism, and occasional rumor-fueled conspiracy. There is often some element of truth to the rumors, but for salespeople, the most fertile meetings of the 'Jungle Telegraph' can happen in the restroom following sessions in the meeting room."

. . .

On how to grow your sales dramatically in dealing with a dealer network: All markets are different in how you win in those markets, but the single thing I have found to grow the business is to multiply yourself through others. The folks that can help you multiply are key customers you sell, your feed dealers, salespeople employed by the dealer, and counter people at the feed dealership. Your job as a salesperson is how you make that happen. It is what separates a good salesperson from an average salesperson.

On building a connective culture for organizational retention: If the premise of *'the most important decision you will ever make is who you hang out with'* is remotely true, it is a wise investment to attract the best talent you can. The skill you train and have to compensate at over market rate often looks for more than compensation in a career decision. People want to hang out with good people. One of your roles as a leader is creating an environment beyond the job to help keep team members connected. That is why you see activities such as those that foster family engagement. People who only work for a paycheck will leave you for the next bigger one. People that work for and with families are more likely to grow a career with you. I have heard it said that building that type of culture is impossible today. I don't think those folks are trying hard enough. It takes work and creativity to develop a working family. A personal warning to leaders trying to establish that culture *is careful not to neglect your personal family in pursuit of a family work environment.*

On how culture is achieved in an organization: Culture is what the customer and the employees view it to be. The 'headwaters' of the characteristics of culture most often starts with leadership.

However, the end result of leadership is most accurately interpreted by your customers, not by organizational leaders themselves. Culture in an organization, like a society, takes a long time to root; but if it is a significant one, it will withstand the storms of the occasional ineffective leader. At some point, you or your organization will have an underwhelming leader. Events and activities that reach the heart of the employee fertilize those roots that help make for a productive workplace.

On how to deal with seasoned employees: When I was twenty years his junior, A wise older employee was asked (told) to work with and report to me. He was not delighted and told me something that has always stuck with me. He said, *"Sometimes, when you have the most to offer an organization, it is when it has the most contempt for you."* My experience working with him was accurate; he had much to offer. My experience was that the more I used his wisdom and expertise, the more successful we all were. Use the knowledge and experience that you have in your organization. You have paid for it already, don't ignore it.

On how long to stay out and socialize with your teammates or audience: **I would give you the rule** to beat at least half of your audience to bed. It would be best if you were fresher than they are.

16

MASLOW MEETS THE JACKALS

The sun rose and used the mirrored reflection of Coeur d'Alene Lake to adjust its guise for another day. Shane observed its every movement from the deck of his hotel room. The deck was composed of eight-inch-thick concrete the size of a pickup bed. It supported Shane and his outdoor chaise lounge eighty feet above the lake. The lake was so smooth this time of day that it looked like the surface of a deep blue bowl of Jell-O.

Shane was practicing the first three minutes of his presentation, which would build his confidence for the next forty. He could hear his buddy Fronk, the Wheat Gangsta, whispering subliminally to him not to over-prepare for this.

Shane took his advice, and after a shower, hair prepped, and sporting a white dress shirt and mortar-board tie, he headed to the meeting room early with his charts under his wing.

Mary Tempo was the only one there. She was preparing elements for Dreamweaver's meeting. The cassette player was tossing out country music for ambiance.

"Look who is the first one to the room," she remarked.

"Wanted to get a feel for the arena."

"Smart. Did you get that dance in last night with Ethel?"

"No, I avoided all the senior Fly Girls last night," Shane replied. He continued, "I sure hope she won't be too distraught."

Mary giggled, "Most likely devastated. However, I have confidence in her strong ability to rebound."

"I see you have your presentation with you," Mary affirmed.

"Battleship ready," Shane proclaimed regarding Mary's advice on weddings and battleships as he saluted playfully and clicked his heels together.

Giggling through her response, she said, "You don't forget much, do you?"

Shane just smiled. He was much more comfortable with Mary than when they first met. She helped him get his charts on the stand and commented on the great calligraphy and strips that covered the different elements of the presentation. She was unsure when Mr. Gilmour would have him present, but as she said, better have it ready to go at any time.

Breakfast for the sales team was a 'straggle in' freestyle affair in the Rodina room. None of the spouses were present. There were varying levels of alertness and enthusiasm in the room. Coffee and sustenance would hopefully provide rallying essentials for those who overdid the fermented beverages the night before. All were smart enough to be sure their condition and attitude were in a sprinter's stance when Gilmour brought the meeting to order.

The Brooks Lilly conference room where the sales meeting was to be held began to fill with the sales team. The music emanating from the cassette player took an unusual turn. The painful tone and tempo of the unmistakable Tammy Wynette were next as she bayed her song "D-I-V-O-R-C-E."

This was the catalyst the room needed as Choppers hollered to Mary Tempo, "Hey, M.T., turn it up that there is America."

Like neighborhood crooners on a street corner, Choppers, Noel Bowman, a sales guy they called 'Commander,' and the two Arizona sales ladies pulled their heads together cheek-to-cheek and were sarcastically and loudly savaging the song with imperfect harmony. Soon the whole room was mocking the song content and exaggerating the spelling lesson this grief anthem brought. The song's premise is that a mother is spelling out some words that her young, clever son Joey would know if he heard them but didn't know how to spell. The second stanza brought similar sorrow but even more amplified chanting, "Me and little J-O-E are going away."

Gilmour didn't join in the warbling, but he was happy with its effect on a team he imagined to be quite hungover and listless following the previous evening's social. As the team wound the final verse to a close, they screamed and applauded their handiwork.

Gilmour stood in the front of the room, clasping his hands in front of him, smiling and scanning the room as they settled into their chairs. Mary Tempo had removed the music because she could tell her boss was ready to open the meeting.

Pausing and scanning for additional effect, he paced about ten steps, and as he sauntered, he began, "I must say I was in deep fear that you would not be your articulate selves this morning. I pictured our group as a kennel collection of lounging bassets and bloodhounds. However, thanks to the genius of Tammy Wynette, you all were like an organized troop of ravenous jackals at a smorgasbord."

The team hollered, clapped, and cheered their accomplished praise like they were at a high school pep rally.

Mr. Gilmour had several topics to address with the team in the areas of dealer tools, financial training, and, of course, his favorite, new distribution and how to find new dealers. At the end of each of those discussions, he asked one of the sales team members to summarize to the group what they heard and what they needed to do with the information or training they received. The uncertainty of who would be called on caused the attention to be elevated. He told Shane later that this was also a way for him to understand how the group was assimilating the messages he was providing.

After the break, about ten in the morning, he decided it would be unfair to Shane to put him on the program in the afternoon with this sleep-deprived crowd and following a heavy lunch. He asked Shane if he was ready and replied, "Sittin' on G waitin' on O."

Following a praise-infused introduction by the Dreamweaver and thanks to all who had helped him in his summer program, he turned the program over to Shane to enthusiastic clapping.

Shane had a metal chart stand strategically placed at the front of the room for maximum exposure to his audience. A blank page covered the pages behind it.

Shane thanked everyone for a memorable and educational summer experience. He was complimentary of everyone he rode with, and the faith Mr. Gilmour had put in him to have this opportunity. He then flipped the blank page to the first of Elk's calligraphic artwork.

He quickly mentioned each of the summer program objectives and hoped it provided the backdrop for the rest of his presentation. The chart looked like this...

MY OBJECTIVES AS OUTLINED FOR MY SUMMER PROJECT:

"Learn something new every day."

1. Gain a strong understanding of Alumni Feed dealer needs and how Alumni Nutrition can benefit from meeting those needs. (Survey questions were included). A mandatory presentation was required at the end of the project.

2. Assimilate as much learning about the Alumni Sales Force roles as possible.

3. Create a wrap-up summary of your project to be presented to the Alumni Sales and Management team.

4. Have fun and be able to tell your story at WSU next year.

Several sales team had lit a cigarette just after their break. Shane asked the audience to take a memorable trip with him back to college. Hooting, and hollering proceeded as the smoke made him think more of a comedy club than a sales meeting.

"The college trip I am talking about was the trip back to the prerequisite Psychology 204 class that almost all of you had to take. You remember the pretty sorority girls swooning over the grad student with the ponytail teaching the class. He was the one that donned the 'I don't care wardrobe' because I have deep intellect. He occasionally wore sandals, sometimes corduroys, but always Bohemian."

The sales team smiled, chuckled, and nodded in memory as they listened for what was next. Shane had their attention.

Shane grabbed the chart stand and flipped to the next page after his objectives. The page flip revealed a pyramid, and Shane asked, "Who remembers this and its significance?"

```
                    SELF-
                 ACTUALIZATION
                   Creativity,
                 Problem Solving,
              Authenticity, Spontaneity
                     ESTEEM
              Self-esteem, Confidence,
                   Achievement
                  SOCIAL NEEDS
                 Friendship, Family
                SAFETY & SECURITY
          PHYSIOLOGICAL NEEDS (Survival)
            Air, Shelter, Water, Food, Sleep, Sex
```

Maslow's Hierarchy of Needs

From the third-row table, the old-timer they called 'Coach,' who reminded Shane a lot of Mr. Howell on Gilligan's Island, hollered out "Maslow." Giggling followed. Coach trailed that comment: "I used to be *'that grad student'* teaching *'that syllabus,'* and I made *'that outfit'* look good."

One of his peers hollered out, "Coach the Bohemian." Fellowship laughter followed from around the room.

The Dreamweaver, who was highly engaged in the set-up, hoped Shane knew where he was going with this. He saw Shane grab the wheel.

"So Coach, since you were the ponytail man, if you would please give the group a basic understanding of the diagram and the significance of the varying levels, I would appreciate it."

Dreamweaver smiled from the back of the room at Shane's simple but crafty recovery.

Coach stood next to the chart stand with the diagram, cleared his throat, rolled up his sleeves for effect, and explained in a dignified scholastic tone to the group. "*Dr. Abraham Maslow from Columbia University created a psychological health theory predicated on fulfilling innate human needs. In priority, starting with basic needs before moving onto social and emotional needs culminating in self-actualization.*" He then finished with an exaggerated deep breath.

The momentary silence, driven by disbelief, erupted in an assortment of boisterous applause laced with a hint of sarcasm. This riotous merriment was triggered by the skepticism that Coach would know anything about this. He took a bow which extended the raucous show of appreciation. Shane asked, "Coach could you simplify those comments for us?"

"Yep." He pointed to the bottom of the pyramid and said, "If you have been in the desert for a week with no food and little water, you would rather have a can of tuna fish and a beer... than..." He then pointed to the top of a pyramid and completed his thought..., "Than to take a violin lesson in a Cadillac."

The crowd roared again and gave him a cynical but appreciative standing ovation as their colleague proudly paraded back to his seat.

Shane giggled as the crowd settled down and said reflectively, "I am pretty sure that in the history of all academia, the explanation of the hierarchy of needs never received that reaction." The crowd chuckled in agreement and settled in as Shane thanked Coach.

Shane followed, summarizing that Maslow's work pointed out that the bottom of the pyramid was the most important to the person at the time. Once that level was met satisfactorily, people moved their needs up the scale.

Then, to reinforce the idea that some categories of people may have different steps and criteria in their satisfaction ascent, he gave an illustrated comparison of the college student's hierarchy of needs. He flipped over the chart to reveal a similar pyramidal diagram.

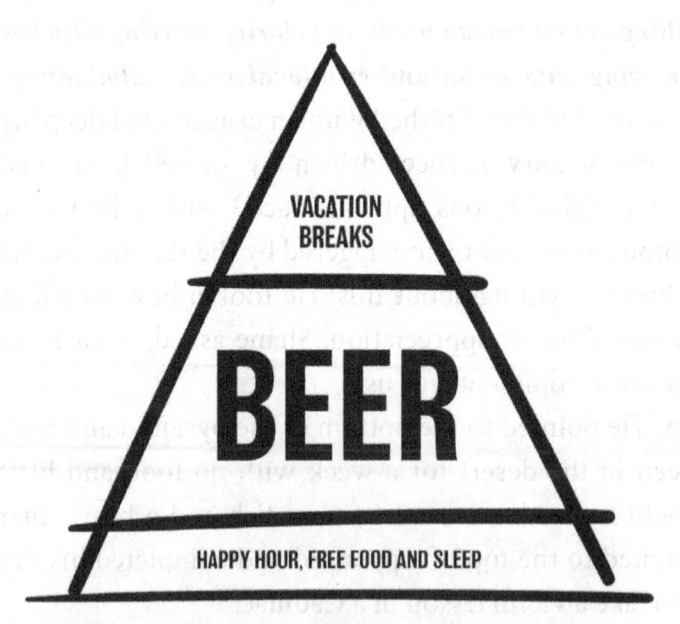

```
            /\
           /  \
          /VACATION\
         / BREAKS  \
        /----------\
       /            \
      /    BEER      \
     /                \
    /------------------\
   / HAPPY HOUR, FREE   \
  /  FOOD AND SLEEP      \
 /_____\
```

College Student Hierarchy of Needs

Shane's example was able to recalibrate the group, which was smiling with head nods around a little bit of humor that they could relate to and would help direct the following discussion. He was most concerned in presenting this list, hoping it would not start a clash over whether something to do with sex should be added.

What he did next was to outline what he wanted to present to the team. He had learned this information from the summer dealer survey discussions and some insights he picked up working with feed dealers.

"Because of the academic foundation presented by Coach, I would like to use the same Maslow modeling in thinking about Alumni Feed dealers. Like college students, feed dealers have a hierarchy of needs as well. In my discussions with over fifty dealers, these identified needs must be met to grow their business with a feed supplier. OK, to proceed?"

Audience heads bobbing like an engaged rowing crew, and a few smiles were apparent in anticipation of where this was headed.

Shane returned to the chart stand. He flipped over the college hierarchy of needs to expose a sheet with strips of blank paper strategically attached with scotch tape to cover the subject matter.

Dreamweaver was leaning in with a curious but encouraging grin. In a supportive, reassuring shout out to the room, 'Choppers' pointed to the chart and said, "Flapper Dress." Laughs lubricated the moment to start Shane's glide path.

Shane acknowledged the comparison and removed the bottom cover strip to reveal:

Alumni Feed Dealer Hierarchy of Needs

Shane followed, "As I stated earlier, there is a dealer set of needs, and like Maslow, they start at the bottom and ascend once the lower needs have been met."

He then moved to the next cover patch and removed it to reveal the bottom of the Pyramid.

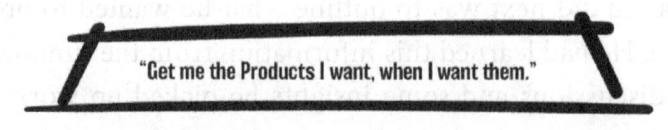

"Get me the Products I want, when I want them."

Alumni Feed Dealer Hierarchy of Needs

Shane said, "The quotes summarize comments I heard or interpreted from the data I pulled." Dreamweaver looked across his table at Mary Tempo, and they mouthed something to one another that had smiles and head nods supplementing their conversation. Shane saw this as a green light.

"Dealers told me that what frustrated them most was not getting the products they ordered. This was especially true for those far from the manufacturing facility because they would have to wait another week or until the next order cycle to get needed products. The more specialized and unique the animal, the greater the impact of the shortage. As a dealer from Boise told me, "There is nothing like dealing with an angry primate owner who is waiting for a unique diet that can't be obtained elsewhere." Shane said the dealer said, "You just hope they don't have your home address."

When an audience asks for clarity, that is a good sign. 'Messkit,' who covers Western Montana, asked, "Did they indicate why it upsets them so?"

Channeling his learning from 'Dan, the chainsaw man,' Shane said, "A great question, sir. If I could get more context to your question, I can probably help target my answer." Dreamweaver smiled like he just found that one parking spot at the mall while Christmas shopping.

Messkit added, "Yes sir. Were most of it supply chain or a complexity issue in general as to why they were disappointed in us?"

"That was very helpful, thank you. Dealers gave examples of several things. Losing the sale, unproductive usage of time dealing with the replacement of the product, tracking invoicing to be sure they are not charged, but maybe the biggest issue I heard was appearing incompetent in front of a dissatisfied customer." Shane paused and asked, "Did that get you what you sought?"

"Yes, sir, and as you can imagine, everyone in this room feels those same issues. I also want to thank you for recognizing *our* biggest frustration." Messkit was becoming a Shane fan and finished with, "We sure do spend a bunch of our time chasing air when our dealers don't get what they order."

Coach jumped in with a supporting comment "You can't sell from an empty wagon."

Shane announced, "This next one is directly connected to the comment Messkit made about invoicing," as he pulled off the masked paper.

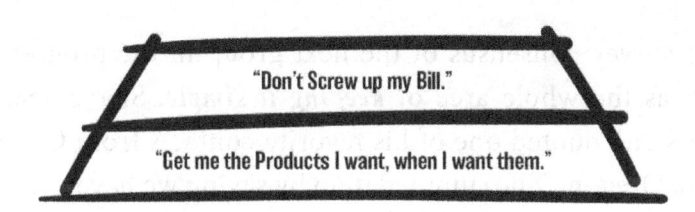

"Don't Screw up my Bill."

"Get me the Products I want, when I want them."

Alumni Feed Dealer Hierarchy of Needs

"Billing errors were the second most repeated response, often related to shortages." Shane continued, "Jodie Borsellino from Coos

Bay told me that if it takes longer to process the order than it takes to order it, you probably have a problem."

Expanding on this designation, the dealers mentioned that at some of the busiest times of the year, over forty percent of the orders had some flaw that needed correcting by calling Alumni Feed's order department. And don't forget that time is a premium for these dealers. This inconsistency required hours of accounting review and unproductive work.

Endorsing the data, the 'Marlboro man' hollered in support, "Tell it all, Maslow!" Generous jungle sounds of approval ensued.

Shane collected the group's attention, and with a bit of Vanna White theatrics, he unveiled the next tier of the dealer's needs.

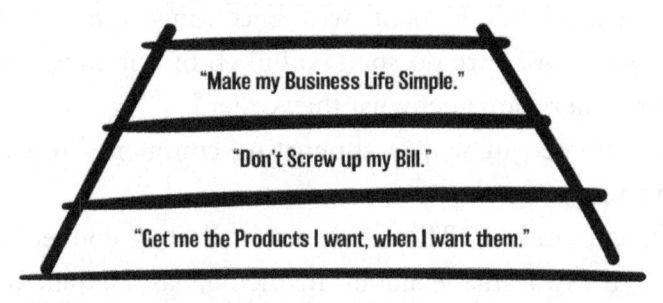

"Make my Business Life Simple."

"Don't Screw up my Bill."

"Get me the Products I want, when I want them."

Alumni Feed Dealer Hierarchy of Needs

The survey consensus of the next group in the progression of needs was the whole area of *keeping it simple.* Shane shared the numbers and quoted one of his favorite contacts from Grodt Feed in Bend, Oregon, "She summed it up by saying we have over 10,000 SKUs in our stores, and we are supposed to know something about how to administer or use all of them." She capped it off by saying, "We don't have time for extra complexity from whom we buy."

Mr. Gilmour wanted more definition of what the dealers

regarded as complexity in dealing with Alumni Feed in today's market.

Shane didn't feel confident enough to ask the boss to clarify. The chainsaw man, Dan, would have seen this as the right move.

"Sure. First, the ordering process is complex. A dealer gave me a price list from Alumni Feed and asked me to decipher how to use it. It took much coaching and was not intuitive. The promotional activities are overly creative and often result in too many steps. Several supply chain rules that are less dealer-focused than an advantage to Alumni Feed were brought up. However, they pointed out that the people they work with at the Alumni order centers and feed plants were great at ensuring they corrected issues for customers. Max Fisher from Grangeville Co-op said that much of the service policy eclipses common sense."

Shane followed with, "Did I answer your concern?"

"Unfortunately, there is little surprise in what you are sharing. The familiarity adds to your survey validity."

Shane beamed. That was as close to a pat on the head as he would get from Gilmour.

Shane shifted from business simplification. "The next area you think would be the most important to dealers is profitability. When dealers discussed the profitability of their overall organization, it took an unexpected twist. Dealers overwhelmingly shared that it is not any supplier's responsibility for their profit success but their responsibility as an entity. However, many did point out that if they didn't make money on a supplier's products, they would either remove them from their offering or de-emphasize support of those products." Shane removed the covering.

"Help me Sell Profitable Items."

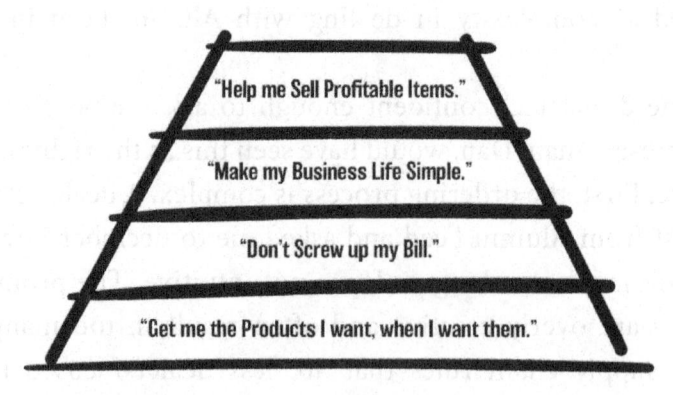

"Make my Business Life Simple."

"Don't Screw up my Bill."

"Get me the Products I want, when I want them."

Alumni Feed Dealer Hierarchy of Needs

Shane explained that dealers gave examples of dog food brands sold in multiple channels like grocery and discount stores as loss leaders. Those brands often have demand, but because of competitive pricing strategy to draw foot traffic, Alumni dealers would steer customers away from those brands. They could make more acceptable margins on other brands. The same could be said about some Alumni products if too many dealers offered them in the same marketplace. Dealers collectively noted that all they ask is that the dealers that handle Alumni products should be bold and charge for their products.

Shane provided an example from a dealer. "Mr. Bone, from Western Washington, commented that one of the reasons the Alumni products need to bring more margin returns to dealers is that they cost more, to begin with. They offer a better value to the customer because of performance, convenience, and security. He also mentioned that by selling the customer these better, more expensive products, they can receive a longer-term return or an *annuity* for selling the animal owner Alumni products."

No audience argument here.

Shane continued, "The next one could be classified as a softer issue but appeared very important to the dealers." The paper was removed to reveal.

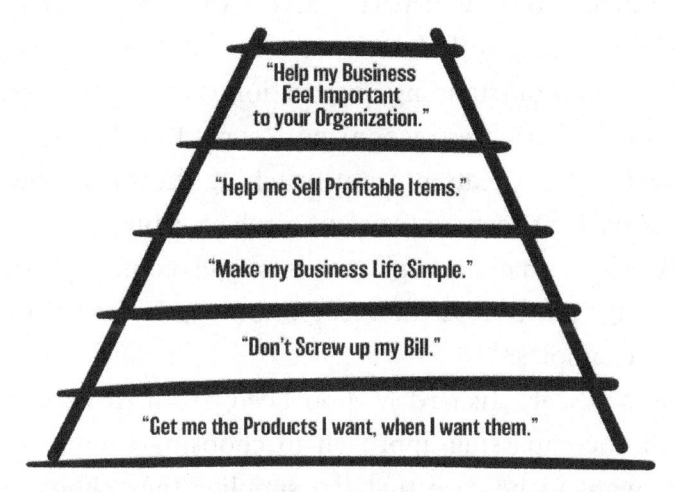

Pyramid (bottom to top):
- "Get me the Products I want, when I want them."
- "Don't Screw up my Bill."
- "Make my Business Life Simple."
- "Help me Sell Profitable Items."
- "Help my Business Feel Important to your Organization."

Alumni Feed Dealer Hierarchy of Needs

"I found it interesting that dealers brought up some of your competitors as appealing to their needs in this arena."

One of the Marlboro men, who was chain smoking like a snowmobile in need of a ring job, asked for specifics about the comment exhaling smoke as he spoke.

Shane questioned him before answering, "Are you looking for competitors or examples of the tactics I observed?"

"Both."

"Ok, I had at least six dealers on the West Coast tell me that they were the third largest Ballam rabbit feed dealer on the West Coast."

Several of the audience chuckled, and a few shook their head at the claim.

Shane followed with, "We know they are not *all* the third largest; however, they were proud enough, no matter the truth, to tell me about their proclamation. Almost all dealers display various awards and recognition in their offices or hallways. I don't think the simple recognition can be discounted as unimportant."

Gilmour had been whispering across the table to Mary Tempo and decided to step in before it went in a different direction and said, "That is an outstanding observation that someone outside of our day-to-day activities recognized. We get too close to it. It's like living next to the ocean and not watching the sunset because we are too busy. That costs so little but can have a big impact. We need to think about that among ourselves and come up with some simple things not to lose the recognition war. Shane, do you have any other examples?"

"Well, a dealer, Rishard Mahoo Feed, from Arizona, shared a rather all-encompassing approach to choosing suppliers. He told me they want to be sure that the supplier they choose may not always be the biggest."

"Curious as to why?" asked Gilmour, keenly interested in this topic.

"He said he wants to ensure their business is important to the supplier's success, not a rounding error. He said if they call their supplier with an issue or request, they want them to show support and action because they know it is important to keep their business."

"Another interesting perspective. Any feel for how we are doing in that arena?" queried Gilmour.

"For the most part, I would say it is good. The exceptions I am bringing up were ones outside of the many compliments I heard from dealers. It is near the top of the pyramid, so it is not their biggest concern."

"Thank you, that helped. Proceed."

Shane then prefaced the next category by saying you would think this would be lower on the list, but the other areas were brought up with more frequency. He removed the strip to reveal the need for product demand.

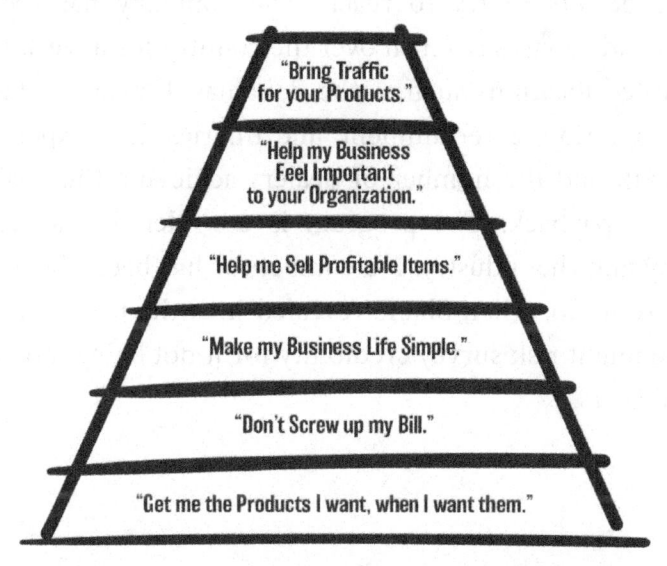

```
                    "Bring Traffic
                   for your Products."
                  "Help my Business
                    Feel Important
                 to your Organization."
               "Help me Sell Profitable Items."
              "Make my Business Life Simple."
                "Don't Screw up my Bill."
         "Get me the Products I want, when I want them."
```

Alumni Feed Dealer Hierarchy of Needs

"I know this is a bit of a head-scratcher because I have been around most of you and others in the company, and we think a lot about brand demand. While it is important to the dealer, it is not the most important thing to them. They love to have it, but there are many more important things, like consistent product availability and their relationship with a supplier, than foot traffic from your brand. They also realize that the 'farm gate sale' is the best way to create demand for both of us. The more of your time and help they get, the more important you are to them and their salespeople."

No argument.

The last area may cause some controversy. Alumni Feed has a

program for its highest-performing dealers to be recognized with once-in-a-lifetime trips and recognition. The 'Summa Awards' program reflecting the collegiate award genre, has a yearly growth goal for dealers to try to reach. The company has recognized winners and spouses from all over the country for a week in exotic and coveted locations such as the Bahamas, Hawaii, or Las Vegas with recognition, entertainment, and fineries. It is expensive, but the growth and the number of dealers achieving this make for a handsome payback. The program is considered a jewel of the company and the industry. No competitor has been able to rival it or imitate it. So, when Shane revealed it as the top of the list, he knew he might risk survey credibility for it not being more important to dealers.

```
                    △
                   ╱ ╲
                  ╱AWARDS╲
                 ╱AND TRIPS╲
                ╱───────────╲
               ╱"Bring Traffic╲
              ╱ for your Products."╲
             ╱─────────────────────╲
            ╱   "Help my Business    ╲
           ╱      Feel Important      ╲
          ╱      to your Organization." ╲
         ╱───────────────────────────────╲
        ╱  "Help me Sell Profitable Items." ╲
       ╱─────────────────────────────────────╲
      ╱    "Make my Business Life Simple."     ╲
     ╱───────────────────────────────────────────╲
    ╱         "Don't Screw up my Bill."            ╲
   ╱─────────────────────────────────────────────────╲
  ╱  "Get me the Products I want, when I want them."   ╲
 ╱───────────────────────────────────────────────────────╲
```

Alumni Feed Dealer Hierarchy of Needs

When he removed the last cover, it generated a couple of grunts, catcalls, and hisses.

Gilmour weighed in calmly to settle the disturbance, "Hey, let's hear what he has to say. Proceed, young man."

"It is where it is because you need to remember that self-actualization, as Coach talked about, is only achievable by very few. If they view it as not achievable, then it becomes less important. To the 4-5 % that achieve this award, it may be the most important item on this list after getting the first two at the bottom right."

More head nods of approval as Noel Bowman spoke up, "I have many dealers who don't pay any attention to the program because they know they will never be able to achieve it. One dealer, Lynn

Mattocks Feed, would miss their daughter's wedding to go to this event and has a chart on the wall to track their monthly progress; for others, it is like a pink unicorn that they won't be able to feed."

Shane followed, "Noel summed up what the survey says, don't get rid of it; it is doing exactly what it is supposed to do for those it is supposed to do it for. As you think about the rest of the dealers, they must also feel loved. What they say is potentially missing in the *feeling important category* for the smaller but still significant dealers."

The room murmured among themselves, and most of the hushed discussion was the agreement with the premise that this may be an opportunity the team might be missing with smaller dealers.

Shane added a point to his presentation that would help folks know there was more content to his summer's work than a pyramid on a chart stand. He held up more than a hundred pages of survey notes and said, "I wanted to let you know there was more to this than the summary I provided today. I will have the multiple-page report Mr. Gilmour requested, and if there are specifics you seek, ask."

Coach spoke up with a concise comment, "This is excellent work." Lots of 'here-heres' circled the room, with some clapping and plenty of smiles.

"Thank you, I hope the data is helpful."

Shane grabbed control to share his wrap-up. "Mr. Gilmour would ask me if I learned something today, almost every day."

One of the salespeople shouted out, "Welcome to the club." Laughter followed, and Gilmour was smiling with gratified guilt.

Shane followed, "So I want to share one more chart to illustrate what I have learned during the summer. Before I do that, I want to thank many of you for your cordial generosity in helping me with my project and answering my ridiculous questions this summer.

FEED YOUR LIFE

This, of course, includes your own Mary Tempo." Grateful clapping and cheers followed from the team for her underappreciated work. She smiled, nodded at Shane, and silently mouthed, 'Thank you."

Shane threw out more appreciation. "I also want to thank Mr. Gilmour for his willingness to take a chance on such a chunk of raw material."

Gilmour smiled and said, "I'll have some comments when you are done."

Shifting gears back to the wrap-up, Shane constructed a narrative about how he had learned so much from the feed dealers he worked with this summer. He pointed out his affection for their work ethic and championing their customer's ambitions led him to ask the question of himself, 'What makes a feed dealer great at what they do?'

After that setup, Shane flipped the page over to reveal these four letters down the left side, with paper strips covering the rest of the content on the page.

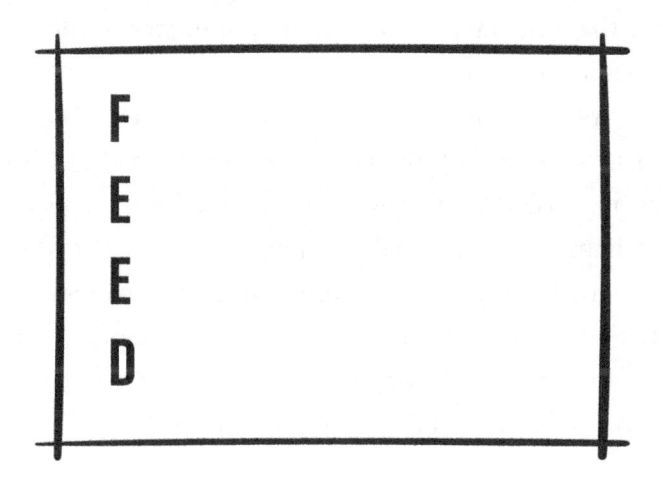

```
F
E
E
D
```

"I have some select words or phrases that describe my learning about what makes them successful with their customers. If you think I am on the right track, please give me an acknowledgment after each." He then reached up and removed the first paper strip to reveal:

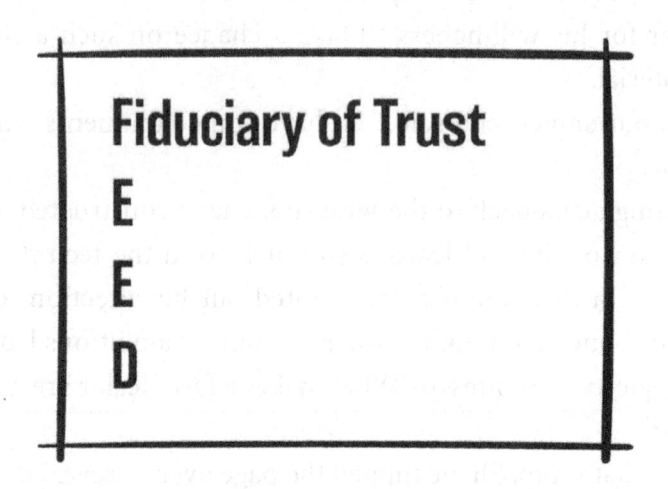

```
Fiduciary of Trust
E
E
D
```

"It all starts here. If the customer or prospect does not trust a feed dealer, they won't have them long. As one of the dealers remarked, the 'fiduciary' in the security industry is the gold standard of obedience to the truth."

Shane explained an abbreviated version of the 120-gallon man and the trust that Gerritt, the Dutch Dairyman, had in Cap and his organization. Trust is necessary for something productive and robust to happen. Great dealers know how to cultivate and not erode that trust by doing the right thing in business situations, even though occasionally, those situations are not profitable.

"Amen" hollered out Choppers.

Shane moved to reveal the next word on the list,

> **Fiduciary of Trust**
> **Expertise**
> **E**
> **D**

Shane expanded, "Expertise is most often applied to the problem or opportunity the dealer helps solve or conquer in the customer reach their goals. The word *expertise* is closely associated with the word *experience*, which directly correlates one to the other."

Shane spoke about how a Sand Point, Idaho, dealer demonstrated the magic of simplicity in providing that expertise. The dealer illustrated that if someone came in and wanted a sandwich, you would ask them the details of what kind of bread, meats, or cheeses and condiments they would like and provide them with a finished product. However, someone with no regard for complexity in the quest to make the sandwich might say something to the effect of: "The wheat used to make the bread in this sandwich was fourth generational, hard red winter wheat foundation seed, planted with four-inch spacing on a northern facing hillside, using ninety pounds to the acre of NH3 fertilizer, harvested with John Deere equipment that was purchased at General Willett Tractor town, handled through single source farmer owned home storage, processed using number three stone grinders and parabolic screening equipment, expanded with Egyptian-aged yeast and baked in Kollemeier stone hearth ovens." The sales team giggled.

Shane said, "The feed dealer would have said, 'Is whole wheat bread OK'?"

Shane summarized, "A feed dealer told me that simplicity and expertise are the primary coordinates to success." He said, "Your job as a feed company is to make good products; our job is to make them great through our expertise and application recommendation."

"Tell it all, brother," yelled Messkit.

The third strip was removed to expose:

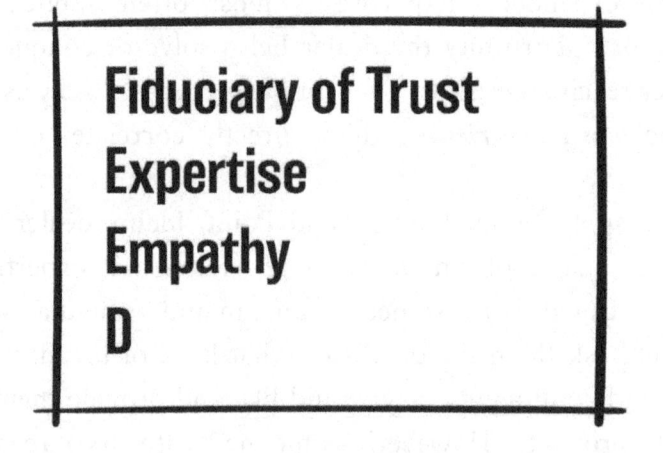

```
Fiduciary of Trust
Expertise
Empathy
D
```

"An example one of the dealers shared with me around this subject was enlightening. She told me that **Empathy** for knowing what a doctor's patient is going through and acknowledging their concerns is often the difference between an effective and ineffective physician. Feed dealers are the same way."

Shane shared that empathy is not always visible but shows in times of difficulty. An example he gave is the dealer mobilizing a harvest or planting a jamboree for the family of an ill or fallen farmer. Support by helping animal owners diagnose and fix herd or specific animal issues demonstrates empathy.

"Stumpy, from Devo's Southern Gentlemen Feed in Bakersfield, told me that **humor is the world's best salve for issues of concern.** A good feed dealer knows how to use their humor deftly to help diffuse adversity and help build a road back toward success."

"Amen" was resounding from the crowd.

"Before I move on, it is appropriate and right to acknowledge the words and the insights of Don (Cap) Wiggin's dad, Harry, when he said the most important three words to practice *empathy* in the feed industry are '*THEE BEFORE ME.*'

"Yes sir, you got us a tent revival goin' on there now, Preacher Intern!" yelled Coach.

"Well, pass the plate there, my man," teased back Shane. The Dreamweaver was beaming, and the room had forgotten their hangovers.

The last area is two separate words— one is a given, and the other is an observation of how the successful feed dealer acts:

> **Fiduciary of Trust**
> **Expertise**
> **Empathy**
> **Desire and Deference**

Shane said, "Whether it is being a major league shortstop, fire chief, or successful mother, **the *DESIRE to achieve*** something eclipses luck and talent on nearly all occasions. One of my key observations over the summer was that the desire to succeed as a feed dealer is driven by one key thing... **LOVE**. The dealers I visited with that are hugely successful absolutely **LOVE** being in the feed business.

Head nods and "Amens."

"The last area of observation surrounds ***DEFERENCE***. Successful feed dealers don't like to do an extravagant 'end zone dance' when they score a touchdown. They like their customers to get the credit for their success, and they don't like to show off opulence or abundance." Shane pointed out that the manager of Jim Jackson Feed told him, "If I live in the largest house in town and place gold bars in my pickup bed for traction and stabilization, I will have a tough time getting customers to see my recommendation as good for them. Humbleness is a sacred creed. A boastful display of success can potentially destroy customer trust."

"An absolute halleluiah!" Shouted Noel Bowman.

"I again want to thank you all for the chance to be a learning member of your Alumni team. I can tell you all one final learning: Being with you this summer wins the prize over cleanin hog barns."

Cheers, applause, and a measure of sarcasm led to a standing ovation to acknowledge that their summer mascot was part of the pack of jackals.

Shane blushed and turned away from the crowd, almost embarrassed about all the attention. His turning around made the camaraderie cheers escalate. As he turned around, a smiling Gilmour sauntered to the front of the room and put his hand on Shane's shoulder.

The recognition died down long enough for Gilmour to ask, "Didn't he do a great job?" More sincere applause followed.

Gilmour said, "Shane, do you remember what I told you my doubts were when we interviewed you at Washington State?"

Looking down sheepishly, he responded, "I might. I think you said you didn't think I could sell."

After awkward laughter and appropriate comedic timing, Gilmour dryly responded, "Well, the good news is... I can see you've forgotten all about that." Elevated laughter followed from the group.

Gilmour asked the group, "So, was I right?"

Booing, catcalls, and hissing ensued. Gilmour continued by saying, "All I know, young man, is that whatever your plans are after graduation, this team and I hope to be involved in them," shaking his hand through the applause.

"Amen" hollered Coach.

Shane's Learnings

On how to approach your speech preparation: Spend most of your time practicing the first three minutes of a presentation which would build your confidence for the remainder of the presentation. Make sure to prepare for a presentation that is designed to be conversational.

On group review following critical presented situations: At the end of each discussion, Mr. Gilmour asked one of the sales team members to summarize to the group what they heard and what they needed to do with the information or training they received. This uncertainty of who would be called on would cause the attention to the subject matter to be high. He told Shane later that this was also a way for him to understand how the group was assimilating the messages he was providing. It was also used most frequently on the weaker sales team members. The theory is, *If that person understood it, the rest of them more than likely got it.*

On using Maslow's theory to evaluate customer's and prospects' needs: The premise of analyzing your customers to develop a list of actionable innate customer needs in ascending order is an excellent exercise no matter what industry you are in. There will be significant differences in the hierarchy of needs by industry. Thinking about these will make you a better supplier, salesperson, clergyman, or family member.

On what truly makes those in the industry they serve the best: This, too, will be different by industry or profession because their customers are all different. I will venture to say that those who excel most of the time, regardless of sector... *love* what they do. Figuring out the other success attributes can provide a road map for interacting more successfully with those in that industry.

17

CARVING A TOTEM POLE ON A TOOTHPICK

There is no handbook on how to re-enter a herd.

Shane had survived most of the summer, living a regimen of feather beds and happy hours while his family endured a steady helping of fourteen-hour days, dense fingernail grime, and TV dinners. To help him re-assimilate, Shane was assigned specific unenviable morning tasks before manning the combine. These duties included hand-digging the septic tank access to extract twenty-five years of family accumulation. This was that rare day Shane missed the hogs. He thought it interesting how they ignored this task all summer until Shane had adequate time to conquer it. Message received.

Shane returned to a regimen of perpetual days of 'combine surfing' for the final trimester of his family's harvest season while one of his brothers prepared the harvested pea fields for next year's wheat rotational crop.

The foreign nature of a hectic schedule and the constant discovery during the summer had worn down Shane's energy. Like a prize fighter following a landmark fight, he was mentally expended. Contouring the hillside in a John Deere was a mission of rejuvenation. It provided hours of minimally interrupted reflection on what he had experienced in the last eight weeks. He also occasionally drifted into what may lie ahead in the future. Right now, the overall focus was to complete harvest, have his wrap-up meeting in Spokane with the Dreamweaver; and then head back to Pullman to finish his senior year at Wazzu.

He realized that what he missed most this summer was the connection with his family. The 10:30 p.m. dinners during harvest; the 6 a.m. combine servicing; the verbal sparring and mental 'Dutch Rubs' he got from his brothers, sister, and Uncle Bo. He missed it all.

The final acreage was harvested, and Shane spent two days blowing off and pressure-washing the combines before they were to be stored until the following season. Next, he would fertilize ahead of the drill to seed next year's winter wheat. He had moved the fertilizer rig to another field. His dad, Boxcar, picked him up to take him to the fertilizer-hauling truck, so he could take the truck to town to pick up a new supply of crop nutrients.

As the two of them bounced along in the green 1950 long-bed Chevy pickup hauling a 100-gallon diesel tank that supplied tractors and combines, the squeaks and creeks of the frame broke the silence. The trails they followed through the field had been punished by grain truck tires that came and went with the recent season's harvest. The silt was so deep in select spots that it felt more like tobogganing through fresh powder than driving a pickup. Boxcar broke the conversational impasse, "So a guy named Don Wiggins, he called himself Cap, phoned the other night."

"Cap called? Did he say what he wanted? Do I need to call him back?" Shane questioned. This information fired an ember of stimulus to know more, considering how much he admired Cap.

"No, he actually wanted to talk to me."

Shane's mind was in overdrive with investigative anxiety and a mild case of conspiracy theory. Why would Cap call his dad? He could feel three quarts of blood rush into his cheeks in anticipation.

Surprised and expecting the worst, in a monotone voice, Shane asked, "Do you mind if I ask what he wanted?"

Boxcar hastened the pace of the straight six in the pickup as they approached a hill that required additional RPM or would result in an unwanted downshift to make it over the top. The pause to focus on the slope was characteristic of his dad rather than delivering what Shane was after.

"He said you were a great kid and that I should be proud of the great job you did working for him this summer."

Shane was momentarily silent, most likely due to the smile he displayed as he looked out the opposite window.

Boxcar and Shane talked for the next twenty minutes, fifteen of which happened after they reached their destination. They spoke about his summer, what he had experienced, and if he liked that kind of work. These conversations are rare with the restrained Boxcar. He was focused on the 'yearly farm cycle' but took some time to understand what his son was thinking.

"Cap also told me that some guy named Ron Gilmour, the guy from Alumni, was also very impressed and was probably going to offer you a job and that if he didn't, Cap himself was going to." Shane was glowing on the inside but expressionless, as he predicted that the whole reason for the discussion was to get a feel for what the family farm labor pool would look like in the future. Shane said nothing.

Boxcar offered a disclosure Shane hadn't expected. "I don't want you to decide your future based on what you think we need here." He continued, "I farm because I love it. I would want all my kids to love it as much as I do, but I know that is unrealistic. As I have thought about it over the last few months, I hope all of you kids find your passion, which may mean a different direction you will follow."

Shane didn't know what to say, so he said something he had never said before. "You are a good dad, Pop. Thanks for all you have taught us."

The uncomfortable silence was the response Shane expected, signaling that Boxcar got the message.

"Thanks for coming back to help us for the rest of the summer," Boxcar said as Shane climbed out of the pickup to herd the fertilizer truck toward town.

"Anything for the family." Shane walked away with a thumbs-up.

The Mission Impossible phone machine had likely grabbed one of its last memos of the summer. Shane got the playback of that familiar smooth and smoky voice. MESSAGE ONE: *"Hello, Shane. I hope this finds you well and that the harvest was safe and bountiful. This is Ron Gilmour. I wanted to call to schedule your summer wrap-up of the program sometime this week before you head back to school. Give me a call and let me know which lunchtime you would like to schedule here at the Spokane plant. You did such a great job on your presentation that a couple of the sales guys got the FEED hierarchy of needs tattooed on their personals.* His patented crescendo laughter followed.... *Give me or Mary a call to set it up. I hope you have a good week. Also, bring this machine back with you so I don't have to get the sheriff after you this fall....* more laughter." CALL ENDED.

Shane arranged for a Wednesday visit with Gilmour. He also phoned Cap to thank him for the call to his dad. He could not reach him but did talk to Boo-Boo, his store manager, and found out that Cap would be at the Spokane plant at 7:00 a.m. on Wednesday to pick up a feed load. Shane told Boo-Boo he would meet Cap and buy him breakfast while his truck was loaded that morning. Boo-

Boo laughed, "Heck, I might take that load if there is free breakfast. I will let him know."

The rain shower that came through the farm on Tuesday was a welcome break from fall planting and an opportunity for Shane to shine up Emmitt for his trip to Spokane.

He got up well before the chickens finished their dreams and stopped at Brother CR Brock's convenience store to pick up some Zeppelin donuts and Parson's root beer for the distinguished Mr. Wiggins. He arrived at the Alumni plant and parked directly in front of Cap's Kenworth, which was backed into the dock awaiting its load. He heard a familiar voice as he walked toward the dock to find Cap. "I understand you are buying breakfast for everyone here at the plant," said Cap as he sauntered out of the warehouse in pressed jeans, an H-D shirt, and an Alumni Feed hat.

Shane retorted, "As a badge of honor, I thought for sure you would still be sportin' those clothes you were wearin' when you pulled that calf this summer."

"Hell, why do you think I am getting divorced."

That comeback extinguished Shane's banter like a funeral announcement.

"You got time for breakfast?" asked a humbled Shane.

"You know I haven't eaten in two days to ensure I get your money's worth at that breakfast buffet up the street."

As he jumped in Shane's pickup and slammed the door, Shane tossed him a quart size Parson's root beer and slid over the box of donuts.

"Awesome. The third one today," Cap said. He then continued, "What are you all dressed up for?"

"Gotta meet with Mr. Gilmour. Company garb is important, you know." Cap was relieved Shane wasn't wearing his tie to the breakfast palace. This eatery was where truckers and bikers dined in harmony. As they entered, they each recognized Cap as the second dressiest in this pancake cave; Shane was the leader.

They sat in a booth near the window. The fake-marble red Formica table was slightly sticky from previous diners and clashed with the sky-blue imitation-leather seat cushions. The cushions were nearly as sticky. There was no concern that a food critic would arrive to care. The paneling on the walls used to be cream white but now represented the color of sausage gravy. The ceiling was low, and the swamp cooler on the roof was working overtime, providing some cool air, but it delivered more levitating stifling humidity. In the background, the cook listened to the local sports radio announcer criticize the mediocre Mariners and predict a five-win Wazzu football season.

"What will a couple of runway models like you two gentlemen want from our glorious menu to accompany the best cup of coffee in Eastern Washington?" bellowed their waitress. She wore a **Michelle** hand-carved wooden name tag and more tattoos than a shipload of sailors. Her camo tank top provided transparency for the ink gallery on her arms, and the brevity of her Daisy Duke cutoff jeans displayed the additional canvas used for her tats on her well-proportioned legs. Nearly a dozen piercings in her cheek, ears, and nose accessorized her strawberry blond curly hair that was bunched into a loose ponytail at the peak of the back of her head. But one thing was evident; this young lady had **long eyeballs** for Cap.

She sat in the booth beside him, and the flirt-fest was on. "Whatcha gonna order there, you big teddy bear?" as she sarcastically stared lovingly at him with her elbows on the table, head resting on her palms, smiling like a grade schoolgirl with a teacher crush.

"What do you recommend there, darlin'?"

"A back rub and melon balls served in a hot tub," her eyebrows raised as she said it.

Cap closed the menu he had been using as a prop and said, "Ok, we will take two," nodding towards Shane as he said it.

Michelle glanced at Shane and emphatically observed, "He's too young."

Cap was becoming mildly uncomfortable. "How about two breakfast buffets and two Parson's root beers."

"You got it, Snookums. If you change your mind on that backrub, I get off at two-thirty," Michelle invited.

"You are the only one I will call," Cap deadpanned.

"I knew you would be loyal," she countered.

As she grabbed the menus and walked off to her following table of visitors, Shane encouraged Cap when he said, "See, you still got it."

"Yep, I am the Don Juan of agriculture. I think a tackle box blew up in her face with all those piercings."

Shane was unprepared for that sneak attack humor and covered his mouth to muffle the convulsive laugh it generated.

During breakfast, Cap shared details of his wife leaving for the basketball coach from the school where Cap's town high school was to merge their athletic programs. He quipped, "Pretty safe chance that SOB won't be getting the merged head coaching job."

Cap said that he and his wife hadn't been on the same page for the last few years, and the theory about the big house being able to hold the city girl to the country was a complete fantasy.

Cap wanted to change the subject and asked Shane to share some details about his summer, his findings, and his presentation. He did. They laughed a lot.

Shane changed lanes to something that was burning in his mind. "I am curious; why did you do it?"

"Do what?"

"Why did you call my dad?"

"Was there a problem with that?" asked a concerned Cap.

"No, it was wonderful and created an excellent and needed discussion catalyst."

Cap smiled and stared out the diner's window when a Spokane County sheriff's vehicle pulled in. They both felt safer and Michelle, the wallflower waitress, now had a new hot-tub target. She worked her foreplay on the lawman.

Cap spoke about how things did not go as he intended. It inspired him to take a vast amount of time to think and reflect on his circumstance, and he had to reassess what was important.

Cap summarized, "How you feel and act when you lose will determine how long it will be until you win again." This reminded Shane of Troy, the Ag teacher's comment during his Caldwell interview.

Conclusions relating to this reassessment were: 1) His kids will remain his primary focus, and he will continue to be as affable as possible with his wife to help that to happen. 2) Put an additional emphasis on life and work balance. His dad could have been a better role model in this lesson, as it was mostly business. 3) Make sure people that you appreciate…know it.

"Tell me more about the people you appreciate part," said Shane as he poured more syrup on the irregular-shaped pancake.

"Well, I just didn't take the time to do it with everyone I should have. What time did it take to pick up the phone and call your dad? We had a ten-minute conversation, and by the way, he was quite a gentleman."

"One of a kind." Shane quickly added.

Cap expounded, "I have sent handwritten notes to people that I normally wouldn't. Long-time customers, my mailman, the salespeople that call on me, and the teachers at the school that are doing a great job. People hear enough about what is going wrong. The news is habitually made up of the misfortunes of that day. People seem to be starved for recognition of one or two little things they are proud of that the world takes for granted. For example, you will never go wrong admiring a woman's hair or a guy's car or tractor."

"Their hair?" Shane reflected.

"Well, think about it, women will go into debt and spend at least fifteen percent of their lives in front of a mirror to make sure their most visible attribute distinguishes them in the way they want. As part of my trial research on this, I have kept track and have commented sincerely on a lady's hair over a hundred times in the last month. I have always generated a smile, a **thank you**, or an unsolicited explanation of their process to make it look the way it does. Every time with no exceptions."

"Some may think you might have overdosed on the root beer?" Shane asked playfully.

Cap spread the hashbrowns around on his platter without much acknowledgment and went even deeper into his personal reawakening with a more serious tenor. "My good friend Kenny is a mortician, the largest in the county. We call him 'Formy' because of his deep connection to formaldehyde. He and I have reflected on what we are going through, as he recently lost his wife in a car accident. He told me, Cap, I get about four to six customers a week, most of whom are unwilling participants. I prepare them for their presentation to the next world. I have been doing this for nearly twenty years. Ya know, in those twenty years, none of them, not one, have ever been able to tell me anything about what they want me to pass along to someone else they loved, admired, or were acquainted with. He said that he knew there was a lot they would like to voice. He knew it was in there, but they never do. So, Formy and I have adopted it as personal missions not to hold those things back, to give those compliments, send those handwritten notes, those phone calls. We never want to regret that we didn't do those things."

Cap looked directly at Shane and said, "That is why I made that call to your dad."

Shane could tell his role as a listener in this conversation was therapy for someone he admired. He redirected a thought he anticipated Cap would appreciate. "Your dad gave you one more lesson in **Thee before me.**"

After a long pause, "Thank you, I hadn't thought about it that way."

They finished breakfast, and as Shane paid, he commented to Michelle, "I must say I really like your hair."

She created a smile divot in her cheek deep enough that if you stepped in it, you might turn your ankle. "Thank you. You know you may not be too young for me after all. I get off at…."

Shane finished her sentence for her nodding, "Two-thirty."

She giggled whimsically as Shane pushed her tip toward her.

As they walked out the door, Cap smirked and said to Shane, "I hope your meeting with Gilmour doesn't conflict with that."

Mary Tempo met Shane at the top of the stairs in the mill. He reached out to shake her hand, and she grabbed him, hugged him, and said, "Family does this, young man." They caught up on the rest of the summer since the sales meeting. Shane returned the Mission Impossible machine, and the office supplies he had been given. She looked in the box, slid it across the table towards him, and said, "Keep this as a gift from Mr. Gilmour and me. I hope we both use it a lot in the future, and we may need to leave you a message in Pullman next year."

Shane was delighted and surprised and said, "Thank you, Mrs. Tempo."

"Good lord, son, it's Mary," laughing and shaking her head in frustration.

"Thank you, my apologies."

She gave Shane directions to Mr. Gilmour's house in the Spokane Valley, where they were to meet for lunch.

Upon arrival, Shane could see this was a fantastic residence. The newer construction two-story brick home rambled across a few acres of lawn with a horse barn out back that Shane thought most people would like to live in. The three-car garage and attached workshop were nearly as oversized as the combine shed at Shane's family ranch. Gilmour was in a pair of shorts and a tan Hawaiian shirt. He greeted Shane like a potential future son-in-law that he actually liked.

"My, that is a good-looking truck there, Shane." Emmitt was parked on the airport runway-width driveway. As they toured the truck, Gilmour got the whole story of Shane's reclamation of the vehicle.

"Mr. Gilmour, no disrespect to your office at the mill, but this is quite a bit nicer than that," Shane said, staring with his mouth open.

Gilmour belly laughed and clapped his hands together. And with a hint of sarcasm said, "Well, that is one of the things I wanted to tempt you with. Upon hiring, you could make that office your home base to work out of." He laughed heartily.

Shane said, "Ag teaching feels more like a calling every minute." They both laughed.

"My wife made some sandwiches for us to eat by the pool. She was disappointed she couldn't be here as she had to call on some doctors as part of her job as an insurance administrator. I couldn't afford this place alone," Gilmour laughed devilishly.

"Can I take my tie off?" asked Shane, trying not to sound like he was begging.

"Yes. You wouldn't want to get mustard on it." Gilmour deadpanned.

They walked through the modern kitchen and a family room the size of a restaurant. A five-foot waterfall cascaded into the pool opposite the outdoor table set for their discussion. A twelve-foot Alumni Feed umbrella shaded the table—a lovely setting.

During lunch, they spoke about Shane's family harvest, his return to school, and his breakfast with Cap. They agreed on the difficult times Cap was experiencing in his personal life.

The Dreamweaver opened up about his childhood, his career, and the mistakes he had made. Shane noticed he was becoming much more human than the earlier uncertainty and awkwardness accompanying positional power in a boss-to-employee relationship.

The ever-curious Shane, now maybe mildly emboldened with comfort, decided to ask some questions he had been on his mind most of the summer. He may be taking a risk in asking, but he thought the payoff would be worth it.

"Mr. Gilmour."

"Yes."

"Do you mind if I ask a few questions about leadership and career management?"

"Would love for you to ask," said a smiling, proud boss.

"I have tried to observe and learn this summer by asking many questions," reaffirmed Shane. "I will tell you I find you a bit intimidating, but I thought asking made sense."

After a short laugh and recalibration, Mr. Gilmour said, "Never meant to be menacing, but I understand where it could come from. Shoot on those questions and see if we can get answers and relieve your uneasiness."

"So, if you could re-do your career, what path would you take based on what you have learned?"

"A great question and I assume you are thinking about this as you direct your career path?" Dreamweaver sought clarity.

"Yes, sir. But I also really value what successful people think."

Dreamweaver began, "Well, a rock-solid principle I have told my children is that you need a bigger reason to get up and work for however many years than just to make money. Find an organization or make one for yourself that stands for high principles you can enthusiastically support. These high principles will motivate your customers and bond with them as you aspire toward success. It must tie into the history of your company. And you need to find unique ways to live those principles out in your area of influence."

Gilmour stared across the pool and continued as Shane nodded, "I would also select a company that rewards personal achievement but celebrates a culture of helping others win. You'll find many cultures that promote success at the expense of others. These places usually fail over the long term due to the resulting mistrust that forms all around. Adopt a philosophy that **you win when others win**, and you will be surprised at how many people will rally to support you in your efforts. This is the start to building a healthy work environment."

"Great advice, sir. What has changed about the company or the business environment since you started?" Shane asked.

"Good lord, son, this is supposed to be a casual lunch, and here you are makin me sweat." Gilmour smiled, and after a bite of his sandwich, he gave Shane a lesson.

"Companies like Alumni and the dealers you surveyed are organisms. They are alive. They change over time and grow and age in different aspects. Be prepared to reinvent yourself when the company may no longer need the special skills you have been focusing on. That is the time to grab a new tool out of your toolbox. When this happens, it is not the time to pack up your aptitudes and lament that no one cares how good you are at your chosen craft. Pouting never makes you better. Be prepared for the need for skill evolution throughout your career, given how fast things change now. Learn to be a generalist, always adding to the list of your talents ... never stop doing this. It takes an array of skill progressions to succeed. No one has all these skills. Learn early what you are good at and not so great at. Surround yourself with people who are good at what you are not so competent at. That is the essence of building a good team. Everyone has a place. Everyone is dependent on others to perform in their respective specialty. This frees you up to double down on where you really excel."

Shane was silent, trying to absorb information as foreign as organic chemistry. The look on his face made Gilmour add some color to the commentary.

"If I remember correctly, you played baseball, right?"

"Yes sir, since I was eight."

"Think about the teams you were on. Was everyone on your team a good pitcher? Could they all play short? Catcher? As a coach, you try to put players where their skills dictate."

"Where do you acquire these skills in the business you are talking about?" Shane asked.

"Companies like Alumni offer many learning opportunities. BUT I will challenge you that truly successful people will be curious, like you are, and search out personal learning to continue to evolve on your own." Gilmour said, "I do not doubt in my mind that you will be successful because of your abundant purposeful curiosity."

Shane was flush with pride hearing his comments. He ate his sandwich to avoid showing an overconfident beaming smile.

Gilmour asked pointedly, "Do you believe that about your success?"

Shane was smiling, slightly embarrassed and muted, other than a proud giggle.

"It is great to be humble, but don't be afraid to appreciate your talent by being appropriately confident. Make sense?"

"It does, and thank you for the compliment. I do have another question I have wondered about all summer."

"What is that?" asked Gilmour.

"What, in your opinion, makes someone in your role successful?"

This made even the glib fountain of knowledge known as the Dreamweaver pause momentarily. He took a long pull off his iced tea and smiled as he formulated his answer. "Well, of course, the big area is people. You are selecting, hiring, motivating, and knowing when to get out of the way. People are always your biggest asset and your biggest challenge. *If you plant an onion, you get an onion.* Be careful whom you hire and spend the extra money on a great employee; you will never regret it."

Shane nodded.

Gilmour continued, "The second area is managing your assignment. You need to learn to fly at multiple altitudes at once. **Fly high** to see the whole forest to understand what major trends are impacting you and what activities your competitors are engaging in. You must constantly ask, "What can you do better than anyone else?" You will instinctively need to dive down to navigate right above the treetops so you can pick the right things to work on that will contribute the most to your and your customer's success. And be ready to drop down to the ground **to carve a totem pole on a toothpick** to deliver exemplary work when it's time."

"That sounds like a skill that is hard to develop."

"Part skill, but much art. Remember when I asked if the whole team could play shortstop? This is the equivalent of that. Not everyone can play this position because of that," Gilmour emphasized.

Since Shane had never really interacted with anyone like Gilmour, he recognized and acknowledged how rare this was.

Gilmour had one more area to address in his role. "Get good at creating your own personal mental Disneyland to show others you are in control despite an array of symbolistic angry bees buzzing around your head. Everyday work life is filled with distractions, meetings, written and phone communication, supply chain problems, and customer complaints. Learning the discipline to stay focused on the big picture would be best. Remember how the work you engage in each day contributes to the overall picture you are painting of your career. Deal with the urgent, but don't let it consume you to the point you can't complete the important work."

Gilmour could tell by the glassy stare that he had filled Shane's knowledge bucket over the brim. He switched gears to give him some relief.

"So, Shane, what was your biggest learning this summer?"

After a pause highlighting the sound of a neighbor's lawn mower laboring through some overgrown bluegrass, Shane reflected, "That is hard because there was so much. However, the most surprising learning was how much you can learn from each different person. It was a given that I would learn a lot from our salespeople or dealership managers, or owners. Still, what I learned from warehouse folks like Boo-Boo, or characters like Carnivore, Spongecake, and Ruby was surprising. They may not have the most senior or high-profile roles, but they have knowledge or perspectives others don't have. Said another way I learned I can learn from anybody and everybody if I ask and listen."

Gilmour was stretched out in his chair with his feet crossed, pointed toward Shane, and smiling with teeth touching each ear. "That is an insight that most people never figure out. You are right. You had an amazing summer."

"I want to thank you for the opportunity and your guidance."

Shane handed him a handwritten note that outlined his appreciation.

Gilmour opened and read it to himself and said, "Thank you. I only have one more piece of advice and two more assignments for you."

"The advice is to be authentic whatever you do or want to become. Genuine people are easily recognized and have exponential allure compared to a pretending replica. If you think about it, authenticity is some of the easiest but most productive work you can do for your career and life. You are demonstrating it well so far. Don't change that practice."

Shane recognized the importance and reinforced it with an affirming "Yes, sir."

"Now, on the assignment. First, I need you to spread the gospel of your summer at Alumni Animal Nutrition to the other students in Pullman. I need you to find me next year's intern."

"No problem. I head out tomorrow and will schedule time to share thoughts with the career center student days," Shane acknowledged.

"Great, and second, I need you to find the best job and salary with another company."

Shane was now in a tailspin but had more trouble hiding his disappointment with the comment. Had he done something wrong? He decided to ask. "Why would you want me to go get another job?"

"I am sorry I didn't finish my thought. Please go check out other jobs, even teaching. I want you to pressure test whether you would enjoy those roles as much as a job with Alumni."

"I am still a bit confused."

"Well, once you have secured that offer, come back to me, and I will match whatever it is and add fifteen percent to it. You could have an amazing sales career here at Alumni Animal Nutrition."

Shane's concerns were quickly extinguished, and he was grinning like a kindergarten graduate.

Gilmour shook his hand and said, "I will check in with you during the year to see your progress on those two initiatives."

"Glad Mrs. Tempo gave me the answering machine."

Gilmour coyly chuckled, "Don't kid yourself. It is a highly coordinated plan. If you don't come back to us, I will have you arrested for larceny. You don't know Mary very well; she is highly sinister. Now take me for a ride in that pickup."

Gilmour, of course, embellished praise of Shane's work on the truck and its condition. He ran his hand across the gloss white glove box and said, "They don't make 'em like this anymore. You could put a hay bale in that glove compartment and sell advertising on that huge door."

Shane was beaming. He dropped the Dreamweaver off after a quick test ride and went home to pull some belongings together for his trip back to school tomorrow.

You never know which days will be memorable or tragic when you arise. This one started as conventional as the thousands he had experienced, but this day was masquerading as an unexpected journey in resilience.

Shane loaded up his pickup with many things he would need to move into his apartment in Pullman. The fall semester started in two days, and he had some meetings to attend and books to buy. The sound used textbooks was cheaper, and you must get there early to secure them. He was especially interested to see who might appear at some of the Moscow, Idaho, watering holes.

He hugged each of his family members, including Uncle Bo, channeled Cap's comments, and told each of them he loved them. This was an odd and uncommon practice for all the family members. Several moments of joshing accompanied his comments with his brothers, hugs from his sister, and an uncomfortable handshake from Boxcar. After a clumsy delay, Boxcar said, "We love you too."

A showing of affection. A watershed occurrence for his farm family.

And he was off to Pullman for an afternoon meeting with Zim, the Mayor, and the Ag education department head. The roughly sixty-mile trip could be cut by nearly fifteen minutes using a shortcut that Shane and others had taken for years. The **Coyote Trail** was a name his family gave to an unmaintained agricultural route. It was primarily used for farm equipment travel. The road had very little gravel. It was mainly dirt and had seen its share of wheat truck travel. The punishment the road had seen the last few months meant much dust. Shane had covered his belongings in the back with a tarp to protect from the settling dirt, and he would have time to wash his truck after his meeting at the ag department. The extra fifteen minutes were an attractive bonus. Bachman Turner Overdrive's greatest hits added musical inspiration to this day's trip. As he entered the road, he recognized the familiar sign that said NO ROAD SIGNS AHEAD. This was a stark reminder of the reasoning for the name **Coyote Trail.**

He was gliding along, proud yet ignorant, to his time-saving decision. Traveling nearly fifty miles an hour on a gravel road feels slightly uncomfortable. Because of the narrow path and neglect, fifty miles an hour on the coyote trail felt like the autobahn. Impaired judgment, when met with impatient reasoning, can be chaos. He craved that additional time upon his arrival, which kept elevating his unwise decisions. With the dried weeds along the roadside whizzing by as a blur, Shane drew Emmitt to the edge of the narrow road at the top of a hill.

With no warning, an oncoming six-foot chrome grill led an orange tandem-axle grain truck traveling the same ill-advised speed as Shane. T-Rex Farms truck must have had a truckload of '***ass***' on it because they were surely **haulin it**. Shane swerved Emmitt farther to his passenger side of the road in a flight reflex to not be tangled in the rear wheels of this oncoming untethered orange Ford 30-foot-long locomotive.

The funniest things go through your mind in times of uncontrolled mayhem. The words of his driver's education teacher McCutcheon sparked into his memory. McCutcheon's loud and monotone voice would repeat for emphasis in his firm. "What is in the ditch? You don't want to be in the ditch because there are only four things there. HOLES, NAILS, GLASS, DEATH... HOLES, NAILS, GLASS, DEATH... HOLES, NAILS, GLASS, DEATH". Shane was trying desperately to avoid one of those for sure.

With the intervention of a higher calling and the kindness of the properties of physics, there was no collision with the driver of the orange menace, which continued down the dust-filled trail without stopping or changing trajectory. Shane and Emmitt were on a different course.

Shane had put the pickup about half its width up a steeply sloped bank to avoid the tandem. After the truck passed, his pickup overcorrected, and it was tossed back across the road into an even steeper dirt bank, which rejected the rig again. Shane could see nothing because of the jetwash of dust kicked up by the tandem. The same dust behind the truck made it so that the T-Rex truck driver could not see the peril Shane was having.

Shane had been on this road enough times to recall some severe drop-offs on his side of the road with, of course, no guard rails. As chance would have it, Emmitt was thrust back across the trail, headfirst down a steep grade towards the remnants of a little-used gravel pit. He had no control of Emmitt at this point as it was propelled even more dangerously by Shane's unsafe speed. He attempted to hit the brakes. His left front wheel caught a rock the size of a mop bucket. This sent the truck listing to the left, and now

Emmitt was hurdling sideways and into a series of rolls shortly after. The roll happened with rapid repetition. All the tarped items in the back of the truck heading to college were flung randomly like a hurricane had hit a trailer house.

Seat belts are lap belts in a 1967 Chevy pickup and are perceived by young rural males as annoying. As a result of his decision to neglect to buckle up, Shane was now vacillating between the compressing roof and the floor of the pickup and occasionally hovering weightlessly above the seat. He had been rotating amongst flying glass, compressing metal, and now was no longer levitating in the rolls. He was lodged and stuck but still spinning with the truck. He and the truck had rolled three-quarters the length of a football field until he landed, now dormant, at the bottom of the gravel pit.

Gaining your new bearings when tossed around in the universe is not a modest task. The pickup was lying on its roof. Smoke and dust floated aimlessly around the remains of his once-pristine chariot. Shane's medical assessment was that he could feel his legs and arms and move his neck. He was lying across the partially folded seat in a compacted compartment. He hoped it was not his coffin. The rear wheels were still spinning, the engine was not running, but the tape deck was still pumping Bachman Turner Overdrive performing **Don't Get Yourself in Trouble**. Shane was thinking how ironic that was and might be a little late.

While the smell of smoking oil on the vehicle's manifold concerned the trapped Shane, he hoped gasoline directly behind the driver's seat would not ignite. A collapsed and flattened steering column held his legs. As he tried to pull himself loose, the grip on him was like a vise. The gear shift pressed deeply into his ribs, causing severe discomfort with every escape attempt. The glass and the rotational banging in the incident had created a fair number of wounds and surface bleeding. His once prized hair was now a vault for blood, dried weeds, and dirt that had agitated into the cab during rolling. He had one arm free but could not reach the horn button to send a distress signal. The chance of gasoline ignition decreased every minute as the engine cooled. The tape deck was still accompanying the predicament with a BTO background soundtrack.

Evaluation and strategic actions to remedy any situation are necessary starting point. Yelling did no good. As expected, traffic on the Coyote Trail had evaporated, and the gravel pit hadn't had an occupant for weeks. He hoped that the point of his accident on the above road would get a T-Rex driver's attention on a return trip. And that they might look deeper into what caused the foreign-looking tire tracks on the dirt road. It was a long shot. Shane drifted in and out of consciousness most of the day.

When your foolishness imprisons you, you reflect on many things. What if he were to bleed out or dehydrate? He was missing a meeting with Zim, the Mayor. Could that absence be a key to someone finding him, or will it be sluffed off as another immature college student blowing off his professor? Would he see his family again? Was all his learning of the summer going to end on the bench seat of a compacted pickup in the belly of a quarry? The tape deck faded as the battery was wilting with no alternator to recharge it. After hearing *Taking Care of Business* for what seemed like the tenth rendition, he rationalized that he needed to send a symbolic message in a bottle if this was it. The free hand and arm were not his writing hand, but he reasoned he could scribble. Using some of the plentiful blood he could accumulate on his finger, he used the white glove box that the Dreamweaver said could be a billboard. The door to the glovebox was about four inches from his face. He used it as an easel. He drew a heart with the word FAMILY behind it. Then in tribute to his summer project, he wrote F. E. E. D. He hoped it would provide meaning to folks at Alumni.

These moments of hardship make you reflect on what is highly important. Shane had an uninterrupted stretch to think about what was important to him. Family, friends, and his new association with Alumni Feed quickly came to mind. He reflected a bit deeper to contemplate that importance against his current circumstance. When your legs are trapped, and you cannot do what you want, it makes you reflect on one of the more overlooked qualities that we all have living in this country: freedom. When something as simple as your ability to walk around and go where you want has been highjacked, you recognize how much you took it for granted. He started to think about those in other parts of the world who couldn't leave their country freely. Some can't practice a religion they might want. Some can't choose a career they might prefer. Some have been restricted to the number of children they can have. He pledged that if he could be liberated from the bowels of this pickup which had become a human mousetrap, he would never take the splendor of freedom for granted again.

Dusk in the Palouse country during the fall was always Shane's favorite. The coolness caused a temperature inversion that would compress the dust and the pollen closer to the ground. This enhanced the aromas making them more noticeable. A field of late-season third-cutting alfalfa was recently cut for drying. It was located just outside the gates of the gravel pit.

Shane breathed in as deeply as he could, smiled, and manifested as he had in the past, "Agriculture has some incredible smells."

He had drifted off again and awoke to the darkness of night being pierced by the sound of a car engine and tires on rocks echoing off the gravel pit walls. The most welcome vision was the pulsating red flashing light moving its way over the mutilated dash and illuminating the inside of the cab of Emmitt. Shane had always been anxious when being pulled over by a police officer. His pulse would elevate, and his heart rate would be frenzied at the sight of the red flashing lights. It struck fear into him. Not today, this red beacon started a new beautiful chapter.

Shane laughed to himself about the red flashing light and how your attitude and circumstance can make you think completely differently about the same thing.

Shane's Learnings

<u>On success recipe when you lose:</u> "How you feel and act when you lose will determine how long it will be until you win again."

<u>On the value of showing people you appreciate them</u>: As Cap shared with Shane, "Make sure people that you appreciate…know it." People have the desire and the need to feel important and valued. To reaffirm that to others may be one of the more valuable things we can do to make the world a better place. It costs you very little and can take less time than it takes to drink a cup of coffee. Your spouse, employee, clergy, former teacher, and friends have likely positively impacted your life more than the compensation they received. Your affirmation is more valuable than any salary they ever received. You will also find that as you develop comfort doing it, *posi-thanking* can become a habit. Those acts of *posi-thank* can take the form of a phone call, handwritten note, or, most impactful, in-person delivery. Try it. Watch the reaction you get. It is a pure form of "thee before me."

<u>On some key things to look for in an organization to build a career around</u>: Search for an organization or make one for yourself that stands for high principles you can enthusiastically stand behind and support. These high principles can also motivate your customers and create a bond as you both aspire to success. It must tie into the history of your company. And it would be best if you found unique ways to live those principles out in your area of influence. If you find yourself doubting the principles of the company you are working for, you may not be in the right place. Also, think hard about picking a company that rewards personal achievement but celebrates a culture of helping others win. You will find many cultures that promote success at the expense of others. These places usually fail over the long term due to the resulting mistrust that forms all around. Adopt a philosophy that *you win when others win,* and you will be surprised at how many people will rally to support you in your efforts. This is the start of the building of a healthy work environment.

On how to deal with changes in your company and your career: Companies are organisms. They are alive. They change over time, grow, and age in different aspects. Be prepared to reinvent yourself when the company may no longer need the unique skills you have been focusing on. That is the time to grab a new tool out of your toolbox. When this happens, it is not the time to pack up your aptitudes and lament that no one cares how good you are at your chosen craft. Pouting never makes you better. Be prepared for the need for skill evolution throughout your career, given how fast things change now. Also, remember that you are rarely truly ready for your next task. You will get better and grow from it. Just be prepared to accept the challenge of that. Learn to be a generalist, constantly adding to the list of your talents … never stop doing this. It takes an array of skill progression to succeed. No one has all these skills. Learn early what you are good at and not so great at. Surround yourself with people who are good at what you are not so competent at. That is the essence of building a good team. Everyone has a place. Everyone is dependent on others to perform in their respective specialty. This frees you up to double down on what you really excel at.

On the importance of selecting the right people in the right roles: One of the most significant factors in an organization's success is its people's quality. Good managers are concerned with selecting, hiring, motivating, and knowing when to get out of the way. People are always your biggest asset and your biggest challenge. *If you plant an onion, you get an onion.* Be careful whom you hire and spend the extra money on a great employee; you will never regret it. Not everyone can play shortstop or pitch. Select your players to meet the needs of your position.

On the idea of managing your assignment as a leader: You need to learn to fly at multiple altitudes. *Fly high* to see the whole forest to see what major trends are impacting you and what your competitors are up to. Ask what you can do better than anyone else constantly. You will instinctively need to dive down to navigate just above the treetops so you can pick the right things to work on that will contribute the most to you and your customer's success. Be ready to drop down to the ground to *carve a totem pole on a toothpick* to deliver exemplary work when it's time.

On maintaining sanity in your role as a manager or leader: Get good at creating your own personal mental Disneyland to show others you are in control despite an array of symbolistic angry bees buzzing around your head. Everyday work life is filled with distractions, meetings, written and phone communication, supply chain problems, and customer complaints. Learning the discipline to stay focused on the big picture would be best. Remember how the work you engage in each day contributes to the overall image you are painting of your career. Deal with the urgent, but don't let it consume you to the point that you can't complete the vital work.

On Shane's most significant learning: He stated his most extensive learning was how much you can learn from every different person. He knew he would learn a lot from our salespeople, dealership managers, or owners; however, what he learned from warehouse folks like Boo-Boo or characters like Spongecake, Carnivore, or Ruby was surprising. They may not have the most senior or high-profile roles, but they have knowledge and perspectives that others don't have. He learned he could learn from everybody if he asked and listened.

On the value of authenticity: Dreamweaver's advice was, whatever you do or want to become, *be authentic.* Genuine people are easily recognized and have exponential allure compared to a pretending replica. If you think about it, authenticity is some of the most uncomplicated but most productive work you can do for your career and life.

On not ever overlooking the beauty of Freedom: Hard to think of a world where you don't get to choose what you want to do in your life. Neglect of such a bequest could result in you losing it. *Appreciate it and protect it every day.*

. . .

How to deal with each day: You never know which days will be memorable or tragic when you arise. Try not to waste one of them.

On the danger of taking an ill-advised shortcut: Bad judgment can be chaos when met with impatient reasoning. He craved that time upon his arrival, which kept elevating his improper decisions. Seat belts are not overrated.

On enjoying each day: Never waste a day. Because you may not enjoy some of the beautiful smells of agriculture.

Shane's Learning Challenges: (participation will be beneficial)

✓ Building leaders at every level in your organization should be your goal for a few minutes weekly; sometimes most effective when seasoned with humor.

Think about an organization you are involved or work with: What are three things you would do to build leadership at all levels in your organization?.... If you don't at least think about it, it won't happen.

✓ The short course in life's success struggle comes down to three words: "Thee, before me." That exercise can be done with customers, employees, and suppliers.

Selfless acts are the root of thee before me. Think about a time when someone (possibly yourself) put their wants or needs after the needs of others.

Recognize them for doing it and watch their reaction.

✓ A handwritten note of thanks and appreciation elevates anyone's professionalism and can be a more critical keepsake than a tombstone. (In other words, do it before they pass away)

TO GET THE FULL MEANING OF THAT: Pick out three people that had an important impact on your life and write them a handwritten note (not e-mail, text, or typed, but handwritten) telling them thank you for their contribution. I bet you will be amazed at the reaction you will receive in return. The process will take less than 30 minutes, and your learning will rival their appreciation.

ABOUT THE AUTHOR

Brad Schu has spent his 42-year career in the Animal Nutrition sector with the Checkerboard Brand. He is proof that 'Purina can get into your blood'. During that lengthy career, he had the diverse pleasure of working under six different ownerships. Each provided a different set of operating and Go-To-Market philosophies. He had roles in wholesale sales to dealers, sales management, and executive roles leading the marketing teams that created robust product line entries such as Equine Senior Horse Feed, Strategy Horse Feed, Ultium Horse Feed, Antlermax Deer diets, Wind and Rain Minerals for cattle just to name a few that changed an industry. His teams also created Dealer Improvement Programs such as America's Country Stores and Premier Dealer Programs. Over 400 Feed Dealers made substantial improvements to their marketplace locations as a result of these programs. Other Dealer support and demand creation programs his team put together included the Purina Gold Dealer Program, Horse Country Trailer, Animal Makeover TV series on RFD-TV, Business Builder, and Barn Steward. He was also involved in leading the Sales Team as VP of Sales and later Sr. Director of Sales Operations. He served over half of his career on the Executive Team supporting the Purina brand development.

His love of Feed Stores came from personal interactions as a salesperson as well as working directly with organizational leaders on supporting the growth of Purina to their customers.

After retiring from the Feed Industry, he started Idea Sherpa L.L.C. where he consults with organizations in the area of selective distribution marketing, customer engagement, and listening programs. He also fulfills speaking requests sharing the importance of Agriculture and how many organizations can prosper from the unique customer engagements, people management lessons, and the preservation of a "Lost Language" about how you think about people and customers that have been preserved in America's Feed Stores.

He is ever grateful to the prior generations of Purina employees, the hard-working people at Purina, and every feed dealer and animal owner he encountered.

You can contact Brad Schu at Brad@Ideasherpa.net

Made in the USA
Monee, IL
30 October 2024